GERMANY
TODAY

GERMANY TODAY

A Personal Report

Walter Laqueur

Weidenfeld and Nicolson
LONDON

Filmset by Deltatype, Ellesmere Port
Printed by Butler & Tanner Ltd, Frome and London

Contents

PREFACE 1

1 *Angst?* 5
2 *Lukanga Mukara* or Germany Revisited 17
3 Young Germany or the Cultural Revolution 49
4 Intermezzo or Variations on German Folk-Songs 91
5 The Unhappy Intellectuals or *Fin de Siècle*, German-style 99
6 Arminius or Patriotism Rediscovered 143
7 The State of the Economy or After the Ball is Over 175
8 Facing the Future 197
   INDEX 227

Preface

The idea to write this essay on contemporary Germany first occurred to me, I believe, while looking out of the Reichstag building in Berlin on a January morning fifty years, almost to the day, after Hitler had taken power. I was photographing, and the East German border guard, on his watchtower nearby, took an evident interest in me: perhaps he was just bored, perhaps he thought I was engaging in a bit of strategic photography. Berlin and Germany had always been divided for this young man from Eberswalde perhaps, or Cottbus: surely there were more fascinating objects for a bona fide tourist to photograph than a wall and some barbed wire entanglements?

It was a perfectly natural reaction on his part, but my recollections went back a little further, and I was bound to be struck by the changes I was seeing from my vantage point. I had been born in Silesia which was then Germany (but is no longer), and I have revisited the country many times since the early 1950s. I have written on modern German history, but never thought of myself as a German specialist; my main interests as a student of politics and history have been elsewhere.

I became again intrigued by events in Germany in recent years, partly because of the crucial importance of that country in Europe. I was also fascinated by the young generation. Similar manifestations of youth revolt and of the emergence of the so-called 'new social movements' could be watched elsewhere. But nowhere had this process gone so far, lasted so long and been taken so seriously. Lastly, I was surprised by some of what I had heard and read in America and Europe about Germany. It was often at variance with my own impressions.

It is no easy task to measure the pulse of any country, let alone to predict its future. True, the observer now has at his disposal

1

instruments which did not exist in past ages, above all social research data, which enlighten him about every aspect of life. They tell him much about prevailing attitudes, but very little about why things happened, and nothing at all about the future. One cannot begin to understand a country without a long stay, or repeated visits – without observation and conversation. During the last two years I have travelled much in Germany. I thought I knew the country well, but after a while I realized that most of my knowledge was limited to certain groups of people in some major cities. Yet the smaller cities are, in many ways, more revealing and a better source of information than Berlin and Munich, Hamburg and Cologne for, as in all big cities throughout the world, even the mayor and his main aides no longer have a clear idea about what is happening once a city has grown beyond a certain size.

A smaller city, on the other hand, still remains a face-to-face community: people know their neighbours, they have more time to talk and to think. The smaller towns, incidentally, are also demographically important, for most have been steadily growing since the Second World War, whereas the population of the very big cities has been decreasing. So I went from town to town, talking to mayors and high-school students, to doctors and booksellers, to factory managers and workers, to small traders and heads of local chambers of commerce, to officers of the *Bundeswehr*, teachers, churchmen and parliamentarians and, above all, to journalists whom I found exceedingly well informed. I must have talked to hundreds of people, which sounds impressive, but is, of course, still a tiny cross-section considering the fact that Germany has more than sixty million inhabitants.

My gratitude is due to all those who have given their time and who went out of their way to be helpful. I owe a special debt to the Fritz Thyssen Foundation, without whose help I could not have completed this enterprise, and also to the Carthage Foundation which provided similar assistance.

A few more preliminary remarks are called for. Germany is, of course, a smaller country than the one I knew in my youth, let alone the Imperial Germany of my father and grandfathers. But it is still far from homogeneous, and I doubt whether it is becoming more so with time, which makes generalization very difficult indeed. Time and again I had to rewrite sections of this book, for what I had observed in one part of the country did not apply elsewhere. Not long before the French Revolution, an astute observer noted that there was a chasm between

North and South Germany – 'different people, different culture, different customs'.[1] In general terms I was, like most others, aware of this, just as the differences between North and South in the United States or in England are well-known facts. But of the full implications for German politics, for the economy, for social and cultural life, I became aware only as the result of frequent travels from one to the other.

Again, like everyone else, I knew that there is, in the media coverage of Germany, a concentration on the dramatic, the interesting and the extraordinary, on sudden change rather than continuity. They focus on the train which crashes, not on the one which arrives on time. But life, much of the time, is neither dramatic nor very interesting. In Germany, as elsewhere, the picture emerging from the media captures only part of the reality. This is not very dangerous for those who live in Germany; they need only to open their eyes to have an inbuilt corrective against distortions. But those outside Germany have no such corrective, and they are therefore likely to gain the impression that Germany is a country in deep crisis – political as well as economic and spiritual: a house on fire, a society about to disintegrate. The fact that some Germans have visions these days about the horsemen of the apocalypse only strengthens this impression. Germans are perfectionists and in need of order; once things become a little chaotic, once full success is out of their reach, hypochondria is likely to set in. In short, their mood is likely to affect their judgment.

This is not to say that all will be plain sailing in Germany in the years to come. There are serious economic and social crises ahead, the political system will be tested and the young generation will protest. There is the old German inclination to exaggerate in time of war as in time of peace and to act irrationally; once heroism was in fashion, now it is *Angst*. But just as sartorial fashions are seldom universally shared, neither are intellectual fashions such as the *fin-de-siècle*, *fin-de-millénaire* mood. If insecurity is widespread, it is my feeling that there is more level-headedness, more common sense in German politics now than ever before. Things may still turn out wrong, a collective hysteria cannot be ruled out in a time of multiple crisis.

This is a personal book, not only because I am drawing on my own recollections – others may reach different and more ominous conclu-

[1] Kaspar Riesbeck, *Briefe eines reisenden Franzosen über Deutschland*, 1783. Friedrich Nicolai, who published his impressions two years earlier, had reached similar conclusions.

sions with regard to the future of Germany – but I suspect that subsequent events will bear out my (relative) optimism. There is the temptation to give a book of this kind a strong title such as *The End is Near*, *Apocalypse Now*, *Armageddon Tomorrow*. Such titles, I am told, are selling books. For better or worse, I could not afford a title of this kind: it might sell books, but it would have been against my better judgment.

Washington – London
July 1984

1 *Angst?*

'Why do you assume that ten or twenty years from now we shall be alive? My friends and I firmly believe that the end is near.' The conversation took place close to midnight in a little car on the autobahn near Kassel. My interlocutor, a graduate technology student, had kindly agreed to drive me to the hotel from the home of his father, a classmate of mine whom I had not seen for many years. I said, if I remember correctly, that while my own life experiences had not been such as to make me an incurable optimist, I saw no plausible reason to agree with him and his friends.

In the weeks and months that followed, touring in Western Germany, I often heard similar views, usually from young people, but also among older ones. At church meetings the general theme these days more often than not is 'We are afraid' or 'Be afraid'. Helmut Schmidt, the former chancellor, entitled his New Year editorial in *Die Zeit*: 'Don't be afraid', and the choice was quite obviously not made for theological reasons only. In the showcases of bookshops such titles as *The German Neuroses*, *The German House is on Fire*, *The Fears of the Germans* are displayed, as well as novels describing the destruction of West Germany as seen from the government air-raid shelter somewhere in the Eiffel mountains. Anxiety, like sex and archaeology, seems to be a good seller. Fear has entered the language of the young generation – '*kaputt*', 'no future', '*unheimlich*', '*verunsichert*' are among the most frequently used words. Articles in newspapers announce that there is great fear of unemployment, but also fear of too much leisure. There is fear of a nuclear holocaust but also of economic and ecological disaster and a general breakdown. Nothing functions any more. *Der Spiegel*, the widely read weekly, reports that 1.8 million alcoholics have been counted in Germany and there are 2 million cases of cardiac neuroses. There is more free-floating aggression than ever before; many telephone booths are destroyed every day. More Germans talk about emigrating than ever. More young people take hard drugs. There are more suicides than ever and more bankruptcies. Endangered species of plants number 822, and 150,000 hares were killed last year on the superhighways. In short, there is an all-pervasive fear, a free-floating anxiety, the assumption that everything that could go wrong will in fact go wrong. Among writers, painters and film-makers fear is definitely in, and theologians talk about little else. The ancient Greeks had gods personifying fear (Phobos and Deimos); so had the Romans (Pavor and Pallor, who were related to Mars, the god of war). If Germans still believed in polytheism, they would surely have a cult of fear, would erect statues to these gods and pay tribute to them.

According to the journalists and writers, Germany in the 1980s is a fear-ridden country. Fear, of course, means different things; it is part of the human condition; was there ever a totally fearless individual or group of people? It is quite likely, furthermore, that without some fear, no species would have survived over the centuries and the millennia. But there is a difference between what Freud and others called *Realangst* and hypochondria. If it were true that more people commit suicide in Germany every year – and more than in other countries – this would be an important, though not necessarily conclusive, indicator. But a look at the statistical yearbook shows that the number of suicides has actually gone down in recent years; in some other European countries, Switzerland and Hungary, for instance, it is higher. More Germans may talk about emigration, but fewer are actually emigrating. There is a curious perception gap: people think that others are unhappy. When asked whether they themselves were more or less content, the answer of some 79 per cent of all Germans was in the affirmative. But when asked whether they thought others reasonably content, less than 50 per cent thought so.

But are these fears not justified? Is it not true that for the first time in history mankind has the potential to destroy itself, to undo the creation? True, but this does not explain German anxieties either. Why should young Germans be more aware of the danger than others, more certain that the worst is bound to happen? Are they politically more sophisticated and far-sighted, are they more highly ethically motivated than others, is their desire for survival more strongly developed than that of the youth of other nations? There are peace movements and ecological groups in many other countries, but nowhere has the resonance been as strong.

The riddle remains. Pacifism in England, in the United States and in some of the smaller European countries has been strong for generations and not just in the ranks of the official peace movements. Poor Neville Chamberlain has entered the history books as an arch-appeaser, and it is usually forgotten that the great majority of Britons thought like him right up to the outbreak of the war. In Holland, as well as Scandinavia, neutralism and pacifism are also deeply engrained. But in Germany the pacifist tradition has been less developed than in almost any other country. On the contrary, Germany was the *locus classicus*, the land of heroism and hero worship and a heroic lifestyle, of Siegfried and of the martyrs of the war of liberation against Napoleon, of the trumpets of Vionville and Mars-la-Tour (the famous battles in the war of 1870–71), of the heroes of the First World War such as Baron von Richthofen and Otto Weddingen, the submarine captain. Their names and their deeds have inspired generations of young Germans, their exploits described in hundreds and thousands of books and in films. Could it be that the pendulum had swung back from Nietzsche and Wagner to the other extreme, that there had been a delayed shock reaction to the events of the Second World War? This would imply that the German trauma has been much deeper than elsewhere and that others have suffered less, a proposition not easy to maintain. Furthermore, it has not been the generation which lived through these events that reacted with so much anxiety, but the subsequent ones for whom these disasters are only a distant recollection, and who are inclined therefore to use terms such as 'holocaust', 'Gestapo' or 'fascism' rather freely and usually out of context. Some of them have persuaded themselves in recent years that only Germany and the German people will be destroyed in the coming nuclear war, and that the rest of the world will somehow survive. These are unlikely propositions, to put it mildly, but then there is no reasoning with fear which, as Descartes once put it, is a state of the soul which obstructs resistance to the evil which is believed to be near. In German history there has been a tendency to overreact: could it be that the present intense pacifism is a reaction to the lack of pacifism in the past?

Such an explanation would make sense but for the fact that the fears and the anxiety concern not just nuclear war but attach themselves to a great many other topics – anxiety about the future in general, inflation, unemployment, life in the big cities, and even the hares killed on the autobahn. The dangers of nuclear war alone cannot account for this free-floating fear.

One day, not long ago, I had the opportunity to watch some of the best-known leaders of the German 'Greens' in action: gifted people arguing their case heatedly and persuasively. What struck me most about their performances, however, was their excitement and shrillness; they seemed to be driven by some inner demons. One could make a plausible case for such behaviour on the part of someone deeply convinced that the end of the world was near; it would clearly be inhuman to expect inner harmony and moderation, let alone a sense of humour, in such circumstances. How could one react but with shrillness *vis-à-vis* opponents too obtuse to understand the enormity of the peril? But was it the right explanation? Perhaps in another age these people would have fought with equal grimness for another cause; perhaps they would have been driven by other anxieties. Some weeks later I happened to be looking at some of the pictures of Germany's greatest painter, Albrecht Dürer. One is a famous portrait (of Oswald Krell); art historians have drawn attention to his staring eyes, the tension and unease (very much in contrast to the serenity exuding from the portraits painted by Dürer's Italian contemporaries!). Here was a man on the verge of a nervous breakdown.[1] Oswald Krell had every reason to be tense and fearful. Other pictures of the period, those of Hans Holbein for instance, provide at least part of the answer. The world of medieval man – and little changed in this respect in the fifteenth and sixteenth centuries – was a cosmos of gloom and doom. There was the all-pervasive fear of sudden death; the *memento mori in media vita* motive returns time and again in these drawings. There was the fear of pestilence and that horrible new scourge, syphilis. In a letter from Venice, Dürer wrote that he was more afraid of syphilis than anything else. There was the fear of war and civil war, of great fires and floods, the fear of failing to get one's daily bread, the fear of eternal damnation, invoked by itinerant preachers. There was an enormous receptivity for signs from heaven: stars fell from the skies, strange comets appeared, horribly shaped animals were born. There was great ferment among town dwellers and peasants alike, and the authorities were blamed for the many disasters. All these signs pointed to one end:

[1] Kenneth Clark, *Civilization, a Personal View* (London 1982), p. 108

8

the coming of the Antichrist, the appearance of the four horsemen of the apocalypse, the end of the world.

Such visions of the end of the world go back a long time – the old Nordic sagas describe the twilight of the gods in minute detail: how the vibrations of the world tree announced the end, how the sun darkened and eternal winter set in, how the good gods such as Wotan and Baldur were killed and the evil Surter set the whole world on fire, and how eventually the continents disappeared in the sea and the globe was consumed by fire.

These old pagan myths survived in various forms throughout the Christian era, their traces can be detected in many popular tales and superstitions. The other source for the visions of the end was the Christian eschatological tradition which had reached a peak in the early Middle Ages but later lost much of its impact. The year 1000 had come and gone but the world had not come to an end. The church authorities always had their misgivings with regard to this kind of literature and its latter-day advocates and interpreters. The New Testament said, 'But of that day or that hour no one knows, not even the angels in heaven, nor the Son, only the Father' (Mark 13: 32). The church establishment therefore took a dim view of the enthusiasts who pretended to be on more intimate terms with God and have more reliable information about the date of the last judgment.

The age of the Reformation brought a new upsurge of apocalyptic fears: the world was corrupt and punishment would be meted out soon; the various books of revelation were rediscovered. Gog and Magog were conjured up; Sebastian Franck, the great chronicler, wrote: 'I realize that the world is finished' (*Germaniae Chronicon*). Martin Luther, a child of his time, was one of the great believers in the apocalypse and he provided specific information with regard to the date of the last judgment. The predictions varied. On one occasion he said that the world would last no more than a hundred years; on another that the present pope would be the last to be elected; on a third that 'this year's wine was the last we shall be drinking'. 'The world cannot much longer last', Luther told his confidants; 'In our camp there is *summa ingratitudo* and *contemptus verbi* [meaning the word of God]; among the Popists *sanguis et blasphemia*. This is the last straw [*Das wird dem fass den poden ausstossen* . . .].' In November 1540 Luther predicted that the end would come before the following summer; on another occasion he dreamed that it would come on the commemoration of the conversion of

St Paul. These various dates passed uneventfully, the sentence had apparently been suspended for a little while, the ways of Providence were after all inscrutable.

Luther was genuinely afraid but he also put his fear to good use spreading his gospel. As one of his opponents put it:

> Luther believed that by frightening his audiences he would attract them more easily to the new doctrine and this is why he talked so much about the Last Judgment and the coming of the Antichrist. . . . If the wind blew hard, if a tempest made for high waves in the sea, this was obviously a sign that the Day of Judgment was approaching.[1]

Luther, to repeat once again, was merely a child of his time, he did not invent the fears but merely expressed them. The fear was all-pervasive; it appears in Dürer's apocalyptic drawings and the imitators of Dürer who illustrated so many editions of the Bible. It is reflected in the countless *Totentänze* by Holbein and others. Known and unknown writers and poets – even Hans Sachs, not a man ordinarily given to panic or despair – wrote plays in the same vein. Thousands of preachers and thousands of leaflets conveyed the message of *Dies irae, dies illa, solvet saeclum in favilla*, the medieval hymn according to which heaven and earth shall melt away on that wrathful day.

These sermons spread dejection but also helped to increase the resentment against all authority, the belief in astrological nonsense, and all kinds of revolutionary plots. But eventually, as one fatal date passed after another, and as life went on very much as before, doubts began to arise. The new leaflets were quite sarcastic. Where is the Day of the Lord? Why are we kept waiting so long for the Last Judgment? The preachers of fear reacted angrily against these 'Epicureans'. But ultimately they had to accept that the mere repetition of the old threats would result in diminishing psychological returns. 'Objectively' nothing much had changed, the world was still corrupt, men and women disregarded the word of God, authority was still hated, war, sickness, hunger, flood and other disasters still threatened Europe. But the belief waned that all this would bring about the end of the world. Fear did not disappear but it lost its immediacy and intensity.

The mood of impending disaster was not confined to Germany and the adjacent countries, but it was more palpably felt there than elsewhere. The Roman Church had not encouraged it, the Eastern

[1] Georg Wizel quoted in Jean Delumeaux, *La Peur en Occident* (Paris 1978,) p. 211

Church had rejected the apocalyptic propaganda altogether, which may help to explain why its impact in Russia and Eastern Europe has been small over the ages. In Germany, too, the apocalypse gradually lost its appeal, and in later ages Protestant theologians from Adolf von Harnack to Rudolf Karl Bultmann proposed to do away with eschatology altogether.

It was only in the 1960s that interest in apocalyptic moods became fashionable again: God was about to break the existing world order. Those beliefs spread among young people who had little if any contact with the established church. But as a theologian wrote: 'They have after all been brought up under the steady threat of a nuclear holocaust.'[1] Visions of the end became a frequent subject to be discussed from the pulpit, described in novels and depicted on the television screen. And just as clerics had taken a leading part in the sixteenth-century *émeutes de peur*, there were some who followed in their footsteps in the last third of the twentieth century.

The fact that the apocalyptic tradition has strong historical roots in Germany is of interest but by itself it does not explain the apocalyptic relapse which has taken place of late. There has been much less anxiety in (predominantly Catholic) Austria though it belongs to the same *Kulturkreis*. (According to the then fashionable theories – the Nazi past of the parents' generation – Austria should have been a hotbed of terrorism, but there was no terrorism at all.) How to explain it – just with reference to a cultural lag? By and large West Germany has not done badly since the Second World War. Its political system has withstood all strains and stresses so far and its economy, with all the problems that have arisen, is still the strongest in Europe. Its security is no more in jeopardy than that of any other European country. This being so, why should Germans complain about frustration and stress, about general listlessness and insecurity, more than anyone else? Why should there be so much talk about fear and anxiety?

Some have argued that German policy is held together only by economic success and that, in the absence of growing prosperity, the fabric of society may come apart. Others have stressed the lack of a collective identity, the partition of Germany. Yet others have claimed that it is the result of a world getting more complex and alien all the time, the feeling of being spiritually uprooted – and of a retreat into the

[1] Hugh Anderson, 'A future for Apocalyptic?' in *Biblical Studies* (essays in honour of William Barclay) (London 1976), pp. 56 *et seq*. and Klaus Koch, *The Rediscovery of Apocalyptic* (1970) *passim*

11

private sphere which paradoxically creates new fears. But most of these developments are by no means limited to Germany, and as for the specific German problems such as the partition of the country, all inquiries showed that they are not really uppermost in the mind of the young generation. These are grave problems but not of the kind likely to induce acute anxiety.

Few Italians, Frenchmen or Britons are likely to spend sleepless nights worrying about problems of collective identity. But even if this should be more of a problem in Germany, it remains to be shown whether it is not just an outward manifestation of a deeper *malaise*, and whether if this specific crisis were somehow resolved, anxiety would not find another outlet.

Much of the blame for the *Verunsicherung*, the loss of certainty, the spread of insecurity, has been put on the media. There is no denying that the German media – like those in other democracies – have tended to concentrate more often than not on the negative features of contemporary society. German intellectuals – and their impact on the media is considerable – see their vocation in being critics, not in being official laudators. The picture that frequently emerges from novels and news magazines, from television reports and movies, is a very dark one, almost an unmitigated chain of disasters. Everything seems to have failed in their unhappy country. If the kind of German society thus depicted were indeed 'social reality' as is frequently claimed, the deep despair would be only too intelligible. And there would be no particular reason to lament the impending destruction of such a misbegotten civilization: it hardly deserves to be preserved.

But it isn't 'social reality', it is only the product of a 'critical theory' which has gone overboard. There is in German history a tragic *esprit de l'escalier* of useful ideas turning up too late, and out of context. A few German Zolas would have done much good in the climate of self-satisfaction of the Wilhelminian age. But there were no Zolas when they were needed, only some Johnny-come-latelies now, so absorbed with their theories that they have failed to realize that the world around them has changed. They no longer face a surfeit of self-satisfaction but a world of insecurity, a world in need of a little encouragement and perhaps some occasional words of comfort.

This is part of the story, but it would be too facile to put all the responsibility on the opinion-makers and the media. Their negativism has not been helpful, but how important is it in the final account?

The impact of the 'critical' German film-makers on the broad public has been minimal and for every highbrow critical account of the state of the nation there are half a dozen stories with happier endings in the popular media. Even if the German media are perhaps a little more negative than those elsewhere, what prevented the public from shrugging off distortions and horror stories? Could it be that there is a predisposition to be told that all is bad and that the end is near?

There seems to be an inclination to expect the worst among this unquiet people. They have always found it difficult to enjoy life: they have acted as pioneers in many directions but never in the field of *savoir vivre*. Being perfectionists their achievements seldom match their expectations; if they do not score a complete success they are quick to assume utter failure. 'O brother,' (to quote *Titus Andronicus*) 'speak with possibilities, And do not break into these deep extremes.' It is difficult to imagine a more un-German saying. For it is precisely this inclination towards the extreme, this drift away from superficial common sense, from acceptance of banal realities to probing depths, often fathomless, which has been the great strength of German cultural endeavour in ages past, and the fatal weakness of German politics.

True, German politics have been conducted with an infinitely greater measure of common sense than at any other time in the recent history of the country. But deep down there still seem to be the same old anxieties, the intensity, the fear of failure, the inability to relax, the difficulty of keeping things in proportion. This is the kind of mental attitude in which molehills become mountains, and major problems insoluble. Italians, Frenchmen and the British have a great many reasons to be unhappy about the state of affairs in their respective countries. But the *Sinnkrise*, the cultural crisis besetting European culture, will not be among their main worries, nor are they preoccupied with the question of collective identity. They know who they are, or they think they do – not for them the constant German probing of their *Selbstverständnis*, their self image. As for the *Sinnkrise*, they usually argue that it has gone on for a couple of hundred years, that the prospects for finding an answer in the near future are small. If so, why not accept what cannot be changed in any case?

But the Germans do not want to accept it. They seem to feel the shortcomings of their society more acutely than others, they suffer more from abstract and metaphysical pains than other less philo-sophically minded nations. They want to know where they have come from and what their ultimate destiny will be. They want not just relative prosperity and relative security and justice and freedom and equality – they want them now and they want them *tout court*. They are still great lovers of the absolute and since, in an imperfect world, it may not be possible to attain total prosperity and security, they feel poor and insecure and unfree, living in an unjust and unequal society.

It would be tempting to end at this point, but it would also be misleading. For what has been established so far is that some Germans talk and write more, and more loudly, about fear and anxieties than others.[1] But the depth and the intensity of the fears remain to be investigated, and also the extent to which people suffer from these fears. Do all Germans suffer, or some, or many? And at this point doubts begin to set in. The psychologists have done their best to work out scales to measure fear but they will be the first to admit that their reliability is questionable. Public opinion polls have shown that almost 80 per cent are more or less happy with their situation; among the young generation, positive attitudes towards the present political system are actually stronger in Germany than in any other country.[2] Where then does one find the great horror, the *mysterium tremendum*, the impending feeling of total destruction? One will look in vain for people suffering the agonies of Tantalus in the department stores or the football grounds or the swimming pools of Munich or Hamburg. One will not find it among the people in the streets, the buses and the railways of contemporary Germany.[3] The mood of the crowds and the individuals seem to be like everywhere else; some are obviously happier than

---

[1] The terms fear, anxiety, hysteria and hypochondria have been used interchangeably as various forms of neurotic behaviour. Greater precision should have been used but unfortunately little is known about their etiology and there is no agreement about their definition. As the author of a recent standard work on hysteria put it: though it has been known since time immemorial, it has been next to impossible to portray it; like a globule of mercury, it escapes the grasp.

[2] *The Young Europeans* (EEC, Brussels 1983)

[3] A recent comparative study on *Patterns of European Diagnoses and Prescriptions* by Bernie O'Brien (London 1984) reaches the conclusion that 'it is noticeable that the Germans represent the European paragon of mental stability, being the only nation not to register neuroses as a leading diagnosis' (p. 9). This is very much in contrast to Britain and France which score very high on anxiety and neuroses. But once prescriptions are scrutinized the picture changes: German doctors prescribe far more tranquillizers despite the alleged absence of neuroses than their British colleagues (Digitalis is prescribed more than ten times as often, and also much more frequently than in the United States). German doctors hold the European record for producing diagnoses and prescriptions. This may be in part the result of the German system of administering medicine in which the physician is paid according to 'action' taken following the patient's visit. But it is also connected with German patients' expectations: a visit to the doctor must result in one (or several) diagnoses and in one (or more) prescriptions.

14

others, but this again should come as no great surprise.

Perhaps in our quest for the great fear we have looked in the wrong places. But one does not see and hear it among the politicians in Bonn either, nor in the churches (hard as some Protestants are trying) or trade unions. The students do not seem particularly dejected either, and even at the very demonstrations where the 'We are afraid' banners are displayed, one feels no particular accumulation of stress, tension and anxiety over and above the so-called normal strains and stresses. In fact, many people seem to enjoy the occasion, the togetherness, the solidarity in the battle for a good cause.

Thus the casual visitor from far away is likely to conclude that the great fear is nothing more than yet another manifestation of radical chic, *Literatengeschwätz* – the idle prattle and the attitudinizing of some journalists and littérateurs who have run out of other subjects of conversation. Or, if he has an interest in collective psychology he may regard it as a form of abreaction, of catharsis: if the confession of misbehaviour relieves so many people, the talk about fear may have a similar function, providing a release, reducing the feeling of isolation.

There is some truth in these observations and comments. *Fin de siècle* and *fin de millénaire* moods are cultivated and sometimes used for political ends. There is nothing new and startling in this: apocalyptic fears (and hopes) have been exploited for a long time. But it is a general feeling of insecurity rather than some deep *Urangst* causing sudden horror and panic, an insecurity for which there are many good reasons given the tenuous character of human existence in general and the present state of the world in particular. Why have there been demonstrations in Germany bigger than elsewhere, why has a 'Green' party emerged only in this country? Perhaps because this country more than others needs order and certainties. Does past history alone explain this strong need? One cannot answer this with total assurance. But it seems about as close as one can get to an understanding as we set out on our exploration of the mood of present-day Germany.

But the mood of a country like that of an individual is given to change. When I began to write this book there was much talk about the omnipresent, paralysing fear; because of nuclear war, of economic and ecological crisis and for a dozen other valid reasons. As I finish, the demonstrations have ceased, the Greens are in disarray, the last houses in Berlin that had been seized by the rebels of the welfare state are surrendered to the police, and even normally sceptical captains of industry and banking declare that the prospects for the coming years are less than catastrophical. Only yesterday many voices had prophesied that the stationing of Cruise and Pershing missiles would lead to an unprecedented deterioration in relations between the two Germanies, perhaps to a final rupture. But the skies did not fall in: in fact, relations had never been so cordial as in the months after; West German politicians from the Left and from the Right hurried to East Germany and were handsomely received. East Germany received massive new credits and gave tens of thousands of permits to those of its citizens who wanted to move to the West. Even a new term was invented to describe the new improved relationship between the two Germanies – *Verantwortungsgemeinschaft*; a 'community of responsibility', one of those very German terms which sound impressive and whose meaning is quite unclear.

Objectively, little or nothing had changed: the threatening missiles were still stationed on both sides of the Iron Curtain, there was still disaffection and insecurity among the young generation, and the basic economic problems had not been solved. The wall opposite the Reichstag mentioned at the very beginning of this report had become a little higher: from a mere 9 feet it had grown, I was told, to 15 feet. But both sides played it down: it was said to be a purely technical change without any political significance. Perhaps so, the new mood is certainly more upbeat, there is much talk about German unity in the air, a vision much at variance with yesterday's 'no future'. How long will the new optimism last, and will it not be followed by another wave of dejection? These changes in mood are bound, of course, to continue; they have to be registered and taken seriously – but not too seriously as if each constituted a radical new departure and would last for ever.

2 *Lukanga Mukara* or Germany Revisited

When the members of the German youth movement met round their campfires in the 1920s they listened to readings from their cult books: Rainer Maria Rilke's *Cornet* for example, or Hermann Hesse's *Zarathustra's Return*. These are still read today, albeit not with the same intensity and faith. But there was yet another book, equally popular but now forgotten and waiting for its resurrection: *Lukanga Mukara*.

Written a few years before the outbreak of the First World War, it described in a series of letters the impressions of an emissary from an East African tribe sent by his chieftain to Imperial Germany. The idea and even the technique were not exactly new: Montesquieu's *Lettres Persanes* are probably the best known example of the genre. It is not one of the *chefs-d'œuvre* of world literature, but its entertainment value was beyond question. Lukanga Mukara was perplexed by the habits of the Germans, most of which he found strange and sometimes very funny. Why had everyone to work in order to be happy? Why did they walk about with a watch, permanently under pressure, why did they have to count everything and to write each other perfectly unnecessary letters? Why did they have to travel much of the time from one place to another without any cogent reason? The author, Hans Paasche, was a founder member of the movement for 'Life Reform', which favoured abstinence, no smoking and vegetarianism. Paasche, who had served with the navy in Africa, was killed soon after the war by the *Freikorps*, the paramilitary bands of the extreme Right.[1]

[1] He was, in other words, a precursor of the present-day 'Green movement'. His book is now exceedingly rare: the only copy I found in the US was a microfilm in the Library of Congress. It bore a stamp which showed that it had originally been in the main archive of the NSDAP, the Nazi party. Since then I have seen pirated copies of the book (*Raubdrucke*) printed in post-war Germany and I have been told that Paasche's heirs have sued the publishers. Some of the themes of Lukanga Mukara reappeared in the fairy-tale bestsellers of the 1970s such as Michael Ende's *Momo* (Stuttgart 1973).

A visit by Lukanga Mukara's grandson to post-industrial Germany would result in even greater confusion. Even the few certainties reported by his grandfather no longer exist. The German tribes, though normally not nomadic, have moved a few hundred kilometres to the west: so has their capital. It is no longer a global tribe, no cultural Mecca. He would find the new Germany smaller than Norway or Finland (or Gambia or the Ivory Coast); its biggest city is no larger than Ahmadabad or Guadalajara. All but a few of the city centres which Lukanga Mukara the Elder knew have disappeared, some as the result of the air-raids of the Second World War, others through the activities of city developers. If Lukanga Mukara the Third would like to get a feeling of the old, the real, Germany, seen by his grandfather, he would have to tour East Germany, or perhaps some of the smaller towns near the Eastern border which, being off the beaten track, have changed less than the rest.

Lukanga Mukara the Elder had many stories to tell about the German villages. The grandson in his quest for the German peasant would have to search for a long time. There are far fewer of them, their lifestyle has changed more radically in the last seventy years than in the preceding seven hundred. The old-style *Dorf* has all but disappeared. Like a Western anthropologist in his quest for a vanishing African tribe, Lukanga III would have to hurry to see some of the surviving species. 'Bonn' is not 'Weimar' according to a well-known essay published in the 1950s. Equally, Germany is no longer Germany, and while it is true that all countries have greatly changed since the early years of the century Germany has changed more than most. Changed in what way?

Its ten biggest cities at the beginning of the century were (more or less in this order) Berlin, Hamburg, Munich, Cologne, Leipzig, Dresden, Essen, Breslau, Frankfurt and Dortmund (or Düsseldorf). This order, broadly speaking, still applies, but Berlin is divided down the middle; Breslau has changed its name and now belongs to Poland; Leipzig and Dresden are in East Germany. A wall has been built to emphasize this point.

A closer look brings further surprises: Essen was Krupp, Ruhrkohle and Ruhrgas, heavy industry, the capital of the Ruhr, the armoury of the Reich. Krupp and most other firms are still in Essen, but not a single ton of steel is produced in this town. For old historical Berlin one has to look beyond the Wall, but there is hardly anything left there either. The inner parts of Hamburg, Cologne or Munich have changed even though some of the destroyed buildings have been faithfully reconstructed. The suburbs are largely new. The 'old' *Ratskeller*, more likely than not, was rebuilt twenty years ago and, next door, Mr McDonald is selling his hamburgers. Not only have the cities changed, but their inhabitants have too. Once upon a time Wedding and Gesundbrunnen and (to a lesser extent) Kreuzberg were the heart of working-class Berlin, the Berlin of communist demonstrations, quarters which before 1933 the SA did not dare enter. It was the Berlin of the painter of working-class life, Heinrich Zille. Today it is Little Ankara.

If Lukanga were to get lost in Frankfurt's inner city, near the main railway station for instance, a knowledge of German might not be of much help; there are schools in this city in which only one child out of ten speaks German at home. Ironically, some of these schools are within a few hundred yards of 23 Grosser Hirschgraben, where Germany's greatest writer was born and lived for the first sixteen years of his life.

When Germany was mentioned abroad in Lukanga's time, what were the first, the most frequent, the obvious, associations? 'Alt Heidelberg, dear city with honours crowned and rare', the Lorelei, factories covered with soot, the Prussia of militarism and large estates, Nuremberg, the jewel casket of Dürer, the *Meistersinger* and gingerbread; St Nicholas and German Christmas; Black Forest cuckoo clocks, the casinos of Baden-Baden, the palaces and parks of Potsdam, the wines of the Moselle valley, the German forest complete with Hansel and Gretel and the old witch, old castles (some of them in ruins), romantic views, the country of *Dichter und Denker* and, above all, composers; a mill by a rivulet, sausages and sauerkraut.

It was, of course, a gross simplification but still vaguely rooted in reality, a reality which those now under sixty will know only from stories they were told, or from books and exhibitions. The sausages are still sold, wine is still grown along the Moselle and the Rhine, the Black Forest has not disappeared and Christmas is still celebrated. But pre-war Germany has gone for ever.

Some years ago I took part in a conference near Bonn, in the same hotel in which Hitler and Chamberlain had met on the eve of the Munich conference. The proceedings, as so often on such occasions, were not very exciting, and I was looking out of the window scanning the river, peaceful to be sure, but a dirty grey. My neighbour, an old gentleman named Staudinger who had followed my glance, whispered that when he had studied in Bonn – had it been in 1900 or the year after? – the Rhine had been blue, at least on certain days.

My own first memories date back to a much later period, but there are similar impressions of changed scenery: a vivid recollection of walking in the forest, of a specific smell which I no longer find, of wild strawberries, of mushrooms, of bilberries which tasted quite differently from the ones now commercially grown. It is difficult not to sympathize with the intentions of the ecologists even though they tend so often to be foolish. They complain not only about lead and cadmium in Germany's rivers (which is justified), they are also saddened by the disappearance of the aurochs and certain rare eagles, even though these lovely animals have not been around for a long time now. The climate changes, as does nature. If some species vanish, new ones tend to appear. The beaver, the lynx and the mountain ibex have actually been revived in Germany, the rivers have been cleaned up, fish have returned to places where they were not to be found for many years.

But it also seems true that wild flowers once very common have become rare. Only yesterday the fields were full of red poppies and blue cornflowers; what popular love song did not mention them? There were plenty of forget-me-nots, marguerites, broom and gorse. They have not disappeared altogether, but the boy Goethe mentioned in one of the most famous poems of the German language would have to look hard and for a long time to find a rockrose (the *Heideröslein*).

The big cities have not grown any larger in recent decades. On the contrary, there has been a movement out of the inner cities to the suburbs as in other industrialized countries. Satellite towns have come into existence, some at a considerable distance from the centre. Almost everyone has a car, which is to say that nature is never far away. On a fine summer weekend there is a mass exodus out of Hamburg to the Ostsee, and out of Munich to the lakes and the mountains. But 50 per cent of the population still live in 7 per cent of the total area, the big conurbations. And those who leave the cities for a few days will not venture far from railway and car, from camping sites and ski-lifts.

Once upon a time Germany was the country *par excellence* of sentimental voyagers; Sterne had coined the term but the Romantics popularized it. City dwellers of the plains, they discovered the beauty of the mountains which previously had been regarded as a nuisance, making life difficult for travellers. The Romantics were ecstatic about ruins of old castles, they called the Bamberg Dom a 'symphony in stone', they also discovered the German forest. Willibald Alexis, a post-Romantic, wrote in a travelogue that the quality of a forest was understood more fully in Germany than elsewhere. Madame de Staël was not a Romantic and Mark Twain even less so. But the former was deeply impressed by the utter silence in nature, and the latter compared the darkness of the forest to the interior of a church. Such silence still existed when I was a child even though Germany was criss-crossed by a network of railway lines and highroads. But one could still walk for hours in certain parts without meeting a single human being and without hearing a sound but that of the birds in the sky, the wind and perhaps the rain. There were few aeroplanes, they did not fly at night and did not make much noise.

Among the few books I took with me when I left Germany, less than a year before the outbreak of the Second World War, was Mr Baedeker's guidebook. It is a book of great wisdom, a mine of information; it induced me in later years to collect old editions of Baedekers on various countries. It is also a deeply conservative book as I discovered when a little while ago I bought the most recent volume (1983) covering West Germany. The very first sentences reminded me of something I had read before:

> Germany is a land of infinite variety extending from the mountains to the sea, from the Bavarian alps down to the low plains bordering the North Sea and the Baltic. . . . Many small provincial towns remote from the traffic of the machine age, still preserve the aspect of a bygone era. In the north, old brick buildings testify to the wealth of the Hanseatic League that once commanded the seas. The old towns of Central and South Germany, free cities of the empire or seats of princes and bishops, still have splendid cathedrals, palaces and town halls of a stone architecture whose style betrays the change of the times in outlook and economic conditions.

This text has not changed for decades. The Empire, the Republic, the Hitlers have come and gone, borders have changed, the wayfarer will look in vain for a single room costing eight marks in the Berlin *Adlon* or *Kaiserhof* – in fact he will not find either hotel, hard as he may try. But Mr Baedeker still tells us about 'diverse kinds of settlement', the isolated farmhouse and the old Germanic 'grouped village', the stately castles and the walled towns. Baedeker, of course, does not lie. Germany still is a land of great variety, replete with isolated farmhouses, castles and old churches. Mountains and rivers are still there, average summer temperature, average snowfall and the time of apple blossom have not significantly changed. The mean average monthly temperature is still 51 degrees Fahrenheit compared with 50 in Britain and 57 in the US; average annual rainfall is still 26 inches compared with 42 in the US and 23 in Britain. But almost everything else has changed, even the administrative structure, something not easily done in such an orderly society.

The *Bundesrepublik* consists of eleven *Länder*. With the exception of Bavaria, and the two city states of Hamburg and Bremen, they are all new creations. The status of West Berlin is different again. Germany is a federal republic, the *Länder* have much wider authority than the administrative regions had in the past. The Allies wanted to create a counterweight to the centralist tendency in government which had been so strong ever since Bismarck. This has created some problems, mainly of inequality. Some *Länder* are rich, others relatively poor. But on the whole the new set-up has worked.

In the 1920s Hans Grimm wrote *Volk ohne Raum*, a mammoth novel which forcefully made the point that Germany was overpopulated and needed colonies – preferably in Africa. The title of the novel became an important political slogan, and the belief in overpopulation was shared by many who were in no sense followers or admirers of Adolf Hitler. Germany, like Ireland, was a country of emigrants *par excellence*. Some six million left their homeland during the nineteenth century, mainly for the United States. When Grimm wrote his novel the density of population was about 170 per square kilometre. Today it is in excess of 250 but there have been few complaints about overpopulation. In fact, the density of population in the new Germany is even greater than these figures suggest. In large parts of the country such as the North German plain or in South-East Germany it remains as low as ever (20–50 inhabitants per square kilometre) whereas in the big conurbations known as RRU (Rhine Ruhr), RMA (Rhine Main), SX (Stuttgart), HH (Hamburg), M (Munich) and RNE (Rhine-Neckar) it is about 1,500 per square kilometre. In these conurbations, which also include the Nuremberg and Hanover regions, the Saar and Bremen, almost half the people of West Germany make their homes.

Between 1945 and 1973 the population of Germany increased from 46 to 62 million, partly as the result of one of the great migration waves in modern history, the influx of millions of refugees from Eastern Europe and East Germany, and also because of the arrival of some four million 'guest workers'. Natural growth, once the post-war 'baby boom' had passed, steadily declined. Since 1971 there have been more deaths than births, and since 1974 the population has decreased in absolute figures from 62 to 61.5 million. The German birthrate is about the lowest in Europe; if the decline continues the total population will have fallen below the 60 million mark and the two Germanies taken together will constitute no more than 7.8 per cent of Europe's total including the Soviet Union by the year 2000. Within the big conurbations, there has been a significant movement from the centre to the periphery. While the populations of Hamburg and Lübeck have declined, there has been a substantial increase in the number of people living in between these two cities. The population in the area around Munich, say about 50 kilometres in each direction, has grown substantially. The picture is the same virtually everywhere.

Present-day Germany is no longer a country of young people; more than 75 per cent of the population is over eighteen years of age. In certain regions such as West Berlin and the spas (Baden-Baden), as well as the resorts in the foothills of the Alps (Garmisch and Berchtesgaden), the presence of an aged population is even more striking. As the result of the territorial changes in 1945 the numerical ratio between the confessions has been affected. The old Germany had been predominantly Protestant, but immediately after the war there was a Catholic majority. The number of Protestants increased again following the arrival of expellees from the East. But the difference between the confessions is less felt now than in the past. Few Germans would be able to give the correct answer – except by accident – if asked whether Ludwig Erhard, the second chancellor, was Catholic or Protestant. (His father was Catholic but he was educated in the Protestant faith of his mother.) The statistics about membership in religious communities do not however tell us much about the intensity of religious belief. Church attendance is lower now than before the war.

Like my contemporaries I grew up in the belief that the great majority of Germans were either workers or peasants. Such belief was solidly rooted in fact. Working-class neighbourhoods dominated the scene in the north and the east of my home town as in many other German cities. True, there was also the army of the unemployed – congregating in the streets, in front of labour exchanges, political party headquarters and newspaper offices, endlessly discussing or just waiting, a sad and disquieting sight. After 1933 they disappeared and a great many uniforms took their place.

'Working class' was not just a statistical term, it was a way of life: these neighbourhoods had their specific sights, smells and even noises. Before my departure I worked for some months in a modern textile factory, and there too no strong gifts of observation were needed to realize that there were pronounced class differences. It immediately appeared in the way the workers dressed both during work and afterwards. Some mechanics probably owned a car, but I never came across one who did. There were richer and poorer villages, but by and large, despite the introduction of electricity, there was still much of what Marx had called the idiocy of rural life.

What was true with regard to the class structure of the German people in the 1920s is no longer true to day. The number of manual workers in the present area of the *Bundesrepublik* was almost 16 million in 1925. It is now below 12 million and in some fields the decline has been even more striking, quite apart from the fact that many of the manual workers are no longer Germans. In the 1960s the number of those employed in coalmining declined by more than half. Most pronounced was the fall in the number of those employed in agriculture. In 1850, the year my paternal grandfather was born, 85 per cent of the population of Germany worked on the land. Even between the two world wars and immediately after the second it was still 25 per cent. It is now 6 per cent – between 1960 and 1980 the number was halved, falling from 3.9 to 1.7 million. Even the current figure may not give an accurate picture, for the species 'agricultural worker' has all but disappeared. Farming is carried out almost exclusively by the owners and their families; wives and children help but on a part-time basis only. Other employment has grown. In 1933 the term 'tertiary sector' had not yet been invented even though the thing itself did, of course, exist. Even when my father was born so few people were engaged in administration of one sort or another that the concept did not figure in the social statistics. It first appeared towards the turn of the century. Today the tertiary sector employs more people than industry, and this applies not only to the country at large but to all big cities, including industrial centres like Hamburg, Düsseldorf (the 'secretariat of the Ruhr'), Munich, Cologne and Stuttgart. In 1950 about a million people were employed by the central government, the municipalities and local councils in various administrative capacities. By the mid 1970s their number had more than doubled and this trend in all likelihood will continue.

These figures have been adduced to prove different, sometimes diametrically opposed, theses. According to some there has been a general levelling, large sections of the working class have, in fact, acquired the income and the lifestyle of the lower middle class. Others, on the contrary, argue that German society is still far from equal, class conflicts still exist and will continue.

These issues can be discussed *ad infinitum*. Only the blind could fail to see the difference between the homes of the very rich in, say Blankenese or Harvestehude (in Hamburg), Sollin (a wealthy suburb in Munich) or Berlin-Grunewald, on one hand, and on the other in the Kreuzberg section of Berlin. Few manual workers or their wives will be seen in the most expensive boutiques of Munich or Hamburg, in the luxury restaurants or on private yachts by the shores of the North Sea or the Baltic Sea. But it is equally true that social class in the traditional sense has become less important than in the past. Even residential area is no longer a reliable class indicator. Millionaires are still unlikely to pick Wolfsburg (vw) or Siemensstadt (in Berlin) or Gelsenkirchen as their place of residence. (But local elections show that the Right by no means always polls its greatest majorities in well-to-do neighbour-hoods.) Few workers retire to Starnberg or Bad Homburg. But an attempt to classify people according to the car they drive or the suits they wear, or their hobbies, or their summer holidays, may lead to wrong conclusions. The cultural and social distance between a British factory worker and general manager is infinitely greater. They frequently speak a different language, they are not even interested in the same sports. The differences in lifestyle in the 'socialist' countries and, *a fortiori*, the Third World, are more marked than in 'capitalist' Germany.

There are substantial differences in wealth and income between various sections of society and also, incidentally, between various regions. Relative purchasing power is about half in the poorer agricultural areas of the Eifel, in the Bavarian forest, and in the low-population-density districts near the border with East Germany, in comparison with Stuttgart, Frankfurt or Hamburg. But the differences are still less pronounced than, for instance, those between the South of England and the North.

I had frequently stayed in German villages as a boy; my maternal grandfather owned a mill and a granary. He was on friendly terms with

25

many peasants in the vicinity, we were invited to their homes, we brought them presents at Christmas. But we were also the recipients of geese and chickens, and baskets of apples and plums. On some summer holidays I went, for whatever it was worth, to help with the harvest. The German village, as I knew it, had its own specific sights and smells, a mixture, not unpleasant, of dunghill, stable, of bread freshly baked, apples stored under the roof. The peasants were people of few words, sometimes stolid, their fashion of dressing (and even more markedly that of their women) was at least a generation or two out of date. They were almost wholly preoccupied with their own work and did not greatly care about what went on in the big cities. They aged early, frequently they suffered from a variety of crippling diseases, despite the alleged advantages of work in the open. One of the reasons was, no doubt, that they had to work very hard indeed. In later years I had a chance to compare manual work in agriculture and industry. I found the latter often monotonous but seldom as strenuous as carrying sacks weighing 200 pounds, spending hours kneeling or bending down, planting, weeding, reaping or digging eight to ten hours a day with spade or hoe. In later life I had little sympathy for gardeners extolling the virtues of work in the fields; there is a world of difference between a hobby and the real thing.

This then was the German village as I remember it, not, on the whole, a very joyful place. Many years were to pass before I again had the opportunity of seeing German agriculture at close range. Frequently I had seen rural landscapes, farms, grazing cattle and fruit trees from the window of a fast train, or looking out of a plane. I had heard about the new agricultural revolution, but I also knew that change in agriculture usually takes much longer than in industry. In short, I was quite unprepared for the shock that awaited me in a village between Kassel and the border with East Germany, where I spent part of a summer in the early 1960s. (The experience repeated itself in later years in other parts of Germany.) Rodenau (as I shall call it) was not particularly prosperous, yet my first and last impression was that the new German village had even less in common with its pre-war predecessor than the German town. The young men and women (and also their elders) were dressed exactly like their contemporaries in town, the shops had a surprisingly rich selection of goods, there were public callboxes at the corners, television aerials on every roof, car ownership was universal and many also had a truck or a van. Only two people in Rodenau still kept a horse, 'for the children', they explained. The backbreaking work is now done by machinery. I met one successful farmer, owner of a substantial herd of dairy cows, who confessed that he did not know how to milk a cow by hand. I could have shown him, but my knowledge was now irrelevant.

To choose another example. In nineteenth-century travelogues, the Lüneburg Heath appears as a poor, inhospitable region, inhabited only by savages and a few hungry ravens. Heinrich Heine compared it to the bosom of a lady of his acquaintance – flat and desolate. It is a very German landscape, it has been called rough, dreary and mournful. But the flowering heather covering the moorland, the pines, the junipers and the birch trees along the roads always had their admirers – the poet Hermann Löns, for example, who is buried here. He wrote the songs about this *wunderschöne Land* and *'Grün ist die Heide'* which was sung by three generations of young Germans and which, despite recent protestations about *Heimat-Kitsch*, will probably be remembered for some time to come. Until fairly recently much of this area was not even cultivated, it was the country of bees and above all of the moorland sheep. But most of the beehives have disappeared; once there were some 750,000 sheep, a few years ago only 10,000 were left. The heath has very much shrunk, part has become a nature reserve, visited by millions each year, another part a training ground for British tank units. One section is now a German Disneyland, complete with dolphins and real crocodiles. Inland tourism is the most important source of income.

Only a few people now work in agriculture, but those who do produce much more. The average size of an agricultural holding is now twice or more what it was, which may still be less than the optimal size. Agriculture has become scientific, it is no longer run according to custom and tradition. Some crops such as potatoes have declined, mainly because of dwindling demand. The output of most other agricultural products including milk, meat and even wheat has undergone a spectacular rise. High yields are now common in fruit, vegetable and wine growing. Far from being a *Volk ohne Raum*, there has been a growing tendency during the last thirty years to leave fields fallow which are perfectly fertile and on which wheat or other crops were grown in the past, simply because the owners have found better-paid work. In certain regions such as the Saar, the Spessart and the Taunus (to the north of Frankfurt) 10 per cent or more is now fallow

27

ground: grass and weeds cover these fields. For even if agriculture has become mechanized and is now run according to scientific principles, productivity was still three times higher in industry in 1970; annual productivity increase seems to be faster in agriculture but it still has far to go to catch up. The working day is longer in agriculture, there are no free weekends, and holidays can be arranged only with great difficulty. In these circumstances, and also in view of cheap agricultural imports from neighbouring EEC countries, the exodus from agriculture continues; furthermore, every second holding is run as a sideline. The Nazis (and not only they) dreamed about a renaissance of the peasantry which they regarded as the main pillar of society. Nazi ideology was based on the *Blut und Boden* concept, and they never really accepted the industrial revolution of the nineteenth century. But even Hitler eventually realized that agriculture was not a sufficient basis for creating enough wealth for a population of 65 million, let alone carrying out global dreams of conquest. Agriculture has not become unimportant and never will, but it is now an industry in which a few people can produce all that is needed.

The effects of the post-war agricultural revolution have been dramatic and far-reaching; the changes that have taken place – and continue to take place – in industry are probably in the long run even more important, but they have proceeded at a slower rate. Near the town in which I was born there were two major coal-producing regions. As a boy I frequently saw the miners streaming out of the pitheads at the end of their shift – dirty, tired, blinded by the sunlight after hours in darkness. I recall the great dumps of slag and rubbish, and on one occasion when a major disaster had occurred, hundreds of wives and children waiting, silently and anxiously – a scene out of *Germinal*. Not that much had changed since the heyday of the industrial revolution even though the miners were among the best-paid workers. It was still a dangerous, difficult and unappealing job. For many years Polish workers had been mobilized to work in the German mines; the same was true for the coalfields of Belgium and Northern France. By a strange quirk of history, for which I believe there is no satisfactory explanation, soccer prospered above all in the mining regions of Germany (as in France) in the 1920s and 1930s. The forward line of the leading clubs of the Ruhr such as *Schalke 04* and *Fortuna Düsseldorf* – which was frequently identical with the national team – read like the Warsaw telephone directory: Czepan, Kuzorra, Kobierski, Tibulski, and so on. This too has changed: *Schalke 04*, so often German champions, was relegated at one time from the *Bundesliga*. How have the mighty fallen – no one had ever heard of *Bayer Uerdingen* (a suburb of Krefeld) but it is now among the top eighteen, and what has become of yesteryear's heroes, of *Hertha BSC*, of *Holstein Kiel*, of *Spielvereinigung Fürth*, of *München 1860* and so on? There are still, or again, quite a few foreign names in the leading teams, but they are likely to be Yugoslav, Turkish or even Thai rather than Polish.

Coal production reached a high (128 million tons) just before the Second World War, it has since fallen to 80 million. It had been even higher in 1913, but this referred to the pre-First World War borders. Many mines have been exhausted and closed, other sources of energy are used and the mines which are still worked have been mechanized and the character of work has changed greatly. The production of iron ore has fallen even more sharply in the post-war period – from 19 million tons in 1960 to less than 3 million by the late 1970s. West Germany is still a major steel producer, though not in the same league as the United States, Japan and the Soviet Union. But the quantity of steel is no longer the yardstick for economic power. There is worldwide overproduction of steel, as new non-ferrous metals such as aluminium or synthetic materials have taken its place. Germany's largest aluminium plant was built after the war not in the Ruhr, the traditional industrial centre, but in southern Bavaria on the river Inn, near a new major water reservoir.

Only twenty-five years ago the Ruhr was described by travellers as something akin to an inferno with the horrible noise and smoke emanating from the factories, the satanic blast furnaces, people suffocating for want of air. The river Ruhr is now one of Germany's cleanest, and the mighty old industrial structures put up by Alfred Krupp, August Thyssen, Peter Klöckner, Hugo Stinnes and their contemporaries have been destroyed or become exhibits, museums for the history of industrial art. The Ruhr still houses the head offices and many of the biggest plants of West German industry. But for the location of the newer industries one has to turn to the south; they are found along the Rhine and the Rhine-Neckar axis. The chemical industry, needing a great deal of water, was always situated along this river, from Duisburg and Leverkusen (Bayer) in the north, to Höchst and Ludwigshafen (BASF) in the south. Once upon a time most of these giant corporations were part of IG Farben. The Allies decided that this trust had become too powerful and split it into several segments, none employing more than 10,000. Today each of them is bigger than the old IG Farben.

The old heavy industry – iron smelting, rolling and steel making – came into being in the Ruhr, and to a lesser extent in the Saar, mainly because of the presence of coal and ore and in view of the good communications system provided by the Rhine and the Saar. Today the raw materials needed by heavy industry are largely imported. Its location is therefore more a matter of choice, as it was in engineering and the electrical industry from the very beginning.

The early German car factories were in Frankfurt (Opel in Rüsselsheim) or in Stuttgart (Daimler-Benz) by historical accident – the founders happened to live there and opened their workshops there. Today the biggest plants are in Cologne (Ford) and in Wolfsburg near Hanover, sites chosen, no doubt, mainly for the availability of labour. For similar reasons BMW is now concentrated in or near Munich. The new electrical industry, and *a fortiori* high technology, is dispersed all over the country. When Emil Grundig opened his little plant with sixty employees shortly after the war, there was no particular reason why he should do so in Fürth (Nuremberg's sister town, and Henry Kissinger's birthplace) but for the fact that he happened to live there.

The most significant trend in the location of post-war German industry has been the migration to the medium-sized cities. Since the end of the war the traditional major industrial centres such as Essen, Duisburg or Gelsenkirchen have hardly grown or actually lost population. Small or medium-sized cities, on the other hand, have doubled or trebled their population. Ingolstadt on the Danube was a small town of some 28,000 inhabitants before the last war; once it had been a fortress and people went there mainly to admire its churches and the various fine examples of Bavarian Rococo. Today it counts three times as many inhabitants, with major oil refineries (Adria Pipeline), a major car plant (Audi) and other industries. Giessen and Oldenburg (once the capital of a Grand Duchy) were sleepy cities before the Second World War. Now their population has doubled and they house a variety of industries, almost all of them new. Before the war Göttingen had a well-known university: for two decades it was the Mecca of mathematicians and physicists from all over the world. As an industrial centre it did not exist. Today the number of inhabitants is 130,000, almost three times as many as pre-war, with an important engineering and optical industry.

Bielefeld at the foot of the Teutoburger Wald was best known for its linen before the war and had just about passed the 100,000 mark, which is to say that it had officially become a *Grossstadt*. Today it has more than 300,000 inhabitants. It still produces linen but it is far better known as a centre producing sewing machines, bicycles, cash registers and, of course, houses the Oetker food-processing factory. With next-door Gütersloh (where Miele washing machines have their head-quarters) it is a publishing centre. The internationally used catalogue of available gramophone records bears the name Bielefeld.

The trend has perhaps been most pronounced in the south-west. Cities such as Esslingen and Reutlingen, not far from Stuttgart, have almost trebled in size. True, there was some pre-war industry such as textiles in this area but nothing even remotely comparable with the post-war influx of machine-tool and automated-process machinery. Some of these cities engage in highly specialized production, others are branches of Bosch in Stuttgart or one of the many new firms which have established their headquarters in the capital of Württemberg since the end of the war (including IBM and Kodak).

Certain general trends emerge from what has been said so far. Much of the immediate post-war reconstruction took place in the traditional industrial areas like the Ruhr, but with the structural changes which took place in German industry, the raw material base became less important for the location of the new sites. At yet a later stage automation in industry reduced dependence on the labour force as well and the infrastructure – accessibility by road, rail or river – became a factor of paramount importance. Mention has been made of the movement of industry from the big cities to medium-sized ones and from north to south. The post-war development of the German electrical industry clearly reflects this pattern. This was one of the growth industries *par excellence* until it ran into trouble in the 1970s. Most of the big pre-war electrical companies such as Siemens, AEG and Telefunken were located in Berlin. After the war, partly as the result of the political situation, part of Siemens moved to Munich, AEG-Telefunken (they merged in 1967) to Frankfurt. While some plants remained in Berlin, and while, generally speaking, there was a fairly wide dispersal, South Germany by the 1970s accounted for more than half of the output of this industry.

The German traffic network was not bad before the Second

31

World War. 'The condition of the roads in Germany is almost universally good', Baedeker said. Statements of this kind are always relative: it was good in the sense that one could safely drive in a car or a truck without fear of breaking one's neck. The highroads were sufficient for the existing cars and trucks. Germany was not motorized to the same extent as the US or Britain. The highroads were certainly not fast: I remember travelling a distance of a hundred miles by bus to a sports competition because it was the cheapest way. But the trip certainly took three hours and sometimes even four without stopping once. Germany had a good and relatively cheap railway network; far more people and goods went by rail than by road. But with a very few exceptions it was not fast either.

Then Hitler came and his much-touted scheme of the special motor roads – the *Reichsautobahnen* – was launched. It was not strictly speaking Hitler's scheme, for the first such superhighway, from Cologne to Bonn, was opened the year before he came to power. Up to 1939, 2,150 kilometres of the superhighways had been finished. They were part of a general scheme to build two new axes from north to south and from west to east. But the schemes were far from complete by 1945 and some sections had been destroyed in the fighting or as the result of air raids.

Today the *Autobahnen* extend to 7,300 kilometres, but the number of motorcars has risen at a much faster rate from about 500,000 in 1950 to 4.5 million in 1960 and to 22 million in 1980. (The number of trucks and vans has not risen in recent years.) In the same time the rail network has significantly shrunk as well as the number of people employed by the *Bundesbahn*. Much of the goods and even more of the passenger traffic has been lost to the roads. If at the beginning of the century the German railway was a highly profitable institution – the Baedeker of 1900 announced proudly that rail transport was less expensive in Germany than in most other parts of Europe and that the second-class carriages 'with sprung seats' were sometimes as good as first class in England – it has been losing many billions of marks since the war. The long-term prospects for rail are somewhat better for, with new high-speed trains and the development of container transport, the railway may again become competitive.

Domestic air traffic is not of great importance whereas most Germans, of course, take a plane for more distant destinations.

Shipping, on the other hand, has played a growing role as far as the transport of goods is concerned, partly because of the rise in the price of oil, partly because of the development of a network of canals mainly in northern Germany but also in the Saar and the Main–Danube canal, as yet to be opened. The character of this kind of transport has changed: once upon a time there was something romantic, even adventurous, about going down the Rhine watching the beautiful scenery passing by. The Lorelei was always likely to bewitch the tourists if not the sailors. Today the standardized Euroships carry as much as a railway train of 50–60 carriages; river traffic is regulated by means of television and something akin to an automatic pilot. There are few surprises in store, the ships are usually steered by two people, frequently a husband-and-wife team. They will not cast a second glance in the direction of the Lorelei.

So much then about the output of industry and the shipment of goods. The changes in living conditions have not been less far-reaching. Before the Second World War Germany prided itself on being a modern country and it is certainly true that amenities such as central heating or elevators could be found far more often in the 1930s in German houses than in British or French. It is also true that Weimar Germany was a pioneer in city planning and architectural design. Examples of the new style of office building were the Deutscher Ring, a high-rise building in Hamburg, the Sprinkenhof and the Chilehaus, also in that city. The Sprinkenhof had (and I believe still has) about sixteen entrances; some six thousand people used to work there during the day. The eastern edge of the Chilehaus resembled the bow of a ship, a fitting allusion for a building in this great port. Other famous examples were the Columbus Haus in Berlin in the Potsdamer Platz, built by Erich Mendelsohn – the Gestapo, alas, moved in there after 1933. There was the huge IG Farben complex in Frankfurt near the Palmengarten with its unheard-of dimensions, and above all the massive Stuttgart central railway station and some of the buildings adjoining it. These were widely (and rightly) praised as examples of a modern, functional architecture. But they were few and far between simply because many of the older buildings were still in good working order and, in any case, there was not that much money to be invested in new buildings in the Weimar Republic.

The great change came after the end of the Second World War. True, there was even less money now. But in most of the inner city areas – not only the very biggest towns, but also in places like Mainz, Freiburg or

Hildesheim – many of the living-quarters had been destroyed and had to be reconstructed in any case. The rebuilding had to proceed rapidly with 500,000 apartments built each year. Sometimes it was done in good taste and with much foresight: Hans Poelzig's early buildings in Duisburg or the Dreischeibenhaus in Düsseldorf. At other times it proceeded piecemeal, in a chaotic fashion, resulting in indifferent or deplorable 'modern' buildings and quarters. Examples of imaginative reconstruction could be found in Hanover where provision was made for parks, in Münster and in Bremen – the Neue Vahr suburb in the east of the city designed by May, one of the leading city planners of his time. Hans Scharoun, who had also belonged to the avant-garde in the 1920s, built high-rise apartment blocks in Stuttgart with original names such as 'Romeo and Juliet' and 'Salute'; he also designed the highly praised Berlin Philharmonic building next door to Mies van der Rohe's fine National Gallery. High-rise and other modern buildings sprouted all over Germany. Before the war, Kaiserslautern in the Palatinate Forest had been a city of some 60,000 inhabitants, a market town with a fine industrial art museum. Its history was somehow connected with Emperor Barbarossa. After the war the adventurous city fathers decided to erect the highest municipal building in Europe (84 metres). Similar daring was shown elsewhere, sometimes misplaced, but always modern. Today every self-respecting major corporation from Ludwigshafen and Frankfurt to Leverkusen and Hamburg has at least one skyscraper. Even in Munich, where churches had dominated the skyline, the high-rise buildings of Bogenhausen crept up until they dwarfed the towers of the Frauenkirche.

In recent years post-war town planning and architecture have come in for very harsh criticism. The modernists of the 1950s are now elderly people and they have been succeeded by a younger generation of traditionalists. The traditionalists claim that their predecessors went too far in their reaction against the monumental architecture of the Third Reich; they thought too much in terms of expansion, their building was too much influenced by technological optimism, they destroyed too much of the still existing substance of the old cities. The cities were cut by too many superhighways, and the old Corbusier concept of dividing homes and places of work was carried out the wrong way. As one critic of the monotony of technical functional architecture complained back in 1960: apartment blocks look like schools, schools like office buildings and office buildings like factories.

The criticism is frequently justified, but then town planning and architecture always express the *Zeitgeist*. The reaction against old-fashioned formalism and monumentalism was quite natural; above all, the builders of the 1950s were operating under great pressure and with limited means at their disposal. They did destroy too much, not only in Berlin which, together with Frankfurt and Hanover, became the laboratory of modern German architecture. Since the late 1970s the traditionalists have had their hour of opportunity, but it is too early to pass judgment on their contribution. They seem to be too much enamoured of the concept of restoration. But in the end it may well appear that the differences between them and their antagonists are less fundamental than one was led to believe in the heat of the argument.

The visitor, taking a stroll in a German city after many years' absence, is bound to be surprised by other new developments. Before the war, outside Berlin there had only been a few cities with underground railways, such as Hamburg where work had begun as far back as 1906. After 1945 the existing subways were expanded and new ones built, most prominently in Frankfurt. Many new parking garages also came into being, but even so the growing motor traffic threatened to suffocate the inner cities. As a result, pedestrian zones had to be established in business areas like the Hohe Strasse in Cologne, the Zeil in Frankfurt or the section between Stachus and Marienplatz in Munich. Some of the shopping centres went underground but most remained at street level.

Almost everything about these shops has changed. Before the war, and well into the early 1960s, the German street scene was dominated by groceries, bakeries, butchers' shops, tobacconists and, of course, dairies, as well as drug stores selling soap, perfumes and some non-prescription medicines (*Drogerien* in contradistinction to pharmacies). These have been all but wiped out; according to an investigation in Berlin, the number of dairies in that city fell from 869 in 1962 to 99 thirteen years later. Most of their business as well as that of the bakers and the other food stores was taken over by the big department stores of which there were now a great many, catering for almost every taste and pocket, and with parking facilities for thousands of cars. The first emerged in 1964 south of Frankfurt, others near Bochum and Coblenz followed. (New hypermarkets were opened outside the big cities.) The little corner shop, to which I had been sent as a child to buy a four-pound loaf of bread or a few eggs and half a pound of butter, could be found now only with an effort, in some of the older suburbs. Those that have survived do not seem to prosper. There was a special contraption at the door of our apartment where the baker would leave freshly baked rolls in the morning, except, of course, on Sundays. Now most bakers have gone out of business and those who remain have no apprentices to make the rounds. Once there were a lot of tailors and shoemakers and other craftsmen, but only a few seem to have survived. Some shops have disappeared altogether, especially those mysterious places located in cellars where ice-blocks could be bought, and the nice old-fashioned laundries with enormous mangles. The women of the neighbourhood used to congregate there for a chat. Today virtually everyone has his own refrigerator, and those who do not have a washing machine use the launderettes in the main street – reading a magazine or simply looking bored while waiting for the machine to stop. Once upon a time icemen with horse and buggy made their rounds announcing their arrival with shouts, a bell or creating some other kind of noise; so did the coal merchant and the rag man. (The beer carts, come to think of it, and the enormous furniture removal vans were also drawn by horses, and what horses!) The old-fashioned laundry and the coal dealer were part of the popular culture and quite prominently at that: *Komm hilf mir mal die Rolle drehen* . . . and *Mutter, der Mann mit dem Koks ist da* were sung or hummed for decades. They seem to have vanished with the world which produced *The Gipsy Baron, The Count of Luxembourg* and *The Merry Widow.* A few lending libraries still exist in the less affluent quarters; and the kind of books taken out seems not to have changed that much: it used to be John Knittel, now it is Konsalik. But there were few paperbacks before the war, and there are a great many now. It seems only a question of time until the last such library will disappear; their place has been taken by shops lending video tapes.

There are still some street vendors about and even an occasional organ grinder, and, of course, modern street musicians. There are some beggars, but not many. The number of bookstores has decreased except in the vicinity of universities, but there are many more places selling radios, televisions, records, stereo equipment and cameras. There are about as many flower shops and hairdressers as there used to be; prostitution has largely moved indoors except that of the cheaper kind; and drug dealing, which formerly was not visible except in Berlin, can now be seen in many places. Other kinds of establishments are now much more common than they used to be: banks, restaurants, boutiques, antique shops, travel agencies, interior decorators and shops catering to sports and hobbies – all these, of course, signs of growing affluence. Much of this is, admittedly, a world-wide trend: there are fewer movie theatres because of television, and no one would dream of building the kind of movie palaces these days which appeared in the 1920s.

Other new developments seem to be specifically German. Have German streets become more like those in other European countries? Well, yes – a street in Frankfurt, Düsseldorf or Stuttgart has more in common with one in a contemporary city of similar size in Northern or Western Europe than one in Stuttgart, Frankfurt or Düsseldorf in 1900 or even 1930. Stuttgart has not become Bordeaux, nor has Hamburg become Stockholm, but in some respects they have grown more similar, just as the tastes of young people in Germany resemble those of young people elsewhere in Europe more closely than those of their parents' generation.

Whether German cities are now more like each other is a question more difficult to answer, except in such areas as the Ruhr where, according to a grim saying, they were exchangeable. Cities usually have a character of their own in accordance with geographical location and the kind of people living there as well as some other circumstances. They have all changed, but each has gone its own way.

Berlin before 1945 was not a beautiful city but it was vital and dynamic and it left few visitors indifferent. Everyone agreed that it had grown too fast in the century before. But the Romantics paradoxically were attracted by it; 'More a continent than a city', Jean Paul wrote, and Clemens Brentano: 'Perhaps the only city in Germany where the so-called geniuses are not thought to be mad.' Even Goethe commented on this 'daring species of mankind'. Foreigners sometimes disliked it; 'He who decided to build a city there must have been possessed by the devil', according to Stendhal, and Dostoevsky also reacted surlily. But he apologized later on: he had been very tired when he first arrived after two days and a night in the train from Petersburg, hence the impression that this was a place like the one which he had just left. He later admitted that his judgment had been at fault. Gottfried Keller noted that the 'good old Berlin humanism' was giving place to megalomania and that, generally speaking, parochialism was prevailing. Mark Twain called it 'the European Chicago' but made it clear that this was high praise: 'A rest to the eye, a thoroughly well governed, a free city.'

There was nothing parochial about Berlin in the 1920s when it was the second city of Europe after London. Many thought of it as the cultural capital of the world. What happened to the city during the war and its aftermath is known. Hitler announced that in ten years no one would recognize Berlin and this, quite literally, was the case. In 1945 it was thought that it would take at least fifty years to remove the rubble – 75 million cubic metres of it, eight times as much as in Munich. But when I first revisited the city after the war in June 1953, a few days before the rebellion in East Germany, the rubble had already disappeared and Berlin made a lively impression, more quickly recovering from its scars than many other parts of Europe. The division of the city was not that much felt, there was no Berlin Wall yet. True, the old Berlin had largely disappeared: only with an effort could some remnants of the Berlin of Wilhelm Raabe and Theodor Fontane still be seen in the eastern sector. West Berlin was a new city, and in some ways it again seemed a very important place, not a political centre where important decisions were taken, but a good vantage point to take the pulse of the world.

There was still (or again) a great deal of industry, such as Borsig, parts of AEG and Siemens, and a new fashion industry. Berlin has the largest department store in Europe, and the largest university in Germany with 50,000 students and 13,000 employees. The underground railway network has doubled since 1953. The theatre and the opera are among the best in the country, the architecture of the Hansa-Viertel is interesting, and sitting on a nice summer evening in one of the coffee-houses on the Kurfürstendamm (which Thomas Wolfe called the 'biggest coffee-house of Europe'), say at Kranzler or Möhring, there certainly seems to be more prosperity than in the so-called Golden Twenties, the creative and tortured years of the Weimar Republic. There are now some 5,500 restaurants, bars and coffee-houses in Berlin and those who want to walk or to swim or to sail can still do so. One doesn't really feel constrained, as if one were on a small island most of the time. There are conventions, *Festwochen*, international seminars. In January it is the turn of music, in February of the cinema, in April of the fine arts and so on, all the year round. Literary dialogues take place for much of the time – 'Workshop Berlin' – and a great many artists from outside are in residence. Never mind that this cultural activity does not always seem spontaneous: the arts have to be subsidized in any case. One day there may be great praise for those who supported artistic life, showing courage, initiative and imagination when the going here became a little rough. It is certainly too early to write a requiem on this city. Cities have a long life, and one should not even try to predict what the position of Berlin will be in a hundred years' time – not, after all, a long span in the history of Germany or mankind.

But right now it is a melancholy place, a city of old people. It has the highest percentage of people above sixty-five in the *Bundesrepublik*, and the lowest below twenty-one, but it also has the highest rate of marriages. It is a city of 'guest workers' who have not been integrated into German society and seem to have no particular interest in such integration. It is the cradle of the students' movement of 1967, one of the main centres of the German psycho-scene and the alternative subculture. It could be argued that all cultural and intellectual history is the history of fashions and seen in this light the recent fads are perfectly legitimate. Legitimate they may be, but not particularly interesting or appealing; it is difficult to imagine that much of the present scene will endure.

East Berlin is also depressing but in a different way. Expectations are not high in the first place, since it is known that metropolitan life cannot develop under a Communist regime. Furthermore it has little competition to face. It may be boring, but East Berlin is still pulsating with life compared with Cottbus or Karl Marx-Stadt – formerly Chemnitz. It is one of the myths of the post-war period, difficult to eradicate, that East Berlin suffered more than West Berlin as the result of war damage and the dismantling of its industry. In fact, about 75 per cent of West Berlin industry was destroyed or dismantled, as against less than 50 per cent in East Berlin.

West Berlin does have plenty of competition. The political centre has moved to Bonn, its exposed position has prevented the growth of major new industries, the banks are now in Frankfurt, and even its cultural eminence is contested by Munich. During the last fifteen years Berlin has become a sideshow, a less dangerous place no doubt than in the years when the reverberations of every little crisis in West–East relations would be registered here: both flashpoint and seismograph of the Cold War. Now everything has become much quieter. As the soldiers in the First World War gradually put up with the no-man's-land between the fronts, the Berliner seems to put up with the Wall and the death zone. After all only a few people each year get killed trying to cross it. It is an outrage, of course, but also the price that has to be paid for an orderly existence. And while people want freedom, they seem to need order even more.

A generation has now grown up which does not know that the Brandenburg Gate and the Reichstag were not the border but the very centre of the city, which does not remember that the railway and subway stations, now disused and overgrown with grass, resembling abandoned mining towns in the western United States, were once hardly able to cope with the enormous metropolitan traffic. I just about remember it from my very first visit to the city, when I was taken to the Brandenburg Gate, the emblem of the city, the Column of Victory and the nearby Reichstag with its majestic façades and greenish cupolas. When I next visited Berlin the Reichstag had burned down. The Nazis did not bother to rebuild it for they had no use for a parliament. The Nazi Reichstag continued to meet once or twice a year to listen to a speech by the Führer. For this purpose an opera house, the Kroll Oper, was perfectly adequate.

The Reichstag was rebuilt after 1945 following further destruction in the fighting during the last days of the war. Today it serves as a museum and for occasional conferences. The Bundestag no longer meets there as it is too inconvenient and the Russians could take offence. It is right on the border: if some repair work has to be done to its eastern wall, the East German authorities have to be asked for permission, for the ladders have to be put on their territory. As one looks out of the windows of the Reichstag the Wall is literally at one's feet, with slogans painted on it in German and Turkish, usually on behalf of some left-wing sect. At a distance of fifty yards there are watchtowers manned by East German border police, watching us through their binoculars. Poor people, they look exceedingly bored; they seldom have anything exciting to report. The desolate, enormous open space in front was once the Pariser Platz; this was the very end of Unter den Linden, the main promenade of the *flâneurs*, the street of diplomats and generals, of the best coffee-houses and the great museums: the French and British embassies were located right here and, a couple of hundred yards away, the buildings housing the offices of the president of the Republic and the Reich chancellor.

A further five minutes' walk along the Wall brings one to another shapeless open square; difficult as it now is to accept, this was once the Potsdamer Platz, the busiest square in Germany, perhaps in the whole of Europe. Beyond it there was the Leipziger Strasse, Berlin's most important shopping street with expensive shops and also the leading department stores such as Wertheim, built around the turn of the century in the brand-new modern style, using plate glass. I last saw the place in early autumn 1938. Austria had already 'returned to the Reich', in the parlance of those days. I had no money and stayed with a friend in Wilmersdorf. What a bustle in the streets even at a late hour, but my friend did not share the general elation. We had just graduated from school. What next? Well, he said with some resignation, two years at least in the army and then, who knows, university or a war? My friend was among the lucky ones, he came back from the war ten years later and minus one leg. The Nazis said that to be young in the 1930s was bliss; they did not say anything about middle age and after.

There is a danger of getting absorbed in recollections as one looks over the Wall, a temptation to be resisted, particularly in this city. The wrong turnings in German history have been made, opportunities missed, fatal errors committed, and there is no way to turn the clock back. One day, perhaps, the Wall will come down and the desolate places will disappear, even children may play again in this no-man's-land. But it will certainly take a long time. In the meantime, the Berliners devote their attention and energy to the urgent problems of daily life, a sensible attitude and one that has much to recommend itself from the point of view of mental hygiene.

With all its problems, Berlin is again a perfectly liveable-in city. The problem is in part one of perception: those who knew the city as it was should perhaps be advised not to revisit it, for it may be depressing. Melancholia is less likely to occur in the new Munich, not because it is a 'great city with heart' (*Weltstadt mit Herz*) as the enthusiasts claim, or Germany's 'secret capital'. It certainly is not the new political centre, for while Franz Josef Strauss is very popular in Bavaria, he has too many detractors abroad. Munich's economic importance has greatly increased because of its many medium-sized firms, even more than its giant corporations. But it cannot compete in this respect with Hamburg and the conurbations of Rhineland-Westphalia. As a cultural centre, on the other hand, it has no equal, with its forty museums, its eighty private galleries, three symphony orchestras, its many theatres and unrivalled libraries. It is the trend-setter, the avant-garde. Most fashions, sartorial or philosophical, good, bad or idiotic seem to emanate these days from Munich. Munich was never a cultural oasis: even in the last century, the Wittelsbachs, unlike their Prussian

41

cousins, were more interested in building than in playing soldiers. When the young Thomas Mann came to Munich from his native Lübeck he was overwhelmed ('Munich was *shining*') and chose to live there. The local bohemians were always second only to those of Berlin, and in some respects their equal. The old Munich was a curious mixture of philistinism and the avant-garde, never particularly proud of its writers and artists who were thought to be, at best, marginal figures. Only after the war did it realize that Schwabing was not a Munich district but, like St-Germain-des-Prés, a state of mind and, taken in connection with the German Museum, the Old and New Pinakothek and the major beer gardens, it had enormous tourist potential. The nice young people swimming naked in the Isar or walking naked through the Englischer Garten were also promoting the city.

Munich was not destroyed to the same degree as Berlin, but as a result of some seventy air raids on the 'capital of the [Nazi] movement' half the churches were heavily damaged or destroyed and one third of the population lost its homes. The great upsurge in rebuilding Munich took place in the 1950s and 1960s when the population almost doubled and the centre of the town between Stachus and Marienplatz was closed to traffic. A bit further to the east is the Feldherrnhalle, another of the monumental buildings erected by Ludwig I in the last century. It is a good place to ponder missed opportunities in German history for it was here that Hitler and his friends collided with the forces of order on 9 November 1923 in their first unsuccessful coup. Max von Scheubner-Richter, who marched next to Hitler, was shot and killed. Hitler was exceedingly lucky and again escaped injury when the next serious attempt on his life was made. This, ironically, took place a few minutes from the Feldherrnhalle, sixteen years later to the day, in the Bürgerbräukeller, one of the traditional major beer halls. But Hitler began his speech earlier than announced, talked only for a few minutes, and when the bomb exploded at 9.20 p.m. he was already outside, on his way to the railway station.

The Ludwigstrasse, which is to Munich what Unter den Linden was for Berlin, begins at the Feldherrnhalle. This was, after all, once a royal city: there even was a Bavarian war ministry in this very street. Further on the Ludwigstrasse changes its name and becomes the Leopold-strasse, the centre of Schwabing. This is the Munich of students, art studios, small galleries, restaurants and coffee-houses. It has served artists and writers for more than a century. Hitler lived here and

Oswald Spengler's *Decline of the West* was written in Schwabing. Before them Lenin had edited *Iskra* in this place and Trotsky stayed in one of the side streets. Bertolt Brecht and Thomas Mann, Paul Klee and Wassili Kandinsky lived here, in the golden days of Schwabing. In the 1950s it became the place where the action was thought to be; ice-cream parlours, more boutiques and bars mushroomed, artists hawked pictures and *objets d'art*, various strange types made their appearance, embodying the 'real Munich'. Sometimes it seemed as if they were all taking part in a modern play, in which everyone, including the public, participated.

With the commercialization of Schwabing it became too expensive for the real bohemians who moved out to Haidhausen on the other side of the Isar. Their place was taken by McDonald parlours, pizzerias and more boutiques. Tradition is important in Munich. The inner city was rebuilt according to the old pattern, there is a Munich 'society' (very much in contrast to Cologne or Frankfurt) which consists of scions of the old aristocracy, representatives of big business but also show-business people, for Munich is also the capital of the German cinema.

The great majority of present-day Munichers was not born here, and one out of five is not even German. The Munich dialect is no longer widely spoken, but the 'indestructible genius loci' (to quote Thomas Mann), is still much in evidence, the constant grumbling, heaping abuse on everything and everybody, which is thought to be the favourite pastime of this city. Those who love Munich praise its tolerance; its detractors say that it simply means that the native could not care less about his neighbour. The critics have many harsh things to say about their city and about each other, but they still prefer it to any other.

Munich's character may be far from admirable, but at least it has character, unlike Frankfurt, a city which could be anywhere in the world. Once upon a time this was a solid town with a tradition many centuries old of *Bürgersinn* (inadequately translated by 'civic sense'), a centre of culture as much as of commerce. It was the town in which German emperors were crowned and also the capital of German liberalism. It has transformed itself into a curious and not very pleasant mixture, a mongrel city. The Frankfurt Stock Exchange is still (or again) the most important in the country, the biggest banks have their head offices here, the airport is the largest by far and there is, of course, the annual book fair. But of the culture and the *Bürgersinn* little has remained other than a respected newspaper. Its post-war history has been unhappy with many demos and broken windows but few impulses reminding one of Frankfurt's great past.

Some German cities have done better than others since the war and it is not always easy to point to the reason. Some which suffered heavily during the war had a spectacular recovery, others which were hardly damaged have stagnated or deteriorated. In some cases effective leadership or local initiative made a difference; sometimes the favourable geographical location helped, and sometimes it may have been simply a matter of accident.

So much then about the new cities which, on fine weekends, are deserted by millions of their inhabitants eager to return to nature, to climb mountains, to swim or sail, or simply to enjoy a change of scenery. Those living in the north-east are likely to congregate in the Teutoburg Forest; this is the real Germany, here Arminius the chief of the Cherusci defeated the Roman legions. Today the forest is no longer wild and if perchance the visitor comes across an elephant, a lion or even a hippopotamus, both will be equally confused, the animal having escaped from 'Safariland', a wild-life park and one of the main local attractions.

Those in the far south are likely to turn to Lake Constance, bordering on Switzerland and Austria. One recent summer I joined the pilgrimage to Mainau, the flower island; it was, alas, Mother's Day and there were far too many people to enjoy the tropical vegetation. Along the shores of the lake there are many fine cities dating back to the Middle Ages or even Roman days – Constance, Lindau, Überlingen, Meersburg. For students of architecture this is a paradise; one finds examples in nearby castles, churches and town halls of every style – Gothic, Renaissance, early and late Baroque. But again, as in the Teutoburg Forest, this has become densely populated and I found it difficult even to envisage the heroes of my youth – Ekkehart the monk and the Truchsess of Waldburg – in this civilized neighbourhood.

There were more windsurfers and sailing boats on the lake than there ever were *Landsknechte*. Constance, where they burned Huss at the stake, now has industries and even a university. Friedrichshafen, which claims to get more sunshine than any other place in Germany, has played an important role in the history of German aviation from the Zeppelin to Dornier and the Maybach engine. It suffered more war damage than any other place in this region. On the lake steamers of various sizes are plying the waves; one can buy a ticket for a coffee trip, for dinner, a dancing excursion and even a trip 'into the blue' – the destination will not be announced beforehand. But there are not many possible surprises; the passengers may be taken to the casino in Lindau or perhaps to Reichenau island, a place of great historical tradition famous for the old wall paintings in one of the local churches. Today it is mainly known as the *Gemüseinsel*, the vegetable island.

Lake Constance, in short, is a lovely place with its picturesque cities; the Säntis, the imposing massif on the Swiss side; the abrupt rocky slopes. But it recalls picture-postcard scenery rather than a romantic landscape and those who want to get away from the crowds will probably turn to the sublime Black Forest, the home of the cuckoo clock, the ornate local garb, and the evergreen firs and pines. But again the visitor will have to move far from the beaten track, preferably to the south. There are not that many trees in the Black Forest and tourism seems to be the most successful enterprise these days. The traditional home industries, to the extent that they were not radically modernized, have frequently gone bankrupt, for the Far East now produces cheaper cuckoo clocks. And so from Freudenstadt to Baden-Baden, from Badenweiler to Wildbad, the visitors dutifully take the curative waters, go to the pump-room and the bath-house, proceed to the thermal springs, take the water in every shape and form, for it is rich in minerals and low in alkali. They swim in warm waters and in cold, they walk ten times the length of the local promenade, after which they repair to the nearest coffee-house and confectioner's. The local springs, we are told, are good for cardiac and vascular conditions and for gastric diseases, skin disease, sciatica and other rheumatic conditions, and help against afflictions of kidney, liver, gallbladder, against partial paralysis, migraine, male and female disorders – against virtually all other diseases with the possible exception of toothache. No other people, with the exception of the Russians, take their course of baths, the diet, the massage and the poultice so seriously. It is touching to watch how religiously the instructions are observed: to drink four glasses of water, no more, no less; to walk twenty-five minutes in the morning from point A to B. British or American physicians ridicule the belief in the magic of the spas. But certainly it has seldom done much harm. The great post-war boom in the history of German spas began in 1957. In the subsequent two decades the number of beds more than doubled. But since 1981 the public sick funds, the biggest customer by far, have tended to prescribe such courses of treatment less and less frequently; many resorts and spas have been severely hit by this crisis.

Life in a spa taking the waters is continuity and tradition. Little has changed in comparison with the world before 1914 except that the luxury hotels were more imposing then and that the employees used to be German. But this is still not the old romantic Germany; where will the wanderer find it? Perhaps on a little steamer going up (or down) the Moselle, watching its vine-clad hillsides passing by; years ago it was recommended as a cure against lover's grief. Until fairly recently time had passed by the river, for with its countless turnings and windings the Moselle was not navigable for anything much larger than a motorboat. But since the 1960s it has been regulated, and Trier, the oldest city in Germany and the birthplace of Karl Marx, is now a port. Everything still looks charming and ancient. But one should not probe too deeply. Many buildings in Cochem (including the fortress) were reconstructed according to old designs; Traben-Trarbach and Zell, known to every wine lover, are old cities but were largely rebuilt in recent decades. For genuine medieval scenery one must again move off the beaten track to a village like Beilstein, with its two hundred inhabitants and its half-timbered houses and the Metternich castle, all of it now protected as a national monument. Beilstein produces excellent wine, and wine tasting, as elsewhere in this neighbourhood, is a serious business. Millions of pounds of sugar had been added to the wine in contravention of the law of 1971 banning adulteration; the law is new, the practice is not, and the competition with other wine-growing areas is great. How is the wine transported? No longer in the casks and vats made of special wood as it was from time immemorial, but in plastic containers. For all one knows it has no effect on the taste. Thus, if in the end one finds the old Germany, it tends to have become a museum, and even there, inevitably, modernity is catching up. And if at long last I met a nightwatchman making his rounds (was it in Nördlingen or in Dinkelsbühl?) admonishing us in the traditional way:

> Hark to what I say, good people,
> It striketh ten from every steeple.
> Put out your fire and eke your light,
> That none may come to harm this night,

the chances are that our nightwatchman is studying computer science in his spare time.

Contemporary Germany cannot be understood without a great deal of travelling, but there is a limit to one's absorptive capacity. There are, of course, short cuts if one should get tired of the sights, of which there are a great many between Flensburg and Lake Constance, between the Iron Curtain and the French border. Above all the social and cultural indicators tell us many an interesting story: that Germany has lower population growth than almost any other European country and that the proportion of marriages ending in divorce is substantially smaller in the *Bundesrepublik* (9 per cent) than in Catholic France (22), in Britain (30) and the US (50). Germans seem to get along better with each other, or are they simply more conservative? The indicators tell us that Germany has more physicians per capita than other Western countries, but that German life-expectancy is still a little shorter. This may have to do with alcohol consumption, which is higher in Germany (22 pints of pure alcohol per person a year) than in Britain (12) or the US (14). But then the French and the Spanish drink even more and yet live a little longer, so it may not be the fault of alcohol after all. The public sector in Germany employs fewer people than in the US and France, and many fewer than in Britain. Germany spends a little less per capita on defence than France and Sweden, much less than Britain and the United States. But then Germany has national compulsory service which America and Britain do not and these figures ought to be viewed in the proper context. Out of a hundred German households 97 have a television, 96 a camera, 90 a telephone, and 84 a car; the figures elsewhere in Europe are not very different except that the British have fewer cars and the French fewer TV sets (but more cinemas).

Modern society produces exact and detailed statistics, some of them of great fascination. Who would have guessed that 383,000 German women belong to football (soccer) clubs, more than to athletic or swimming or riding or skiing clubs – but fewer than to tennis clubs? But the figures still tell us only part of the story, and usually very little about the quality of life. We do not know, for instance, how many German women actually play football or whether they simply join out of sympathy with their boyfriends or husbands.

Profound changes have taken place in the status of German women since the end of the Second World War. They have gained legal equality, they have organized themselves in militant groups and take a leading part in the so-called 'new social movements', about which more below. German women now have full property rights and there is less dependence and oppression in marriage. While some belong to militant feminist and lesbian groups (the two are very much at loggerheads), most German women have no wish to exchange roles with their husbands and they are quite satisfied with the nuclear family, which, according to the revolutionaries, has become an anachronism.

An end to patriarchal society then and a total change in the role of women? Not quite, because domestic servants have virtually disappeared, because grandmothers no longer live in and are less available (and willing) to help out with the grandchildren. German schools, in contrast to other countries, keep the children only half a day. All of which is to say that the German housewife still faces a fifty- or sixty-hour working week, or perhaps even more. She may no longer be the servant of the husband but she is still the servant of the children. She has much less free time than men and this, in turn, has far-reaching implications for her participation in society and public life.

There is a big step from the absolute certainties of the annual statistical yearbooks to the relative certainties of the public opinion polls. But they still give us much reliable information: that some of the traditional values (such as order, discipline, cleanliness) are now less highly thought of; that in recent years there has been a retreat into the private sphere (but also more interest in politics); that some 57 per cent of those asked prefer to live in the countryside or a small town rather than in a big city (14 per cent). It emerges that they prefer Munich to all other major German cities: Munich is followed, surprisingly, by Berlin and Hamburg.[1]

Forty-five per cent consider themselves as belonging to the middle classes and only 23 per cent to the working class; a majority of Germans have reached the conclusion that religion and the churches have become irrelevant for our age. Some of these trends are worldwide, some can be found, *grosso modo*, all over Western Europe, some are specifically German. Which is to say that in some respects Germany is like the rest of the world but in others it isn't; it is to this specific German change (or lack of change) that we shall turn next.

---

[1] The names most frequently given to German boys are no longer Hans and Otto, but Christian and Sebastian, Michael and Daniel, Alexander and Stefan. Among girls Stefanie and Julie, Christine and Katherine are the most popular, a notable change since the days of Anna, Rosa and Lisa.

3 Young Germany or the Cultural Revolution

At some time or other every visitor to a West German town in the late 1960s or in the 1970s was bound to come across some manifestation of youth protest. While such protest has occurred in many countries, nowhere else has it been so widespread and lasting. The youth rebellion itself became an object of interest to be included in sightseeing tours: buildings occupied by squatters, alternative bookshops or coffee-houses, communes, drug peddling, street demonstrations (weather permitting), have been among the attractions shown to the visitor from abroad by conscientious hosts eager to present not only relics of the past but also a picture of things to come.

The older generation of Germans has been unhappy, needless to say, about an almost unending chain of demonstrations, sometimes violent; terrorist action; the rejection of traditional values, an alternative culture often including the use of drugs, aggressive homosexuality and lesbianism openly flaunted; the resurgence of extreme ideologies, mainly of the Left but also of the far Right; the spread of various Utopian creeds sometimes in quasi-scientific guise and the flowering of strange Indian and Far Eastern religious sects. The generation of fathers and mothers starting from scratch after the war felt bitter about the attacks on their 'consumer mentality' on the part of a generation which never suffered want and always took a certain living-standard for granted. A room of one's own, enough to eat, a free education should occasion gratitude. But gratitude is seldom an outstanding virtue of young people, and young Germans do not wish to be bored by stories about events which, even if true, refer to a period before their birth, almost as remote to them as Napoleon or Frederick the Great. Even if the going was difficult for their parents, of what relevance is this now? And why did their parents fail to build a society more free, just and humane than contemporary Germany? Having failed, why does the generation of the fathers and mothers refuse to understand that large sections – albeit a minority – of youth reject this society?

There has been more youth protest in Germany than elsewhere, but Germans have also worried more about such protest than any other people. When a number of terrorist outrages took place in the 1970s, the authorities and wide sections of the population reacted very nervously indeed, as if they faced a mortal danger to the state unparalleled in recent German history. The reasons for such over-reaction may be rooted in the German urge for order (quite irrespective of political conviction) and the corollary – the apparent inability to live with a certain amount of disorder. Germans are, or were at any rate until recently, people with a sense of history. They should have known that generational conflict is not a rare phenomenon in the annals of mankind, that such protest may take various forms, including terrorist attacks, that similar manifestations of protest were taking place in other countries. They ought to have known that young people, almost by definition, resent the prevailing state of affairs; that tolerance, the willingness to make concessions, mature reflection and a statesman-like approach are not the attributes of youth. Lastly, they should have known that while some young generations are happier than others, the process of growing up is seldom altogether painless. Bitter opposition against the parents' generation may well be a psychological necessity. A collective vote of thanks on the part of the children for the wonderful achievements of those responsible for the economic miracle would have been against all historical and social experience. The protest should have been seen in proper perspective; instead the impression was created that the majority of German youth was involved in terrorism or at least sympathized with it. In actual fact the conspirators were never more than a few dozen. True, many thousands demonstrated on various occasions. But it is also true, as the investigations have shown, that German youth was more satisfied with the way democracy worked in its country than any other young generation in Europe. Even at the height of the youth protest, only small minorities were involved in its more extreme political and cultural manifestations.

But this is not the complete story, for if the older generation took youth protest very seriously indeed, so did the younger. There is in German history a tendency towards exaggeration and excess, a relentlessness, a desire to pursue things to their (allegedly) logical end, rather than to stop and reflect. For this there are few parallels elsewhere. As Hans Magnus Enzensberger recently noted (after practising the opposite for two decades): 'Every good cause becomes false if we think it through to the very end.' When American, British and Italian students had long ceased to demonstrate, when the young French intellectuals developed an elaborate and extreme critique of communism and the Soviet system, German students were still holding aloft the banner of 1968. Once upon a time the great majority of German students had veered to the extreme Right; for the German student of the 1970s there were no enemies on the Left. It was only in Germany of all Western nations that a new alternative, a 'Green party', emerged as a political factor of consequence on the national scene. This may seem excessive publicity for the activities (and moods) of small minorities, but history is full of examples of how determined groups of people, however small, succeeded in influencing the majority. Following the vote of many hundreds of thousands for the Green party, it was no longer possible to dismiss the protest movements as small and inconsequential: the party had certainly benefited to a great extent from media exposure and publicity. But it is no creature of the media: there was an inclination, a predisposition, to begin with, and probably more.

Some observers belittled youth protest altogether: boys will be boys and girls will be girls, it was said – all of us have sown wild oats in our time. Sooner or later they were bound to grow up and face the harsh realities of life and, no longer protected by parents, teachers, society and the state, they were bound to accept reality and act sensibly.

These observers took it for granted that young Germans would become more moderate, conservative, traditional in outlook, as had happened time and again in the past. But it is equally true that there have been true cultural revolutions whose impact on society, institutions, culture and the *Zeitgeist* in general has been lasting. The question arose whether the great ferment of the 1960s and the 1970s was just another form of generational revolt or whether it was a new social movement likely to cause irreversible change.

The student revolt, the first manifestation of the protest movement of the late 1960s, came as a bolt from the blue. The surprise was all the greater because protest seemed so unlikely at the time: there had been virtually no warning. But there had been no warning either on the eve of 'Storm and Stress', the rebel group of the 1770s, or 'Young Germany' in the 1830s and 1840s which had troubled their elders and betters and also the forces of order. There had been no warnings indicating the rise of the *Jugendbewegung* which first appeared on the scene in the late 1890s. This was neither literary nor artistic in inspiration or purpose but consisted of some tens of thousands of very young people who wanted to create a new lifestyle without the benefit of the advice and supervision of adults. Some observations on the *Jugendbewegung* seem to be called for because of certain obvious similarities in both inspiration and behaviour with the youth movement of our own age. It tried spontaneously, if often awkwardly, to alter the human condition at a time when philosophers and sociologists were already writing about the alienation of man and the atomization of society, the lessening of contact between human beings. The academic messages did not reach the young people. But they instinctively felt the anonymity and impersonality in their society and the loss of vitality. They were shocked by the squalor of the big cities and wanted to escape from it. Their leaders and thinkers proclaimed that world history was just beginning and that the young generation had a great assignment to fulfil: to help to change it permanently.[1]

There is no mystery about the inspiration of the 'classical' youth movement: it was romantic, part of the general revolt against the Enlightenment and the neglect of non-rational realities. But it was in no way decadent, *fin de siècle*, and, unlike the Romantics, it was not emotionally egocentric and introspective. Unlike the Romantics it tended to apotheosize the group rather than the individual. It was the expression of a fresh awakening to life on the part of an unpolitical elite, the sons and daughters of the middle class. It was post-materialism *avant la lettre*. These idealistic young people of 1900 were depressed by the conventions, the artificiality and the materialism of the society in which they lived, the absence of human warmth and sincerity. And it was in response to these conditions that they set up their groups as alternative social centres in which they could develop qualities of life to which they aspired: sincerity, decency, open-mindedness and idealism, free from petty egoism and careerism, snobbery and affectation and artificial conventions. 'Their main defects were confused thinking,

---

[1] The youth movement was one of the few aspects of German life which Lukanga Mukara truly liked. Paasche, the author of the book, appeared at its meetings and told all who wanted to listen that the German house was on fire and that the youth movement was the fire brigade. It was a dramatic slogan and was used widely again in the 1970s.

inadequate social courage and responsibility and a profoundly illiberal outlook.' When I wrote these lines in a history of the German youth movement some twenty years ago I concluded: 'Blessed be the land that does not need the youth movements.'

But why did it happen in Germany? For these groups remained limited to the German-speaking nations of Central Europe. Was it because elsewhere there was no 'time of transition', because social roots and cohesion were stronger and the barriers between parents and children, between teachers and pupils less rigid? This is implausible because, by and large, British and French society did not greatly differ from German society in these respects. Were perhaps the short-comings, the discontent more acutely felt in Germany? Perhaps there is a special propensity for youth revolt in Germany. But it could be argued with equal justice that there has also been a traditional longing for authority in Germany.

During the last hundred years Germany has gone through several radical changes of political regime: there was strong opposition among the youth against the relative freedom of Weimar Germany and the *Bundesrepublik*. Conditions were widely considered intolerable and the 'system' was rejected *tout court*. Opposition against the authoritarian Wilhelminian regime, on the other hand, had been restricted to the cultural sphere. And in the Third Reich few complained about the rottenness of the system, about intolerable repression or the crisis of legitimation. (*Staatsverdrossenheit*, discontent with the state, usually appeared when repression was low) Young Germans, it would seem, wanted to love their state, but democracies are usually unattractive. They do not inspire great passions, they do not pose challenges or demand sacrifices, but so often merely cause boredom.

The parallels between recent youth protest and the youth movement of an earlier period are striking when the complaints of the 'Greens' are considered: they are less obvious with regard to political action. (The *Wandervögel* did not engage in political demonstrations as did the students in the late 1960s – against the Vietnam war, against Moïse Tshombe, the Shah, and Vice-President Humphrey's visit to Berlin.) This political movement first developed in Berlin, and it had its first martyr in Benno Ohnesorg, shot by the police on 2 June 1967. Within a short time it spread to other cities. (Among the reasons adduced for triggering off a movement of this kind were the emergence of a new national coalition in Bonn (in 1966) and also the occurrence of a first recession interrupting the post-war German boom.)But this was a mild recession which hardly affected the students, nor is there any obvious connection between the temporary co-operation between the Social Democrats and the CDU and the students' movement.

Events in other countries no doubt had a great impact, above all student radicalism on American campuses and later on also in France and Italy. If the revolution of 1848 had quickly spread from one European country to another, at a time when mass communications were still in their infancy, there was nothing surprising if demonstrations spread even more quickly in an age of jet travel and television.

The protest movement was triggered off by a new generation which had no recollection of Nazism, the Second World War, post-war reconstruction and the Cold War. True, there was much talk even then about fascism, but fascism had become an abstraction and it was far more frequently used in contemporary contexts (for instance 'monopoly capitalism') than with regard to the Third Reich or fascist Italy. Hitler was dead and so was Stalin. If there ever had been a 'Soviet threat', a doubtful proposition in the first place, it no longer existed. The main danger in the 1960s was American imperialism.

The ideological inspiration of the movement was at first anti-authoritarian, an interesting admixture of anarchist and Marxist elements. Soon the more radical among the rebels turned from violence against things to terrorism pure and simple. The *Rote Armee Fraktion* (RAF) was born and up to 1977, the year of its most spectacular exploits and its final defeat, it was one of the main issues preoccupying the media and German politics. Enormous publicity was given to its exploits – the kidnapping and murder of Hanns-Martin Schleyer and Jürgen Ponto, the bank robberies and the Mogadishu hijacking. There is no need to recall these events in any detail, nor does one have to discuss the ideology and the proclamation of successive generations of RAF, the 'Movement June 2nd' and other terrorist groups. The components were not new, only their mixture was, such as the idea that various Third-World strategies, political and military, could be applied in a developed industrial country in Western Europe. Nor was there anything specifically German in their doctrine: but for the bombs and the shootings, no one would have bothered to give serious consideration to this infantile hodgepodge of contradictory ideas. Certainly no one would have bothered to refute them.

Nevertheless the handful of terrorists was taken exceedingly seriously by the authorities, by their own supporters and much of the public. Bonn at times resembled an armed camp, what with armoured cars, helicopters, special units of sharpshooters and barbed-wire entanglements in front of the parliament building. Leading politicians devoted much of their time to calls for national solidarity to face this great challenge to society and the democratic order. Professors invested much learning and critical acumen in the search for the deeper motives of the RAF. Some reached the conclusion that it was somehow connected with the fact that Germany had lost the war. Others pointed to the sickness of German society, the special sensitivity of idealistic young people facing its many imperfections and shortcomings.

It was a disconcerting spectacle manifesting insecurity and confusion. It should have been clear that there was no reason to fear for the survival of German society. One bank was robbed but all others continued to function; one plane was hijacked but all others continued to fly. The democratic order was in no danger, even though the authorities could not possibly safeguard the life and property of every citizen. The confusion was rooted in the German tendency towards perfectionism, 'all or nothing', the assumption that the alternative to total security was total insecurity. If the state could not prevent the kidnapping and murder of one single man or woman, the state had seemingly forfeited all legitimacy. But no society had ever succeeded in stamping out crime altogether, nor was it readily obvious why psychology, sociology, philosophy and other learned disciplines had to be mobilized in the search for the roots of terrorism: it is *a priori* impossible to account for the actions of thirty people (or even three hundred) among sixty million. Terrorism may appear in democratic societies in all and any circumstances. However perfect a society, there are, as experience has shown, always some people arguing that the *status quo* is intolerable, and that it should be changed by violent means. Whether a mood of this kind leads to action or not, as more frequently happens, is no more than historical accident.

Boredom certainly played an important part and those who produced the movie *Tätowierung* (*Tattooing*) (1967) certainly had an intuitive understanding of the problem. This is the story of an orphan (Benno) growing up in a closed educational institution for difficult children. Benno has no easy life; his classmates apply an electrical drill to his breast (hence the title of the film) because he refuses to reveal the hiding-place of the pistol he had recently stolen. Benno is saved by the intervention of Mr and Mrs Lohmann who own a little factory in the vicinity; they become his foster-parents. Benno is not a success in the family, he drifts from one job to another, steals and is permanently in debt. But the Lohmanns try to understand him; enlightened, educated parents, they are prototypes of *Scheissliberale*. They show infinite patience and even welcome the fact that he makes love to their niece, Gabi. Such repressive tolerance is too much for Benno to bear. Eventually he shoots Mr Lohmann. There is an additional twist to this interesting and psychologically convincing story: Christoph Wackernagel, the actor who played Benno, joined the RAF a few years later, became one of the most wanted terrorists and was arrested in Holland in 1977.

Tätowierung revealed more clearly than academic investigations that while terrorism probably had many sources, the most important single motive was inner emptiness and its corollary, the desire for excitement. It also showed Mr Lohmann's all-forgiving attitude was too much for Benno to bear. He expected punishment, and the fact that he did not get it confused and annoyed him. (*Paris s'ennuie*, a prophetic Guizot wrote on the eve of a French Revolution, and the same ennui could be found in German universities in the 1960s.)

But the overwhelming majority of the New Left, as the students' movement of the 1960s was widely if not always accurately called, rejected terrorism. It favoured various extra-parliamentary actions, including clashes with the police. Later on there were frequent occupations of buildings for short and long periods, a practice sponsored by various 'autonomous' and 'spontaneous' groups. By that time (the late 1970s) the old New Left had disappeared from the scene: its anti-authoritarian phase had only lasted a few years. Of the first generation of New Leftists, some turned their back on politics, a few moved into the orbit of the pro-Soviet German communists, a party not known for its anti-authoritarian character. Most joined the Social Democrats and began the 'long march through the institutions'. On the whole they still belonged to the Left of the party, but as they approached the fifth decade of their lives they were certainly no longer 'wild radicals' but had become part of the political (or academic) establishment.

Mention should be made, however briefly, of the small groups and 'groupuscles' on the extreme Left, simply because all of them received some fresh impetus from the influx of students. Among these was the communist *Arbeiterbund*, which transformed itself ten years later into the Marxist-Leninist party; this was a Maoist group, but its ideal was the young, revolutionary Mao and it dissociated itself therefore from the present Chinese leadership. There was also the *Kommunistischer Bund*, the *Bund Westdeutscher Kommunisten* and even a pro-Albanian *Kommunistische Partei Deutschlands–Marxists–Leninists*. Such sects can be found in most democratic societies: they usually combine fundamentalist beliefs, a sectarian approach, frequent splits and a low number of members. Most citizens of the *Bundesrepublik* were not even aware of their existence. But not unlike the terrorists they received publicity out of proportion to their numbers. From time to time they would join forces in violent demonstrations and thus catch the headlines.

In many universities *Spartakus* remained for years the leading organization. This is a branch of the pro-Soviet German Communist party (DKP) and numbered no more than 6,000 members in 1982, about one half of a percentage point of all German students. But in view of its cohesion and internal discipline, and also in view of the fact that the other students' organizations had even fewer members, it played a fairly important role in student politics. While campus politics are unlikely to affect the Bonn government, they are still a factor of greater importance than they were in the Weimar republic, when the number of students ran into tens of thousands, whereas now there are more than a million.

The rise of the Greens

The most important event, however, in youth politics was the advent of the Greens. The majority of those active in politics among the younger generation turned away from the established parties and found a new home in the ecological movement. The Greens achieved a first breakthrough in the Bremen regional election in 1979 when they entered the local parliament. Later on they succeeded in getting their candidates elected in Baden-Württemberg, West Berlin, Hamburg, Lower Saxony and ultimately in the elections to the Bundestag of 1983. On all these occasions the party polled between 5 and 7 per cent of the total, clearly not enough to seize power but sufficient to attract publicity and, in some cases, to prevent stable rule by the two major parties.

While averse, in principle, to entering coalitions, they helped to elect Social Democratic mayors in some key cities such as Kassel, Darmstadt and Marburg. The supporters of the Greens came mainly from the younger generation, as shown by their superior polling in university towns and in student quarters. A public opinion poll in Lower Saxony in 1982 showed – to give but one illustration – that 74 per cent of those aged between 16 and 24 thought that a Green party was needed.[1]

The 'Green' phenomenon reflected the growing discontent with the established parties. By the early 1980s a great many young Germans had come to believe that the quality of life was the major issue and that neither Christian Democrats nor Social Democrats were capable of tackling this successfully. The Green movement grew out of initiatives at local level. Subsequently opposition to the stationing of Pershing II and Cruise missiles became their focus of activity. The Greens advocate a neutral Germany and Europe; thus their opposition is not limited to a Republican administration in Washington. In principle they oppose the Soviet arms build-up too, but they regard America as the far greater menace.

Most members of the Green party consider themselves to the left of the Social Democrats without being Marxists. But this self-assessment is contested on the Left by those who consider the Greens a Utopian and divisive force because they perpetuate the disunity of the Left. They may welcome the Greens as allies in the struggle against 'nuclear death' and NATO, but do not share the negative attitude of the Greens towards the idea of progress. Much of the Green programme can be accepted with equal ease by people from the Right and the Left of the political spectrum. It has not come as a surprise therefore that the extreme Right has been active among them. Anti-Americanism and neutralism are not a monopoly of the extreme Left in Germany or elsewhere in Europe. 'Blind industrialization', 'materialist consumerism', soulless modern society and generally speaking the excesses of modern technology were strongly opposed by the Nazi party, which always stressed the need to return to nature, to a simpler and healthier life.

The great strength of the Greens has been their ability to absorb the discontent of all kinds of single-issue enthusiasts including pacifists, vegetarians, lesbians and protagonists of other causes. It is the party of

---

[1] But a study in 1984 sponsored by the Volkswagen Foundation showed that only 15 per cent of the 16–18 age-group actually supported the Greens; there is a far cry from general sympathy with some of the demands of a new party to personal involvement in its activities.

youth and expects to be trusted by the young generation. But experience has shown that such divergent causes cannot be kept together for long except perhaps by a charismatic leader, which is about the last thing the Greens would welcome. For they are the party of those who demanded 'No Power to Anyone', constant rotation among their leaders, and close control of those elected by the 'basis'. They would like to prove that the iron law of oligarchy does not apply to them. In this respect the Greens have certainly learned a negative lesson from the authoritarian structure of communist parties ('democratic centralism'). But it is impossible to conduct a policy unless the elected represent-atives have at least some freedom of action; and the so-called 'rank and file', furthermore, is no more than yet another elite group, representing the activists but not necessarily the views of the voters.

Thus the fissures leading to splits and certain decline had already appeared in their hour of triumph. Nor was the time of their arrival on the national scene propitious: it coincided with a new technological revolution on the one hand, and on the other with growing unemploy-ment and economic stagnation. An economic policy based on the return to pre-industrial conditions of production is clearly impractical. It may or may not be able to cope with the problems of a people numbering a few million inhabiting a large country rich in resources. But Germany is no such country.

The rise of the Green party can only be understood against the background of the popularity of the causes it has sponsored. But it is one thing to identify a danger, another, far more difficult, to suggest a viable policy to cope with it. The high motivation of this movement is matched only by its muddled ideas. It is certainly an idealistic movement; it feels it has the right to propose – with total inner conviction and from high moral grounds – easy, almost painless, solutions to difficult or even insoluble problems. In its highmindedness and confusion it is a perfect illustration of the state of mind of wide sections of the young generation in Germany at the present time.

Opium for the (young) people?

Youth revolt hovered between rebellion and resignation. While some took to bombs or the barricades others retreated to the private sphere, to various religious cults and sects or to a drug counter-culture. The avant-garde of the late 1960s was Marxist, most of their successors are not political in the narrow sense of the term. But the juxtaposition of active political struggle and passive resignation is partly misleading, for (the late 1960s gave birth not only to anti-authoritarian politics but also to a new youth culture) and the 'unpolitical' 1970s after all produced the 'Green' movement. The political groups base their demands on quasi-scientific arguments, whereas their motivation is quite clearly that of an ersatz religion. The fanaticism of some of the religious sects, on the other hand, recalls the passions of political life.

One of the forms of rebellion against the world of the adults was a religious revival of sorts from which Christianity benefited less than various northern Buddhist (Mahayana) sects which reached Germany via the United States. The emphasis was usually on mysticism, emotionalism and the personality of the guru.

Mystic influences had frequently found fertile ground in Germany; mysticism had been known, in fact, in the early Middle Ages as *philosophia Teutonica*. After the First World War Far Eastern religions had a certain following among sections of the German youth movement, in some other sections of society and in the writings of C. G. Jung and others. But their impact was not wide and certainly not lasting; Hermann Hesse's *Siddharta* first appeared in the 1920s but found its mass readership only in the 1960s. By and large the cults which were successful in the 1970s, such as Ananda Marga (the 'road to happiness'), the Divine Light Mission, Hare Krishna, Scientology, Dianetics (not a Far Eastern sect), Transcendental Meditation and the Unification Church (the Moonies), came into existence only after the Second World War. There are substantial differences between these groups, of which only the major ones have been mentioned: TM and Scientology accept present society but merely provide psychological techniques to individuals striving for 'self-liberation'. Hare Krishna, on the other hand, puts itself into deliberate opposition to the outside world, opting for a monkish existence. The Unification Church is an ideological-political authoritarian organization, hierarchically organized, using massive indoctrination to fight the battle between 'good' and 'evil'. Other groups (such as the 'Family of Love') pretend to offer love and security through a collective religious experience brought about by withdrawal from the outside world.

Only a small minority of German youth has joined these sects. But the very fact that they did find followers at all, and were taken seriously in some circles, caused much concern among parents and educators: what was the attraction of these outlandish and often bizarre cults? One does not have to go far to find the answers: the urge on the part of young people to find certainties in a confusing world which science cannot give, to find love and security which established religion and the family could not provide. It is not a rebellion against repression or an excess of discipline; on the contrary, it is a reaction against a spiritual vacuum, a feeling of emptiness. In Wilhelminian Germany and the Third Reich young people were indoctrinated with traditional values or were filled with heady ideals – perverted perhaps but still quite effective in providing a compass to youth, in overcoming identity crises, in helping the integration of the individual into society. Neither Weimar nor the *Bundesrepublik* had comparable messages appealing to the young generation; they had little to tell youth other than to ask for general support for the principles laid out in the constitution – the *Grundgesetz*. Young people who want to know why to live and how are most unlikely to find moral support in a constitution. They will much rather turn to groups professing firm beliefs, even if it should be Albanian communism as a model for mankind, or the 'witnessing' of the Children of God through prostitution. It is possible that some of the less extreme religious and political sects may have done some good in certain cases – such as providing drug therapy or a social framework for disturbed adolescents. On the whole the cure has been worse than the disease. Underlying this religious revival there has been not true religiosity but regression, the total identification with the group leads a good way towards the total loss of identity. There is, in short, a self-destructive element in most of these cults. Established religion can also be blamed for the success of these sects, for it is well known that such cults grow where (traditional) religion fails. But this does not make the whole phenomenon more positive in character. The spread of sects has been part of the new irrationality which finds converts among young people in need of a message leading beyond the consumer society. They are particularly effective among young people with a weak ego.

If religion, according to one of Marx's most famous *obiter dicta*, is the opium of the people, opium (or one of its derivatives) has become a quasi-religion for some adolescents. It has spread most widely during the last fifteen years. While exact figures are not available, there are indications that experimenting with hard drugs is still rising; that there are no noticeable class differences except with certain fashionable drugs such as cocaine; that first experiences tend to occur at a younger age now; that Berlin is the capital of the drug scene but that drug-taking and peddling has spread to almost all medium-sized and most small cities. Between 60 and 70 per cent of those asked said that curiosity was the main motive for first trying, 44 per cent said that they took it while friends took it – a kind of social drug-taking comparable to social drinking. Almost three-quarters of the addicts have tried at one stage or another to get out of the habit.

Typical is the story of a young girl, Christine F., as recounted in a bestselling book and film. Christine's family had recently moved to Berlin from a village in North Germany. They found an apartment in one of the high-rise buildings in Gropius-Stadt; it looked nice from afar but it was very impersonal. According to Christine the children behaved rather beastly to each other much of the time: playing games was allegedly forbidden. Christine's parents quarrelled and eventually separated. Her mother's friend did not mistreat her but spent most of the time in front of the television set: there was no communication. In school she became a member of a group ('clique') and discovered a new world: 'To be cool' Led Zeppelin and David Bowie. She began to drink and to take marijuana. The clique became the centre of her life; another important meeting-place was the youth hostel of the Protestant church where she was introduced to hashish.

From time to time the social workers told them not to overdo it, but Christine already knew better than to listen to grown-ups, especially to teachers and social workers. In the clique they talked about music and dope and they showed tenderness to each other. 'The Sound' (a discothèque) became her second home. There she met 'types who were fantastically cool'; the term actually used was '*unheimlich*', one of the most fashionable words of successive post-war generations. She had a trip at least twice a week, drank and took drugs almost without interruption. In school she engaged in a long tirade against a teacher who wanted to talk to them about ecological problems: why didn't people behave better to each other? The teacher furthermore should learn to be just to the children.

After a Bowie concert she first injected heroin, just to see whether it really made people as happy as they seemed. To pay for it she became a prostitute. Now aged fourteen or fifteen, she was quite proud since she earned 4,000 DM a month, as much as the head of a big enterprise. She was arrested a few times, but the police were not really interested in her.

Only after becoming a dealer was she put on probation. The woman in the police department dealing with her case would have preferred to send her to prison. She knew from experience that fixers were reckless; they took hard drugs merely out of curiosity and boredom and were invariably surprised when made to accept the consequences. They claim to be humiliated, exploited, outcast by society: everyone is determined to get them, no one is nice to them or gives them a break. In short, it is all the fault of others.

A sad story with some unconvincing alibis: according to Christine's own account she took heroin out of curiosity, not because people were so beastly. The same story has been told by many others. Christine claims that she did not get any help. But what kind of help would she have accepted and from whom could it have come? Would a different social order have resulted in more human housing conditions, would it have saved the marriage of her parents or prevented the children in the playgrounds from beating each other? Many of the teachers and social workers were young, progressive and full of goodwill. But Christine had already decided to hate them. Perhaps they should have paid even more attention, showing even more patience despite all rebuffs. But there is no certainty that the outcome would have been any different. While Christine wanted love and care (and did not get much of either), she did not make it easy for anyone to come to her help. She needed a firm hand, guidance and discipline, and she received even less of these than of love. Christine did not grow up in inhuman conditions nor did she have to face intolerable repression at home or in school. She apparently had no one who greatly cared about her one way or another, a regrettable situation, but not one that can be changed through legislation. No one seems to have tried to inculcate certain values; it was apparently taken for granted that every child had a character which was in no need of forming, certainly not by adults. She drifted into drug-taking not because something horrible was done to her, but because she missed something.

Christine related that taking heroin was not accidental; for months she had unconsciously prepared herself for the experience of graduating from soft to hard drugs. Only a small minority is addicted to hard drugs. But soft drugs and drink were widely taken in the 1970s, had become an essential part of the youth scene. Just as the various factions have their favourite music, they have their favourite stimulants. The Heavy Metal fans love Hard Rock (such as AC-DC, Motorhead and Van

Halen) but drink nothing stronger than beer; the Punks prefer their own special rock (Sex Pistols, UK Rocks) and are said to take about every drug in the pharmacopoeia and some that are not. The Rastas (copying the Rastafari) love Jamaican reggae music (Black Uhuru and Bob Marley) and stick to 'grass'. Fashions rapidly change, every year new groups appear and also new collective experiences. But the general attitude to drugs is unlikely to change soon and it is even more unlikely that music will cease to be a central part of contemporary youth culture.[1] This has been the case from the old youth movement via the rock 'n' roll generation to Woodstock (Music reflects a mood better than any document and it ranges from the search for a new identity to aggression against the adult world and to resignation)

Yet another feature of the new German youth culture is its clothes. The *Wandervögel* and the *Bünde* had their distinctive attire: shirts, cords and neckerchiefs; the youth scene has its distinctive clothes and hair fashions in all lengths and colours of the rainbow; while the Mods favoured army parkas, the Heavy Metal fans opted for blue jeans and shirts of the same material with the emblems of bands and football clubs. Punks and Skinheads wore heavy high boots.

Such fashions are meant to shock adults, appalled when meeting young people with hair dyed blue or green or wearing swastika buttons. Accessories such as earrings and buttons also play an important role. The inscriptions on buttons, posters and stickers are more often than not in English: typical examples are Rocky Horror, Disco Lady, Rainbow Police, Black Sabbath, Earth Wind and Fire. Alternatively they refer to leading figures on the British or American pop scene, from Elvis Presley and Bob Dylan to Led Zeppelin. Such buttons are bought in great quantities, the intention being not to leave free space on shirts, jackets, cars or the walls of one's room. The colours are vivid and the inspiration truly international; the fashions include an Iroquois hair-do, Kamikaze look, Safari and jungle-look T-shirts with abstract landscapes and so on.

The textile industry has been quick in getting into the act of

---

[1] The list of the most popular female singers in 1983/4 was headed by Irene Cara (*Flashdance*) of the US, followed by Kim Wilde who is British. Among the most popular male singers there were Shakin' Stevens, Rod Stewart, Paul Young, Michael Jackson and David Bowie (*Bravo*, 16 January 1984). There seems to be less experimenting with soft drugs now than in the previous decade. Statements on the rating of pop stars are bound to be out of date within a few months; since these lines were written Nena, a twenty-two-year-old girl from Hagen, has risen meteor-like on the German pop scene.

interpreting this taste and catering for it. It has become difficult to know whether a certain new fashion is spontaneous or has been invented by the design department of one of the great department-store chains with a special interest in the youth market. There are boutiques, bars and coffee-houses catering for the young in every German city. But it is not at all clear what is specifically German in these manifestations of a youth style. Most of the inspirations seem to have come from the United States and England. The fashions are copied with great gusto in Germany and linger on long after they have disappeared in their country of origin. But the specific German contribution to this branch of international culture seems to be minimal. Some German music-makers have tried to assert themselves against foreign importations which at one stage almost entirely monopolized the market. Hence the emergence of the *Neue Deutsche Welle* as against David Bowie. But again the inspiration seems to be mid-Atlantic rather than German.

Alternative lifestyles

While drug-taking seems to be fairly evenly distributed among all classes, the cliques with their emphasis on sartorial fashion and their own specific music are predominantly working or lower middle class. Middle-class youth, or those with better than basic education, are more attracted by the more sophisticated forms of an alternative lifestyle.[1]

The idea of a return to a wholesome life – usually on the land – has a long and honourable history in Germany, even if it has been a story of failure. Groups of the extreme Right but also religious socialists of the old youth movement of the 1920s tried it. They should be regarded as the precursors of the agricultural and urban communes (*Wohngemein-schaften*) of the 1970s. 'Alternative' initiatives also produced small publishing houses, a flood of periodicals and even a daily newspaper, *taz*, in West Berlin, a bakery in Wiesbaden, some consumer retail shops, the Sponton electrical workshops in Berlin, a sheep farm in Leutkirch, 'autonomous' theatres and cultural centres. An alternative guide to Berlin mentions six hundred enterprises engaged in various

[1] Which is not to say, of course, that all middle-class youth, or even a majority, has adopted an alternative lifestyle. During the last few years a new conservative mood has made considerable headway among German youth; it is especially strong among the 'teens' and the emergence of the 'Poppers' has been symptomatic. Youth studies unfortunately tend to lag behind events by a few years and Germany is no exception.

forms of manufacture or services.

The occupation of houses condemned by local authorities in Berlin, Cologne, Freiburg (Schwarzwaldhof) and other places, which frequently triggered off street battles, has attracted more publicity than any other activity undertaken by alternative groups. The first major such actions took place in Frankfurt in the autumn of 1970 (*Aktionsgemeinschaft Westend*). They were followed by squatting in Cologne, Göttingen and Hamburg and reached their climax in West Berlin towards the end of the decade. These actions were frequently opposed by the old New Left, which had no sympathy for the mindless smashing of shop windows as a replacement for political action. Rockers and 'teds' meanwhile remained neutral or even attacked the squatters. In some cases there was a genuine need for inexpensive quarters for young boys and girls who had fled from home. Sometimes groups wanted to establish 'autonomous' youth centres. In other instances the squatters were mainly motivated by the wish to defy the authorities and the hated police. Such action provided excitement; the fact that it was also undertaken on behalf of a good cause was coincidental. The following comments by participants seem to be not untypical: 'What a feeling of enjoyment and release when you watch a brick smashing the show-window of a shop', and 'Instead of bathing in champagne I decide to participate in some kind of [violent] action. This is for me also a way of finding satisfaction.'

The seizure of buildings sometimes found support among the public, and in certain cases it was said that while the squatting was illegal, it was not illegitimate. Municipalities, including those headed by the Social Democrats, sometimes tended to approach town planning and housing problems without making due allowance for the human factor. Though the reclamation and the modernization programmes were carried out with the best of intentions, this often led to substantial rent increases, and thus to squeezing out the sections of the population which were unable to afford the higher rents. In certain cases speculators were at work, buying and reselling at considerable profits the land and buildings about to be modernized. Lastly, some groups of squatters on their own initiative invested a great deal of effort in repairing the buildings which had been seized. This was the case, for instance, in the Cuvrystrasse in Berlin-Kreuzberg. Elsewhere only the very minimum (or less) was done to make these houses habitable. Who benefited from squatting? Hardly ever the working class or the poorest of the poor, but young people who had left home and wanted *Lebensraum*. But even more important was the desire to engage in common action in a popular cause, and the knowledge that such action would generate solidarity, warmth and the feeling of power – at least for a while. In the longer run the squatters would quarrel with each other and complain about 'intolerable stress'. Some would work hard and paint the walls, others would refuse to pull their weight. Some negotiated with the local authorities for recognition and perhaps even a contract. Others disdainfully rejected such 'reformist' strategies.

For many squatters the seizure of a building was both a practical and a symbolic action: the conquest of a base, however small, from which society could be changed. The 'reformists' who paved the way for the Greens first developed their theories of alternative (or autonomous) lifestyles at the time of these battles. They advocated the decentralization of work so as to make it enjoyable – suggesting the use of 'soft' technologies. They also envisaged new forms of living in which the nuclear family would no longer monopolize social life. Their efforts were frequently disrupted or sidetracked by the single-issue advocates in their ranks, those claiming that lesbianism or nutritional issues or anti-fluoridation are the most urgent and the most important issue to be given absolute priority.

The alternative proposals and strategies have not yet shown that they are practical on a wider scene. It is one thing to criticize current structures, practices and techniques, and another, far more difficult, to develop new ones, both superior in theory and viable in practice, in a country of sixty million inhabitants, limited natural resources, accustomed to the use of high levels of technology and also a fairly high standard of living. They face such difficulties of education even within their own ranks: the ecologists preach the advantages of walking or cycling over poisoning the atmosphere with the fumes of internal combustion engines. But the motorcycle and the car have still retained their central place in the thought of even the youngest generation.

Young Germans frequently complain that while everyone is doing his (or her) duty by them there is an absence of warmth. It may be true, or true in part, but how to generate such warmth? There are relatively few playgrounds in Germany and relatively many signs saying *'verboten'*. Elderly people in Germany seem to complain more often than elsewhere about children's noise, and it is also true that German children spend less time in school than in most other Western countries; far from being adduced as proof of the humanity of the German system it is interpreted as a sign of neglect. The way to school in Germany is fraught with danger, more children are apparently killed in traffic accidents in Germany than elsewhere. Family life for a variety of reasons is said to be no longer as close as it used to be. German children's books are frequently cruel: in Grimm's Fairy Tales some fifty-six heroes die a natural death, but four times as many are shot, starved, stabbed, smashed, quartered, put on the rack, eaten by wild animals or undergo some other painful treatment before their demise.

These and similar examples are frequently adduced to prove that childhood and adolescence are usually unhappy stages in the life of individuals in Germany. But it is impossible to prove that German children are either more or less happy than children elsewhere even though great attention is paid to children in America, Italy or Russia. But frequently a price has to be paid even for care and attention, and an excess of warmth can also be stifling.

School and university reform: a story of good intentions

The experience of German educational reforms, many of which came as the result of the youth protest of the 1960s, shows the limits of institutional change. It is a story of high hopes and expectations which were not on the whole fulfilled.

Few deny that there was need for reform. The German universities were rather authoritarian in structure and frequently also not very efficient. For example, the rector was usually elected for one year only, hardly sufficient time to initiate and carry out major changes. The professors were supposed to run the university but they did not do it very well. The traditional university was built according to the concept envisaged by Wilhelm von Humboldt some 160 years ago: a place where young people were not only taught, but also engaged in peace and freedom in the search for truth. Science, according to Humboldt, formed not only the mind but also the character; science, as he saw it, was general education, *paideia*, the classical Graeco-Roman ideal, not the urgent issues of yesteryear or today. But the urgent issues could not be ignored and seen in this light the university had become outdated. Following the demonstrations and the riots of the 1960s, the authorities gave their blessing to a series of sweeping reforms which lasted throughout the following decade.

These reforms affected primary and secondary schools as much as the institutions of higher learning. There was a quantum jump; as the number of places in infant (grade) schools rose by 50 per cent within the decade, the number of teachers doubled, so that by 1980 there were more teachers in Germany than soldiers. This was no doubt all to the good, but only a few years later the results of the declining birthrate were felt. By 1983 a large percentage of the newly graduated teachers were unemployed, and there was reason to assume that some of them would never teach.

There had been a first school reform immediately after the war under the auspices of the Allies. By a strange quirk of history the theories of the German school reformers of 1910–25 returned to their country of origin via the United States. Following the second wave of democratization the German schools became the freest in the world, a place where education would be 'collectively imparted without stress and effort'. These in any case were the expectations. The actual results ranged from disappointment to sadness. Far from becoming a place of contentment the schools remained (to use professional jargon) a 'multidimensional field of tensions'. Students were more aggressive and not noticeably happier than before, more teachers were contemplating a change of profession. Frequently the experiences of young teachers were reported who only yesterday had been in the forefront of the struggle for 'emancipation' – the magic word of a whole period – and who now felt mainly frustration and in some cases even feared physical danger.

Conditions in German schools prior to the recent wave of reforms had not been ideal but a certain level of education had still been maintained without too much stress: it could be taken for granted, for instance, that pupils would know by heart a few poems in their native language. This kind of knowledge disappeared not only in the *Länder* most affected by the reforms (such as Hesse) but also in others.

The changes, such as the introduction of a new type of general, unified school with a minimum of streaming (*Gesamtschule*) and the reform of the upper classes of the secondary schools were not for the better. Knowledge that could be taken for granted fifteen years ago at graduation and university entrance no longer existed. The revolutionaries of the late 1960s had referred to some of their teachers as *Fachidioten*, experts who knew more and more about less and less. Ironically the school reforms resulted in specialization at an earlier age and reinforced this tendency. General education, subjects which were of no direct relevance to the subsequent career plans of the student, were no longer in demand.

Humboldt may well have been in need of some reinterpretation, but little was gained by jettisoning the concept of general education altogether. Schools, according to the reformers, were to operate on the assumption that discipline is offered voluntarily without the threat of punishment. But what if patience and tolerance do not have the desired effect, what if vandalism spreads widely? It would be splendid if it could be taken for granted that schoolchildren are sure of themselves and critical, rather than the *Duckmäuser* of the classical old school novel – sneaks fawning on the teacher. But criticism *per se*, the supreme value of the late 1960s, is of no use unless there is also a body of knowledge and experience to which it can be applied.

The theory of radical school reform was based on the fiction of equality, but if there were equality between teachers and pupils there would be no need for education. There is bound to be authority in education and, while it is advisable from a pedagogical point of view not to stress this unduly, there are limits to the tolerance of even the most progressive teachers.

The university reforms, too, were inspired by a great deal of goodwill. The new laws – the *Hochschulrahmengesetz* of 1976 and the corresponding laws of the *Länder* – were based on the assumption that the university would become more democratic, less 'ivory tower' in character and more relevant to real life, by giving the young lecturers and also the students an equal say in running the university. It was assumed that as a result of co-determination most of the problems of running a university would go away. Yet only a few years later it emerged that the attempt had not been a success. Some critics even claimed that higher education had been ruined in the process. Power had passed from the chair-holders to the *Fachbereich*, the group, the department, and almost everyone now had a say on important decisions. But only about 20 per cent of the students participated in the elections. Those who spoke on their behalf more often than not represented a small minority. Democratic procedure can be established by decree, but no amount of legislation can make an institution function according to democratic principles: there has to be a consensus on fundamentals. And even if such a consensus exists, there still is the problem of competence in decision-making: should students, for instance, have an equal say in deciding whether a certain subject should be taught or not? (At most universities, it ought to be added, they do not have this right.)

Alone among all sections of public life, the university became the place where co-determination was tried. No one would have dreamed of carrying out operations in a hospital along such lines, or piloting an aircraft or running a ministry in this way. Universities, in contrast, were considered safe enough for such experimentation. Government showed a great deal of indifference to developments inside the universities and they were quite willing to confirm the appointment of mediocrities, if this was the way of least resistance. The old ritual greeting at the beginning of class (good morning, *Herr Lehrer*) may have been authoritarian and outdated. But quite obviously some discipline had to be maintained and thus, even in the *Länder* in which the most far-reaching reforms had been carried out, the retreat from exposed educational positions began within a year or two after the reforms had been introduced.[1]

Whenever the prerogatives of local authorities were directly challenged – by squatters for instance – even left-wing Social Democrats tended to react sharply. But even right-wingers were not unduly perturbed by the remodelling of the universities: provided the radicals stayed within the walls of the universities and did not ask for more money they were more or less left to their own devices. The laws of bureaucratic politics, as is well known, have their own logic.

Research in the new ('group') university was downgraded. It was still desirable but, compared with other needs, it was considered a luxury. The professors, in any case, doing their duties by the new regulations, had to spend much of their time in committee meetings and administrative functions. A decline in standards ensued: once German universities had been admired and emulated all over the globe. They had attracted ambitious students from the four corners of the world, and everyone knew the worth of a degree from Heidelberg, Jena or

[1] It had been one of the aims of the school reforms to inculcate a new collective spirit among the students. Yet one of the complaints I heard most frequently among those in the higher grades concerned precisely the absence of such a spirit, simply because with growing specialization, almost everyone has a different curriculum. Not a few educators complain that the schools entirely limit their role to imparting knowledge; there is a vacuum as far as the formation of character is concerned. Thus, a decade after the emancipatory wave, there seems to be a new craving for authority, even a 'strong hand', not among the anti-authoritarian teachers, but from among adolescents.

Göttingen. In the 1970s the German universities became something akin to a giant laboratory, but the experiment was not a success. And it was probably no accident that the universities which were most politicized, such as Bremen, declined most.

The road to this state of affairs was paved with good intentions. This refers to the assumptions underlying the 'emancipatory reforms': that students were men and women young in age but mature in spirit, intellectually inquisitive, eager to acquire a maximum of knowledge in a minimum of time. It was forgotten that the learning process is not wholly fun and games for the average student at the best of times. Nor was it taken into account that the universities had to absorb students considerably less well-prepared than before, following the school reforms. Quite frequently the young students were unable to express themselves adequately in their native language, and this was not compensated for by grandiose ideas – how science should be made relevant for society, how all traditional propositions should be approached critically, how greater emphasis should be put on theory rather than the mere collection of mostly irrelevant facts. 'Elitarian standards' and 'repressive tests' were bitterly attacked by the radical students' spokesmen and there were many complaints about the inhuman efforts demanded and stress caused. In extreme cases legal action was brought against universities to lower entrance standards and to raise marks.

After a few years of such experiences not a few professors reached the conclusion that a good student had become the rarest and most gratifying thing in their lives. The majority of students, as these critics saw it, wanted to get by with as little learning as was feasible, to graduate and get a secure job, providing a reasonably good life, involving not too much work and providing retirement on an adequate pension at an early age. Thus behind a smokescreen of revolutionary phraseology an early-pensioner mentality (*Frührentnermentalität*) could be discovered. And behind the attacks against 'bourgeois' science there was no advocacy of proletarian, let alone Marxist, science – but the kind of attitude best expressed in the song of a certain pop group: 'We don't need no education'. Far from becoming truly democratic, the German universities became ineffective institutions in which bureaucratic intervention was palpably felt. Above all, they were places in which neither teachers nor students, neither 'progressives' nor 'conservatives', felt happier than before.

Laments of this kind were widely heard in the 1970s: it was a true picture but it was not quite the whole picture. A decline in the general level would have taken place anyway, quite irrespective of reforms, simply as the result of the enormous expansion of universities over a very short period. Secondly, the impact of reforms was far more strongly felt in some *Länder* than in others, and inside the universities the 'soft' subjects (humanities and social sciences) were more affected than the 'hard' options like the natural sciences. Lastly, the very excesses of the reform and the feeling of failure were bound to bring about a counter-movement, a reaction to the cultural revolution, and this came about even earlier than expected. By the early 1980s the philosophers of the school and university reforms had disappeared from view whereas in the Berlin Free University, a bulwark of the Left, a new president was elected in 1983 who was anything but a believer in the ideas of the cultural revolution.

With all this a considerable amount of damage has been caused. Elementary knowledge has frequently been lowered in school and university and the result has not given much joy to anyone. Not a few German schools have become the scene of political indoctrination: subtle, and sometimes not so subtle. The opponents of the reforms maintain that it is surely not accidental that a nation which once used to collect more Nobel prizes than any other hardly figures now among the recipients. The reasons for this decline have to be traced to a more distant past. The level of German science suffered greatly as the result of Nazism and war, and it was by no means a foregone conclusion that the country would re-emerge after 1945 as a world centre of learning. The Nobel prizewinners of the 1970s were, in any case, the products of schools and universities of the 1930s and 1940s; the reforms of 1970 cannot be made responsible for these failures. The real impact of the reforms will be felt in the years and decades to come, and since awareness of the problem is widespread, the return to research, and even elite research, is only a question of time. The Free Democrats were the first to take up this issue in 1984.

But there yet remains another question to which no satisfactory answer has been found: that of German cultural life and the young generation. Some of the greatest cultural and scientific achievements in Germany in the past were the work of very young people. The issue of *Wunderkinder* quite apart, there have been such examples in every generation. Goethe had written his *Werther*, as well as many poems, and

73

Schiller had published *Die Räuber*, well before they were twenty-five. The same is true for most of the Romantics, for Georg Büchner (who died aged twenty-four), for Heinrich Heine, for many other writers up to Thomas Mann (whose *Buddenbrooks* was written at twenty-four), for Rilke, Hugo von Hofmannsthal, Hermann Hesse (*Peter Camenzind*) and others. Marx was editor-in-chief of the *Rheinische Zeitung* at twenty-six and wrote the *Communist Manifesto* before turning thirty; Einstein published his most important work at twenty-six and Werner Heisenberg at twenty-four. All this happened in the 'pre-emancipatory period', when repression was rife. It is of course known that young people mature at a more advanced age in our period and it is also true that there is no accounting for genius: geniuses are sown sparsely in any time or country. But with all the mitigating circumstances it is still remarkable that in an age of youth revolution with so much creative energy set free it is quite difficult to think of major cultural or scientific achievements by young Germans under the age of, say, thirty-five.

This then was the *Bildungskatastrophe*,[1] the educational disaster. It was brought about by more than one cause. A contributory factor was the softness and the self-pity which spread, the encouragement given by some of the older generation who should have known better to those among the young who came to regard achievement almost as a social stigma. Intolerable stress was invoked time and again, as if it were not the case that young people have suffered nervous breakdowns, taken drugs or committed suicide out of boredom rather than because of excessive homework or fear of examinations. The overall picture would not be complete without stressing again that I found the negative features more pronounced in some parts of Germany than in others and that there have been important changes since the mid 1970s. Common sense has reasserted itself more quickly and more widely than could be expected at the time.

The face of the young generation

Much more is known about German youth today than of any previous generation, partly because more attention has been devoted to the subject than ever before, partly also because the techniques of

[1] The term was coined in the early 1960s but referred at the time mainly to inadequate standards in the natural sciences.

interrogation through public opinion polls have been refined. Few stones have been left unturned, few questions have remained unasked in the course of these inquiries. It is less easy to say with total assurance whether this body of knowledge is entirely reliable, whether opinions and moods are not subject to rapid change, whether, in brief, it is a safe guide for the future.

Looking back, the 'sceptical generation' of the 1950s was followed by an elite committed to political activism in the 1960s. More recently there has been a retreat from politics or, to be precise, from the kind of political illusionism which proclaimed that revolution was just around the corner, and that as a result society would be free and just, personal neuroses would be cured, unhappy people would be content, the plain would be beautiful, the stupid clever, violent people would engage in social work and, generally speaking, everyone would be able to do his own thing, in an atmosphere of mutual goodwill and harmony. Such a description may be a caricature but not by very much. The belief in a brilliant future as the result of political action has largely disappeared, partly because the 'movement' of 1968 ran out of steam, but also because of the failure of the reforms of which mention has already been made. Furthermore, there has been a steady decline of the gods of the 1960s.

Vietnam had then been the great cause and Ho the great leader to whom people looked for inspiration. But Ho is dead, the Americans have left, Vietnam has been liberated. But subsequent events in that country – not to mention in Cambodia – have not been conducive to strengthening faith in either communism or Third Worldism. Afghanistan was invaded and the clamp-down in Poland took place. Developments in the Soviet Union, in China and Cuba have not been encouraging either. The one became 'revisionist', the other militarist, bureaucratic and rather unattractive to exude much fascination. The factions of the PLO have been fighting each other and Khomeiniism has been a major disaster. True, hope springs eternal – Nicaragua may perhaps show the road to a better future. But if US imperialism is still the enemy, it is far more difficult to point to ideals and idols on the international scene: there have been too many false dawns. Even inside Germany most hopes have not materialized: the rebels of the 1960s and 1970s were highly critical about the Social Democrats, and even with the Greens in action today, it is easier to feel enthusiastic about certain single causes (such as, for instance, the anti-nuclear campaign) than about a political party.

Among the first to join the radical movement of the 1960s were the younger writers. But they were also the first to suffer disappointment. For ever in search of good causes to give a deeper meaning to their life, they at long last believed they had found the answer. But the more open-eyed among them had their doubts almost from the very beginning. Nikolaus Born found himself more or less by accident in front of the Berlin Opera at the time of the first big demonstration against the visit of the Shah in 1967. There was a stone in his hand, but he still held it when the demonstration was over. He realized that the demonstrators ('young vicars and organized social workers') were too much intent on *one* truth, and he felt himself incapable of sharing such unconditional enthusiasm. Unlike them, he had no answer to certain questions.

The enthusiasm waned but the distrust of the established parties persisted. They were out to capture votes, it was said; they couldn't care less about people. In fact, the leaders no longer knew, or desired to know, what ordinary people really wanted. The bureaucracy had become all-powerful, the parliament a theatre of the absurd. Such a mood was reminiscent of the anti-parliamentarism of the late 1920s when the *Reichstag* was dismissed by most young people as farcical, a '*Schwatzbude*', and when salvation was expected from new forces outside the traditional political spectrum. The Greens were given a chance by German youth, and there was also a new belief in direct action, such as the citizens' initiatives. Politics at the grassroots level had never been widespread in Germany and these new initiatives seemed worth trying to educate people to take an active part in public affairs. But the assumption that politics on the local level was bound to be positive and progressive by definition was a little naïve: just as local citizens might oppose the building of a nuclear reactor, they might want to keep foreigners out of their town, village or suburb. There was a strange but widespread Rousseauean delusion that the state – the institutions, society – was always the culprit, as if society was not the sum of human beings, as if institutions could possibly be better than the people staffing them, as if people in politics would behave better than in private life and, lastly, as if it were possible to run a modern society without interference in the affairs of the individual and without some regulation.

There was a certain confluence between the world view of the Left and the far Right, which also preferred deregulation. A generation educated on Marxism and Freud should have taken a more realistic view about the perfectibility of mankind in the near future. But then young people needed faith, and if historical experience undermines or contradicts faith – too bad for history and experience. They were encouraged in their aversion to history by some of their elders, who in their wisdom suggested (as did Hesse for instance) that it might be a good idea to abolish the teaching of history in school altogether and replace it by some hybrid new discipline. This downgrading of history is of importance for, when historical standards for comparison vanish, what happened in the past no longer matters, the present state of affairs easily appears intolerable, and radical change seems always possible.

The great majority of student youth certainly did not advocate a Soviet-style system for Germany. Some favoured quasi-anarchist strategies based on direct ('basis-controlled') socialist democracy. Others wanted to go back to the idea of the soviets (councils) which had been envisaged but not adopted in the Russian Revolution. They saw the greater danger in 'aggressive American policies': the fact that America was far away and the Soviet bloc a next-door neighbour did not bother them. As they saw it, Germany would be safe only if it proclaimed its neutrality in the West–East conflict. But was not the West–East rivalry mainly about Europe, about Germany? This was not the way they saw it: the idea of opting out had great attraction and the hard facts of geopolitics seemed fabrications of professional cold warriors. There was an unwillingness to accept the fact that Germany was not a Pacific island, a belief that one could opt out of history and geography if one only wanted it enough: there would be no war if people refused to attend the spectacle.

The allusion to a South Sea island may appear far-fetched but it is, in fact, of a certain relevance. Successive opinion polls have shown that dreams about a life in the sun under palms on such an island (or at the least in a faraway fishing village remote from neighbours) have an uncommon attraction for German youth.[1]

[1] 'The Shangri-La of the generation of the 1980s is a South Sea Island', according to *Jugend '81*, the most comprehensive such study sponsored by German Shell: 'A South Sea Island with palms, sun and many fruits, how much do you want to live there? 55% replied "very much", 32% "much", 10% said "not so much" and 4% "no" or "not at all".' These fantasies also express themselves in sartorial fashions (Hawaii Look, etc.). But would a similar poll carried out fifty or eighty years ago have shown very different results?

The majority of young people profess not to believe in politics. But at this point, inevitably perhaps, contradictory attitudes emerge: 40 per cent nevertheless claim to be very much interested in politics. One-third believes in self-help, three-quarters are in favour of the nationalization of major industries, one-third thinks that all reforms are mere patchwork. The great majority rejects the dictatorship of the proletariat. One-third is willing to participate in the armed defence, if necessary, of Germany's democratic order; 40 per cent are ready to use violence for political purposes but only in defence against would-be dictators, in self-defence, etc.; 20–30 per cent are in favour of 'unconventional forms of protest' but only 8 per cent favour violent action (i.e. terrorism).

Much water has flowed down the Rhine since the young rebels of 1968 regarded themselves as the avant-garde of the revolutionary working class. The rebels of the early 1980s feel no special link with the proletariat and they have asked the generation of the friends of Rudi Dutschke, the left-wing students' leader, to leave the younger ones alone since they fail to understand them in any case. Capitalism is still the main villain for the youngest generation of the 1980s. But radical political and social demands now go hand in hand with a longing for security and hedonism; everyone should have whatever he or she needs to be happy. It is easy to envisage agreement between people from all political camps in all countries and at all times. But how to achieve these aims? They will admit that their propositions involve certain problems and dilemmas, but they seem to be not unduly bothered by internal contradictions. There has to be national security, but the majority opposes the very concept of deterrence and about half the high-school graduates do not wish to serve in the *Bundeswehr*.[1] Of today's students 90 per cent are not interested in established religion and seldom, if ever, attend church. They may no longer believe in God, but many are still superstitious and there is a revival of irrational trends. They do not think much of marriage, and every second person claims that he (or she) will never marry. But most of them will, of course, marry in the end despite the criticism of the nuclear family and its problematical character. There is much talk about the need for love and more tenderness which has become a key concept of youth culture. But concentrated anger and aggression are also constantly invoked. High-

[1] But only 30 per cent of the age-group actually graduate from high school (*Gymnasium*) and with all the ideological reservations the *Bundeswehr* has had more volunteers than it could handle.

school pupils and students say that they abominate manifestations of rabid nationalism, let alone racialism. This by and large seems to be true. But once they face such conflicts in their own surroundings, say in relations with foreign workers and their offspring, much of the goodwill and the humanism tends to evaporate as both the polls and experience have shown.

Most of the discussion so far on the young generation has dealt with high-school and university students predominantly of middle-class origin. But the social investigators have not neglected the rest, which is to say the majority. They claim to have discovered also among them profound changes in values and attitudes amounting to a cultural revolution. Could it be that these changes affect the whole population rather than the young generation? Yes, the investigators say, but the young generation is more affected than the rest; class differences seem to matter less in this context than the differences between the age-groups.

The findings can be summarized as a radical turning away from traditional values such as the belief that work and effort are of crucial importance in society, that one should not waste money but save, that young people should be polite, modest and unobtrusive, that it is important to adjust oneself to one's surroundings at home and at work, that honesty is a cardinal virtue and that even petty thievery at work is reprehensible. These and other basic values, once known, broadly speaking, as the Protestant ethic (but apparently more frequently found in recent decades among the non-Protestants of South Korea, Japan and Singapore), seem to have few adherents among the young: 'ethos is slipping', it is reported. According to other investigations young workers are increasingly saying that they want to enjoy life; spare time and holidays are now more important than work. Some 40 per cent said, in fact, that they would be quite happy leading a life altogether without work. Effort and risk in one's working life are to be evaded as much as possible, since the prospects of improving one's status through initiative and effort seem doubtful in any case.

There is the growing belief that justice and equality are synonymous, and that no special rewards should be given for extra effort. On the other hand the appeal of socialism seems to be declining; it is widely identified with unfreedom and compulsion. Lastly, a growing pessimism has been noted in comparison with the 1950s and early 1960s: life, it is thought, becomes all along more difficult, even though the belief in

79

scientific progress and the marvels of modern technology has not been affected so far.[1] In short, the Germans who idolized duty, who always liked a job well done, who were workaholics, seem to have undergone a fundamental change in outlook: their values and ideals are no longer the same.

But final judgment ought to be reserved. It is beyond question that there have been such trends and they have been most pronounced among the young. But how far will they go? Mankind is now in the first stage of a new technological revolution in which the character of labour in society will undergo profound change, in which fewer working hours will be needed and the working life of the individual will be shorter than in the past. Attitudes to work are likely to change, as past experience has shown. Italy was traditonally the country of *dolce far niente*, yet Northern Italy after the Second World War became the country of hard and conscientious work *par excellence*. There is no accounting for such changes in the national mood, just as there is no obvious causal explanation for the fact that the *fin-de-siècle* mood in France (the belief that the country was degenerate beyond redemption) suddenly gave way around 1905 to a positive attitude, to a cult of nationalism and physical fitness, even though *objectively* nothing had changed in France, except that a new generation had arrived on the scene, bored with the boredom of its predecessors. More recently there was the famous and often quoted vote of the Oxford Union in the 1930s not to fight for King and country. Not many years passed and the under-graduates of that class became war heroes.

All this is not to argue that history always repeats itself, that there is

[1] Young Germans are probably the most investigated group of people in the world. There are reliable data about whether they suffer headaches more frequently in autumn than in spring, whether they prefer to take their holidays alone or together, what they think of Luther, the pill and their mother-in-law, when they drank water from the tap most recently. Their favourite professions are fashion designer for girls and pilot for boys. Much depends, of course, on the phrasing of the question. It has to be recalled furthermore that only now, for the first time in German history, do the great majority of people seem to feel free to answer without political and social constraints. Did young workers feel more positive towards their work in 1884 or in 1934 than at present? Attitudes towards saving have changed for the worse according to the polls. But in actual fact the rate of saving rose from 11 per cent in 1965 to 13.4 per cent in 1980. Equally paradoxically, one of the most influential social investigators, Professor Nölle-Neumann, observed well before the 'cultural revolution' of 1968–75 that only 12 per cent of those asked wanted to accept important and responsible assignments and that soldier and politician were lowest in the scale of desirable professions. While close attention should be paid to findings of this kind they have to be critically examined, nor are they necessarily accurate signposts for changes in views and mood.

nothing new under the sun and that in the struggle between Eros and Thanatos the former will always prevail. But it may well mean that the worst fears that have been expressed with regard to the changes of attitudes towards work among the young generation are misplaced, or at the least exaggerated. If it were true that, to put it crudely, indifference and laziness have replaced the old work ethos, there would be reason to worry about the prospects for a country heavily dependent on exports. But if there was indeed such a change, it was caused in considerable part by the general prosperity of the 1960s and 1970s. The going in the years to come will be rougher, there will be persistent unemployment and it can no longer be taken for granted that the standard of living will improve more or less automatically every year. Realities have a self-correcting effect and while individuals on rare occasions commit suicide, whole societies hardly ever do.

Much of what has been noted so far could be said with equal justification about youth in other Western societies. What is specifically German about the protest movement of the young German generation? In some respects precious little: music, to give an obvious example, plays a central part in youth culture everywhere. A comparison with other European countries shows that as far as their political views are concerned (Left–Right) young Germans up to twenty-five years of age are somewhere in the middle, but those over twenty-five are a little to the right of centre. As far as national pride is concerned young Germans score very low and the same is true with regard to religion (together with the British). Attitudes towards their parents are slightly worse than the European average but not significantly so. What about the post-materialist character of the young generation? There are as many 'post-materialists' as there were ten years ago, but those who were between fifteen and twenty-four ten years ago have again become a bit more materialistic, which may necessitate some revisions in the more sweeping theories developed in the 1970s.

The attitudes of the older generation towards youth protest ranged from welcoming it with great enthusiasm, uncritically hailing every new fad and fashion as the embodiment of wisdom, creativity and beauty, to total rejection. Youth, as Martin Buber once said, was the eternal hope, the *Glückschance* of mankind. The genuflections of the older generation, their ecstatic 'O altitudo' were both comic and embarrassing. But many others, on the contrary, voiced apocalyptic forebodings: civilization, as they saw it, was coming to an end. They

81

failed to realize that youth protest, far from being an unprecedented disaster, has occurred at fairly regular intervals throughout history and that there are in-built limitations even to cultural revolutions. If youth protest in Germany in some respects went further than elsewhere, so did the reaction of the parents' generation. Nor did they show much imagination in trying to understand the motives of the rebels. The world as seen by a very young man or woman in the 1970s was certainly far from perfect. There was the danger of nuclear war with its unimaginable horrors, the gradual destruction of nature, the wastefulness and irrationality of consumer society, the ugliness and the coldness of the cities, the feeling of impotence on the part of the individual *vis-à-vis* various anonymous, all-powerful forces and repression of every kind. The list is long, and the complaints were all justified if one compared the world not with what it had been in the past but with what it ought to have been. Their ideological mentors told them that capitalist society was sick unto death, that it had exhausted its constructive ideas. Thus it came as no surprise that the demonstrators confronting the police in Zürich, Amsterdam, Berlin and Hanover proclaimed: 'We have enough reason to weep even without your tear gas.' What sensitive human being could feel well in the anonymous concrete jungles of the big cities, could be happy in a world in which social ties had shrunk and roots disappeared? Novalis's complaints about the waning of the Middle Ages acquired a new meaning: once upon a time the individual had his or her firm place in family and village; religion, culture and tradition prescribed his or her behaviour; everyone knew where he belonged. A price had to be paid, to be sure, but the reward was security, so palpably absent in the modern world.

This then was the character of the society in which they had grown up and which they had come to loathe. What was to replace it? They discovered Marx and Lenin, and some even read Georg Lukács and Karl Korsch, Walter Benjamin and Ernst Bloch. But these had been critics of society, not builders of a new one, with the partial exception of Lenin.

The rebels complained about the many anxieties besetting them which, as they claimed, had been induced by the unnecessary strains and conflicts of the present social order. They failed to accept that even a tightly integrated society is not free of *Angst*. In fact, in the Middle Ages, let alone in primitive societies, people had been even more riddled by anxiety. In the last resort, the quarrel of the young critics was

ridiculous

not so much with society as with the human condition, the fact that
however much institutions could be perfected, essential features of
human character and of relations between people would remain
unchanged, people would still suffer and eventually die. To accept the
essentially tragic character of human existence does not come easily to
youth; perhaps such acceptance would be unnatural. And so it was only
natural that they should blame authoritarian institutions and economic
and social structures.

Permanent revolution and the 'new social movements'

In the late 1970s it was widely believed that the revolutionary wave of
1968 had ebbed away. There were many indications to confirm this
view. The reforms in the schools and on the campuses, whatever their
other consequences, seemed to have defused the tensions there; most of
the political activists of the late 1960s had joined the established
political parties or sects. Terrorism had abated, a Social Democratic
government was in power in Bonn. True, there had been some
manifestations of unrest here and there against the *Startbahn West* (the
project to expand Frankfurt airport), at Gorleben and other places
somehow connected with nuclear installations. But these demonstrations and clashes with the forces of order were not that different from
similar events in other parts of Europe. Then, in 1981, as suddenly as
thirteen years earlier, there was a new wave of violent demonstrations
which left politicians, parents and teachers shocked and very much
confused. There were some notable differences between the new
revolutionaries, the *Spontis* and the *Autonomen*, and their predecessors.
They had no leaders, in fact hardly any organization. They were
inchoate, sometimes literally speechless. Their motivation was not
political in the ideological-doctrinaire sense of 1968. In fact, the old
APO (Extra-parliamentary Opposition) took a very dim view of these
products of an education which they had helped to initiate, whereas the
Spontis bitterly resented any attempt on the part of the aged revolutionaries of 1968 to join the bandwagon.

What caused this new outbreak? Had Germany entered an age of
permanent youth rebellion? A government committee of inquiry
published its findings in February 1983, and while its report contained
much that was true, it failed to see the obvious in some essential

83

respects. It juxtaposed the 'political' character of the revolt of 1968 and the 'emotional and spontaneous' character of that of 1981. There were differences, but how much importance should be attributed to them? The generation of Rudi Dutschke had expressed its views in Marxist, or para-Marxist, language, and had spent an inordinate amount of time in the interpretation of various radical thinkers, not all of them of great importance. But the underlying motivation was, of course, as emotional and spontaneous in 1967 as in 1981: it was a romantic movement with a rationalist superstructure, which the rebels of 1981 lacked.

The experts in Bonn noted (unanimously, the report stated) that youth protest should be viewed as a response to unsolved social problems and not as a 'classic conflict between the generations'. They saw it as an expression of basic changes in attitudes and mentality not just among youth but in wide parts of society. This, quite obviously, was a reference to the concept of a 'new social movement' first developed in the 1970s. According to this the youth protest was not just a manifestation of generational revolt but a response to the crisis of the industrial system and of representative democracy. It signified the emergence of new social groups, disaffected and marginal, directly hit by the transition to post-industrial society. It was an interesting theory and contained some elements of truth. But it tended to ignore the great weaknesses of a movement of this kind, the presence of so many disparate elements, the anti-intellectualism, the commitment to 'cultures of identity', the quest for 'autonomous spheres', the tendency towards de-solidarization. In short, while the considerable opposition-ist force of the new movement was rightly stressed, it was not realized that a movement engaged in the search for the 'true self' and 'authenticity' could not possibly be a serious contender for political or social power under any circumstances.

'Unsolved social problems' can mean a great many things. Did they perhaps have youth unemployment in mind or repression in school? No, the committee replied, only a few unemployed had participated in the protest and school was no longer repressive; on the contrary, 'democratization' had made parents and teachers insecure. 'Unsolved social problems' always exist and are therefore a popular scapegoat. In this specific case the more profound causes may have to be traced in a different direction – the existence of what, for want of a better term, ought to be called a spiritual void, a *Sinnkrise*, the need for ideals, for post-material values, meaning creativity and a community spirit rather than prosperity.

The young generation's fear of the future has also been invoked, its near despair, and on the other hand the legitimization crisis – the fact that the authorities, the state, were so often not accepted by the young. Despair has frequently been a dominant mood among the young throughout history: not total despair nor a despondency lasting for ever. Legitimization is the Achilles' heel of free societies. Nazism did not face this problem, its legitimacy was not doubted by a majority of young Germans. I have quoted elsewhere the typical reaction of a member of the German youth movement on the day of the Nazi take-over in 1933:

> The fact was that National Socialism offered all that a young man in his most secret and proudest imagination would desire – activity, responsibility for his fellows and work with equally enthusiastic comrades for a greater and stronger fatherland. It held out official recognition, and careers that had been unthinkable before; while on the other side there were only difficulties and dangers, an empty future and doubts in the heart.[1]

All we know about the Soviet Komsomol in the 1920s and early 1930s shows equal idealism, the willingness to undertake great efforts and to make sacrifices on behalf of a cause.

Nazism and communism to be sure provided pseudo-legitimacy and false ideals. They exploited the innate idealism of young people for inhuman purposes. But parliamentary democracy cannot even provide this, it has nothing to offer but relative freedom. And this is not very much for a generation which has never been deprived of freedom. The modern dictatorships have no more an answer to the *Sinnkrise* than anyone else, but they contain a magnetic element absent in democracy. They know how to stage great spectacles, they generate powerful myths and there is no time even to think about a spiritual void.

There is no known cure except the message of a new religion or secular religion. The problem can be assuaged, tensions can be reduced, but there is no solution. But if this is a universal problem, how to explain the fact that Germany should be affected more than other nations?

Mention has been made of the traditional German quest for the unconditional, the *refusal* to accept compromise, to live with boredom and imperfection. Germany has been the country *par excellence* of

---

[1] Walter Laqueur, *Young Germany* (London 1962), p. 202; new ed., New Brunswick, NY, 1984

Romanticism, and also the only country to produce a neo-romantic youth movement. The same tradition may well underlie the present unrest. To some extent the protest movement is global, but young Germans have suffered more acutely and reacted more violently than the rest. Reforms and dialogues will only have a limited effect on a movement of this kind. Reforms may be desirable in any case and dialogues will do no harm, provided that the adults do not try too hard to appear young in spirit, heart, body and fashion. Too much understanding will only cause irritation, for protest is a psychological necessity, an inherent part of growing up. Young people have claimed since time immemorial that their elders cannot understand them and in part they have been right. If so, there is not that much that adults can do when confronting such protest, except do away with obvious social ills and face the movement with some detachment.

There is something unhealthy in the excessive preoccupation with the problems of youth. Never before in history has so much attention been paid to the changing moods and views of youth, and never before has so little been achieved. One of the first to recognize the problem was the Dutch historian Johan Huizinga, who coined the phrase 'puerilism' in the 1930s. He defined it as permanent puberty (or as social scientists would now say 'post-adolescence'), a lack of personal dignity, of decent behaviour and respect towards others, the weakening of the critical consciousness, a semi-voluntary infatuation. Was it not an obvious symptom of decadence or senility, all this combined with the adulation of youth, the abdication of the older generation in favour of the immature? Civilizations at the height of their creative power have loved youth (Huizinga wrote), but had neither spoiled nor celebrated it but demanded obedience and respect. Huizinga deplored the phenomenon but did not blame the young generation, for the young, after all, had not invented the cult of youth.

Karl Jaspers pursued the same theme: when things are in a state of dissolution (he wrote in the early 1930s) youth acquires a value *per se*. Young folk demand what their teachers no longer possess, and the older generation turn to youth, expecting it to supply them with a message that has vanished from the world, endowing it with some fictitious superiority. These views were aired at a time when fascism made its appearance on the European scene. Fascism and Nazism were, among other things, a protest movement of the younger generation. Hitler was Germany's youngest chancellor ever, his closest aides such as Josef

Goebbels and Heinrich Himmler were in their thirties, and some others were in their twenties. The anthem of Italian fascism, it will be recalled, was 'Giovinezza' – Youth.

Parallels with that horrible period of recent German history will be resented. But there are certain analogies which cannot be simply ignored. There is a dilemma which many adults find difficult to face: the fact that, on the one hand, so many valuable and great things in the annals of mankind have been done by young people and that, on the other hand, youth almost by definition lacks maturity, is in need of guidance, education and, on occasion, even a firm hand. It has always proved difficult to steer a middle course between repression and the adulation of youth. Repression does not solve the problem, nor does the abdication of responsibility on the part of the grown-ups. The young generation revolts against repression but it seems to suffer even more when there is no authority, when parents and teachers fail to help them to make sense of a confusing world, showing them how to live and what to do. Such guidance is difficult to come by in an age in which firm beliefs have become rare. Instead youth has been encouraged by some educators to regard itself as the measure of all things and to disregard past experience. Such advice given at the most impressionable age can only lead to severe disorientation; it opens the door to all kinds of charlatans, false gurus and political demagogues.

Germany was not only the country of Romanticism and the *Wandervögel* but also of the Pied Piper. Not long ago, more or less by accident, I found myself in the very place in which the children were led into the mountain which swallowed them. It happened to be almost exactly seven hundred years, to the day, that the disaster had occurred and it was suitably commemorated all over this prosperous city. There is an open-air theatre where the story is re-enacted; restaurants, coffee-houses and many shops recall the events which have entered European and world literature. The experts maintain that the historical kernel underlying the story is disputed to this day: some point to the children's crusade, but others deny this. I watched the proceedings from the guildhall, now the municipal centre. A man in medieval garb appears playing the flute. He is followed by a small army of children dressed as rats and performing the rat dance. But the atmosphere is not one of doom and gloom, many thousands of parents and children obviously enjoy the spectacle. Hamelin's fair, one of the biggest this side of Coney Island, is a permament fixture with its countless merry-go-rounds, candy-floss, hamburger stands and shooting-galleries. Is this all a giant delusion or have the Germans learned their lesson? We have it on the authority of Adolf Hitler that a nation does not burn its fingers twice: 'The trick of the Pied Piper could work only once.' This sounds reassuring but as far as young Germany is concerned the memory of the Führer is receding into the distant past, and in any case there are tricks to be played other than the Pied Piper's.

A German philosopher once noted that he who sees two or three generations is like someone who sits in a conjurer's booth at a fair, and sees tricks which are meant to be seen only once.[1] This is true with regard to 'normal' periods, but the twentieth century has been an age of discontinuity. There was the generation (or cohort) of those like Konrad Adenauer who grew up in the security of the 'world of yesterday'. The outlook of the next generation was shaped by the experience of the First World War. This was followed by those who reached maturity in the late Weimar Republic or under Hitler. After the débâcle there came the 'sceptical generation' and, most recently, two revolutionary generations. As authority weakened, as the self-confidence of parents and teachers declined, youth protest has become something akin to Trotsky's permanent revolution. But like Trotsky's concept it is largely a figment of the imagination: periods of hectic activity on the youth scene are followed by apathy; at one time the emphasis is on cultural change, at others on political demands. There are fairly quick changes in mood and outlook: as these lines are written the demonstrations of 1981 are almost forgotten.

What has been the outcome of youth protest? In its late eighteenth-century manifestations it was largely literary in character; *Sturm und Drang* killed the fathers but only figuratively speaking. The youth movement of 1896 was also mainly cultural in inspiration. During the last decades youth protest in Germany has become increasingly political in character. At a recent meeting of French and German historians a Frenchman argued that recent German history is replete with uprisings of the young generation (*Aufbruch der jungen Generation*), and that invariably it has taken the wrong turning – in 1871, in 1914 and in 1933. In 1968 it turned to terrorism and in the early 1980s to neutralism. It is a provocative statement and probably meant to be taken with a pinch of salt: the foundation of the Reich in 1871 was Bismarck's achievement, not the doing of the young generation. The unfortunate 'ideas of 1914'

---

[1] Arthur Schopenhauer, *Parerga and Paralipomena*.

were rampant all over Europe: war would save the nations from suffocation. Nor is it true that German youth turned to terrorism with Andreas Baader and Ulrike Meinhof; their story is one of pathetic isolation. But there was in the early 1930s a tremendous amount of enthusiasm, unthinking and unreflecting. It was easily guided into the wrong channels. There are such dangers today: historical lessons can be learned too well and the cultivation of *Angst* in our day is largely a reaction to the pre–1945 official heroism. Some Germans find it difficult to accept that there are compromises between wearing jackboots and walking barefoot.

The concern about the politics of the young generation is perfectly legitimate. But youth politics, like youth culture, are subject to rapid changes, and the essence of a young generation is seldom found in its politics and virtually never in its manifestos which, in any case, express only the thoughts of a small minority. There is so much that is attractive in contemporary German youth. Nothing could be further from reality than the assumption that most of these young people are neurotic wrecks wavering between joining a terrorist movement of the extreme Left or of the far Right. In many respects, social and cultural alike, there are no marked differences between them and the young generations in other Western countries.[1] Never before in history has the affinity been so close. If there have been important changes in the attitudes of youth, these have been world-wide rather than specifically German. The main difference is that Germans are great worriers and the youth of today is no exception: apprehensive by tradition, their anxieties have been reinforced by preachers of fear. Like their sixteenth-century ancestors, they are bound to wake up one day to the fact that the prophecies of apocalypse have been premature. In the meantime a certain *fin-de-siècle* ('no future') pessimism will prevail. But it does not go that deep: historical experience shows that such moods are real, but given to sudden and far-reaching change.

[1] Opposition on a massive scale to service in the armed forces would be unthinkable in France and Italy. Since these countries have major Communist parties, it appears that German pacifism is rooted in a different mentality and ethos, or an extreme reaction against militarism – rather than in a specific political orientation. So much has been said and written about the pacifism of the young generation that the impression has been created that the great majority does not want to join the army. But according to the most recent studies (1984) among this age-group (16–18-year-old) undertaken on behalf of the Volkswagen Foundation, 74 per cent had no compunction about joining the *Bundeswehr*. Thus the more negative figures about attitudes among high school graduates earlier quoted seem to be already out of date.

During my peregrinations in Germany I made it my business to visit also the upper classes of secondary schools and even an occasional *Diskothek*, to talk and to listen. As a result I have the growing suspicion that while much that has been said in this chapter may be true with regard to young people in their late twenties and thirties, it no longer applies to those aged seventeen or eighteen. A generation different from the preceding one is about to make its appearance on the German scene, but it is too early to point with assurance and in detail to the character of a cohort that was not even born when Rudi Dutschke unfurled the banner of revolt in Berlin.

4 Intermezzo or Variations on German Folk-Songs

One day not long ago I found myself seated on the pavement in an open-air coffee-house in the city of Detmold, watching the passers-by and pondering the future of Germany. A city of sixty-five thousand inhabitants, it has a number of well-kept castles, a fine theatre, and much visible evidence of the fact that a grand duke once resided here. It is a charming city which Thomas Mann may have had in mind when he wrote *Royal Highness*. The half-timbered buildings are well kept and impressive. On almost every one there are inscriptions in Latin or German. They give the name of the first owner and his wife, and bits of advice of a general kind: 'in all labour there is profit', 'the path of the just is as the shining light', 'righteousness exalteth a nation'.

The centre of Detmold, like that of almost all German cities, has become a pedestrian zone; there are restaurants and ice-cream parlours. In the front of the coffee-house where I am sitting four pleasant young people are making music. They obviously do not expect to be paid; it is agit-prop on behalf of some political cause, probably of the far Left. But this is a very bourgeois city, unpromising for Maoism or the New Left. Walking the streets, I've seen more than a few signs for organizations like 'The Association of Expellees from the East'. If Christ stopped at Eboli, Lenin did not linger long at Detmold – even though the three most prominent citizens of Detmold were all of the Left. There was Ferdinand Freiligrath, the radical poet. There was Georg Weerth, according to Engels 'the first writer of the German proletariat', and the only one with whom Marx did not quarrel. And there was Malwida von Meysenbug, the intellectual lady who knew and was admired by two or three generations of Europeans from Alexander Herzen and Richard Wagner to Romain Rolland and Lou Andreas-Salomé.

The repertory of the four minstrels is wide – there are some IWW (Industrial Workers of the World) songs in English, some Spanish songs of Civil War vintage, and one in German about a capitalist who, having transferred his money to a Swiss bank account, closes down his factory. The patrons don't pay much attention, but there is not much active hostility either. At last one of the singers makes a little speech which I hope will bring some clarification. But my confusion deepens; though the speech is made in German, a language not unfamiliar to me, the meaning is incomprehensible. Then they start singing again – some German folk-songs, a Negro spiritual, then a song about Jesus. Do they belong to a religious rather than a political sect? They are quite common in Germany nowadays, ranging from Ananda Marga (a Buddhist sect) to the Unification Church.

I pride myself on my ability to establish the political motivation of a speaker, or group of speakers, after a few minutes. But that day in Detmold I suffered total defeat. The minstrels were obviously quite critical, even angry. But whether they attacked the state and society from the Left, the Right, some transcendental point of view, or a mixture of all three remained a mystery. Later that evening in the hotel it occurred to me that perhaps the episode reflected the general confusion here.

Next day I returned to my coffee-house and the singers were back too. This time they opened with a fine old song: '*Brüder, zur Sonne, zur Freiheit, Brüder zum Lichte empor!*' (Brothers, turn towards the sun, upwards to light and Freedom!). It is a rousing, spirited song, and it brings up all kinds of memories, of many years ago, of rows of tents somewhere at the edge of a forest, of boys and girls marching behind a banner. Is there a German of any age who does not know this song? It is an optimistic, positive song with its imagery of the endless columns of millions emerging from the night, marching into the glow of a new dawn. (It is notoriously difficult to render the text of songs in another language – more about this anon.) There is also the image of unity, something like Auld Lang Syne, clasp your hands, brothers, defy danger, defy death; an end to slavery, break the yoke of tyrants, sacred the last battle.

It is a fine song, this unofficial anthem of the Young Socialists and the peace movement – but also of countless other groups, and it is probably unfair to analyse it too closely. Who in Germany in this day and age feels that he (or she) is about to emerge from the night of slavery into the bright day of freedom, having lived under the yoke of tyranny? Who believes in that final battle between good and evil which also appears so prominently in the *Internationale* and before that featured in medieval eschatology? No generation in the annals of German history ever grew up in greater freedom; perhaps they sing it unthinkingly, like other old songs; perhaps the text is no longer of much consequence?

But the memories connected with the song are not all pleasant. When I went to school, in the early years of Nazi Germany, '*Brüder, zur Sonne, zur Freiheit*' appeared in our songbooks with a short comment at the beginning: 'Author and composer unknown'. Where did the song originate? Many years ago in a Moscow shop I bought an album called 'Lenin's beloved songs', and here it was, between *Sacred Baikal*, the *Warszawianka* and other Russian patriotic and revolutionary songs.

The rest of the story is quickly told. There are few songs whose origins can be traced with such certainty. The author and composer was a strange Russian – part genius, part Bohemian and drifter, named Leonid Petrovich Radin, born in 1860 in Rauenburg. This place, notwithstanding its German name, is located in deepest Russia, a couple of hundred miles south-east of Moscow. The Soviet Encyclopedia refers to him as professional revolutionary, poet and inventor. He studied chemistry with Mendeleev, the greatest Russian chemist of his time, wrote a chemistry textbook for working-class students and re-invented (or reconstructed) the mimeograph machine which had been built a few years earlier by Thomas Alva Edison. (This machine was put to good use by the illegal Social-Democratic party for printing its underground pamphlets and periodicals.)

He also wrote in 1896, on the eve of the big strike of the Moscow railway workers, a song *Smelo Tovarishchi v Nogu* (Boldly forward, comrades) which, published in the journal *Krasnoe Znamya* in 1900, the year of Radin's death, almost immediately became phenomenally popular. Every young Russian is still taught this song in school or Komsomol and there are few who don't know it by heart. The Russian text is slightly more revolutionary than the German. 'We came out of the people, children of the working-class family; we were kept long in chains and starved. But the hour of redemption has struck.' Later on the song mentions rifles, bullets and bayonets and it ends with a ringing vision of victory: 'With a mighty hand we shall break for ever the fatal oppression, and we shall hoist all over the planet *krasnoe znamya truda* – the red banner of labour.'

Exit Radin, enter Hermann Scherchen. Born in 1891, the son of an innkeeper in Berlin, he opted early on for a musical career, became a disciple of Arnold Schoenberg and took part in the long rehearsals for the first performance of *Pierrot Lunaire*. When the First World War broke out Scherchen, still only in his early twenties, was guest conductor in a seaside resort near Riga. He was interned by the Russians as an enemy alien and spent the long war years, not too uncomfortably, in Vyatka (now Kirov), in the east of European Russia. He founded a children's choir in the internees' camp and later on became the conductor at the local theatre. Scherchen learned Russian, became an ardent supporter of the Russian revolutionary movement, and after his return to Germany served for a time as director of the German workers' *Sänger-Bund*. His subsequent professional career as a distinguished conductor and also as the editor of the periodical *Melos*, the main organ of modern music, is well known.

One day, not long after his return to Germany from Russia, in between rehearsals with the Schubert choir, he had a sudden inspiration and jotted down from memory the song which he had so often heard in Vyatka:

Again, as in Russia, the song was an instant, tremendous success. It was sung not only on the Left but also on the Right, and it became one of the favourite songs of the German youth movement. A literal translation from the Russian was quite impossible, and so Scherchen, rightly no doubt, took considerable liberties with Radin's song while preserving its spirit. It was, even in translation, a progressive song with the emphasis on light, freedom and the vision of a better future; it was revolutionary but at the same time vague enough to apppeal to all those who wanted change, to go forward, quite irrespective of direction – of which there were a great many in Weimar Germany.

Another ten years passed: Hitler came to power and Scherchen emigrated. The marching columns of the SA and the Hitler Youth had no wish to give up a song which was so popular just because it had originated in Russia. In fact, the Nazis had already sung it for years. They adopted it complete with 'slavery', 'breaking the yoke of tyranny', and the 'last battle' – all of which fitted into their political vocabulary. There was a small change in the last stanza – it was not the red flag but the swastika which was to be hoisted over the new workers' state.

But so popular was the tune that several other texts were written to the same melody in the Nazi era. I have tracked down some twenty different variations and for all I know there may be more. But the differences between them are not substantial and they can be summarized briefly as follows. One song is entitled *Brüder in Zechen und Gruben* (Brothers in mines and coal pits); its appeal was clearly to working-class elements in the Nazi movement: 'speculators and racketeers keep the fatherland in servitude, but we want to earn our livelihood honestly. Hitler is our leader, he is the one not tempted by the gold rolling from Jewish thrones. We are faithful to Hitler to death. The day of retribution is bound to come, and we shall be free again.'[1]

Some of the variations went a little further: 'Load your rifles, shoot the traitors, down with the Jewish tyranny!' Yet another, which was widely sung in North and East Germany added: 'Once we were Communists, Social Democrats and *Stahlhelm*;[2] now all of us are National Socialists, fighters for the NSDAP' – which in German happens to rhyme (SPD-NSDAP).

[1] I have perused the following Nazi songbooks:
Deutsche Kampf- und Volkslieder (Reutlingen 1933);
Kampf- und Marschlieder (Berlin 1934?);
Volk ans Gewehr, Lieder des neuen Deutschlands (n.p., n.d.);
Deutschland Erwache, Das kleine Nazi Liederbuch (Salzbach, Oberpfalz n.d. – edition A and B);
Liederbuch (Mainz 1935);
Werkleute Singen, Lieder der N.S. Gemeinschaft Kraft durch Freude (Kassel 1936);
Müller Liederbuch (Leipzig n.d.);
Das neue Deutschland singt (n.p., n.d.);
Lieder der Freiheitsbewegung mit Klaviernoten (Berlin n.d.);
Sturm-Kampf Liederbuch (Berlin 1935);
Was wir singen; über hundert Lieder (n.p., n.d.);
Schutz und Trutz Liederbuch für die deutsche Jugend (Berlin 1934);
Bernhard Priewe, *Nationalsozialistisches Volksliederbuch* (Berlin 1936).

For the Russian origins *Krasnoe Znamya* 3, 1900, and *Revolyutsionnaya Poeziya 1890–1917* (Leningrad 1959) and most recently *Russkie Sovetskie Pesni* (Moscow 1977).

[2] Members of the conservative paramilitary Steel Helmet organization

The other main variant became known as the fighting song or the song of the columns, *Brüder, formt die Kolonnen*:

Brothers, join the columns – the shout of many thousands is echoed – Germany, we shall liberate you in a storming assault. We advance mindful of our victims, Germany needs us, unfurl our flag – red as blood and black as death. Brothers, our slogan: Revolution. Brothers, we create a new, greater, *völkisch* Germany – *Grossdeutschland*.

The main difference between the songs was that the old *Brüder, zur Sonne, zur Freiheit* was set in A flat major whereas the other two were in B flat major.

When the Third Reich came to an end, Scherchen returned to Germany and the old song became as popular as ever before, and it also spread through other countries of Eastern Europe. It became the title of various songbooks and record albums, and eventually reached the peace movement. And why not? Lilli Marlene, after all, originally sponsored by German-run Radio Belgrad, became almost equally popular among the allied troops, and it is of course well known that the melody of the *Red Flag*, the song of British Labour, is that of the German Christmas song 'O Tannenbaum': 'The people's flag is deepest red'.

Tunes are clearly international, and this seems to be particularly true with regard to love songs. But in the case of *Brüder, zur Sonne, zur Freiheit*, it is not just the case of a catchy tune or a love song: how to explain its popularity with such disparate groups as Russian revolutionaries, the German youth movement, the Nazis and the peace movement? After all, they belonged to fundamentally different political camps. How could a political song announcing liberation, revolution, the victory of the forces of light over darkness and evil be sung with only minor changes by people on opposite sides of the barricades, by the extreme Left and the extreme Right, pacifists and militarists, conservatives and progressives? Does it mean that the fighting spirit, the aggression, the longing for the *lutte finale* are politically indifferent – such as, say, food or drink or aesthetic beauty? Closer to the present day rock music has been used by both the extreme Right and the far Left in Germany. It is an interesting and potentially uncomfortable question and the answer has been shirked so far.

The Nazi songbooks of 1933 announced, it will be recalled, that the origins of *Brüder, zur Sonne, zur Freiheit* were unknown. (They said the same about the author of the *Lorelei*.) When the song resurfaced after the Second World War in a songbook sponsored by the 'Working Circle for Amateur Art', an offshoot of the early anti-nuclear movement, the Russian revolutionary origins of the song were mentioned, but no allusion was made to its fate between 1933 and 1945. Another twenty years passed and in 1984 the Catholic youth organization published its *Song Book Two*. Predictably, it included *Brüder, zur Sonne, zur Freiheit*, but by now the Russian origins had also been forgotten and it was introduced as a 'German folk-song'.[1] Like some disreputable character this indestructible song seems for ever destined to hide its past. And it is not, of course, a question of the history of just one song.

Is there a lesson in all this about the state of present-day Germany, the culture and politics of the young generation, or is it just a matter of confusion and general human forgetfulness? Part of the answer may be in another song almost as popular as *Brüder, zur Sonne, zur Freiheit*. This is *Wenn wir schreiten Seit' an Seit'* – 'when we stride together and sing the old songs, reverberating in the forest, we feel that we shall prevail. For with us strides the future, the new age' (*mit uns zieht die neue Zeit*). The second and third stanzas mention birch trees and green meadows: 'how wonderful to escape there after a working week in noisy factories. Mother Nature extends her hands to man so that he may return where he belongs.'

The song was written in the middle of the First World War. The poet was Hermann Claudius, the great-grandson of one of the most famous German poets of the eighteenth century. The younger Claudius made himself a name as an *Arbeiterdichter*, a working-class poet, though he was not a worker. He was thought to be a Social Democratic sympathizer and his songs were published in the anthologies sponsored by the SPD. But they were sung also by the youth movements and by right-wing groups.

In the Nazi era Claudius became very much an establishment figure, a model of what a German writer should be, close to nature, close to his people. His poems were published even in 1944 when paper was already strictly rationed and allocations were made only to books of national importance.[2]

---

[1] *Song Book Two* was withdrawn from circulation after someone had found out that it included more anti-clerical songs than those of the *Te Deum laudamus* variety.

[2] He was not a party member but in 1933 he belonged to a group of eighty-eight authors solemnly pledging to Hitler their unconditional loyalty (*treueste Gefolgschaft*).

Claudius survived the Nazi era by many years, yet there was no longer much interest in poetry of this kind.[1] But *Wenn wir schreiten Seit' an Seit'* remained as popular as ever. It was sung at the Easter marches of the anti-atom-bomb movement and later by the Greens and even the extreme Left. A West German communist songbook in the late 1970s published it with the following comment: 'Despite the indifferent text and the somewhat unworldly and idyllic description of nature the song is still popular, probably because of the first stanza.'

The explanation is quite convincing. There is no arguing with people claiming with such conviction that the future is on their side. But what is the direction of the march of these columns in the midst of which the New Age is striding?

> Do not think of the fruit of action,
> Fare forward.

[1] In 1979, at the age of 101, Claudius published another two books, a volume of poetry and a collection of stories for Hamburg children in the local dialect, probably an all-time record.

5 The Unhappy Intellectuals or *Fin de Siècle*, German-style

For a very long time the world has been familiar with German academics and German writers, German painters and German composers, but German intellectuals are of much more recent vintage. Schiller and Goethe were not *hommes de lettres*, Kant and Hegel were not 'leaders of the intelligentsia'. There were a few intellectuals in the Weimar Republic but their influence was negligible. As a force of some importance in the cultural life, and to a lesser extent in the political life of their country, German intellectuals are a phenomenon of the post-1945 period.

Germany has produced many talents, and perhaps more geniuses than any other country in the nineteenth and twentieth centuries. But it has never been an easy country for independent minds, let alone for eccentrics. Under a surface of dissent there is a good deal of conformism. Nevertheless, it is not at all easy to provide an identikit picture of the German intellectual, and not only because there are now so many of them.

How to define them? It can be stated without fear of contradiction that most German intellectuals subscribe to *Die Zeit* and *Der Spiegel*, to the *Frankfurter Rundschau*, perhaps even the alternative Berlin *taz* rather than the *Frankfurter Allgemeine* (let alone *Die Welt*); that the intellectual's feelings towards Franz Josef Strauss and Axel Springer are not friendly; that he will sign public appeals – against the threatened deportation of a left-wing Turkish émigré, against American intervention in Central America and elsewhere; that he is very much against arms races; that he used to be mildly philosemitic but has no use for Israeli policy now; that culturally Paris and London attract him more than New York, unless he happens to be a scientist. By and large he is now less interested in events and trends abroad than in the past; there is something slightly funny in his excessive preoccupation with theory but as of late he has become a little tired of it (*theoriemüde*); sometimes he shows a certain disdain for common sense and compromise and it does not come easily to him to concede that he may have been wrong.

One cannot feel entirely comfortable with generalizations of this kind: are German intellectuals really more uncompromising, dogmatic and obstinate than others, are they more idealistic, is their sense of justice really more developed than in other parts of the world? Public opinion polls cannot provide the answers; nor is it safe to generalize on the basis of the *obiter dicta* of well-known writers or film-makers, of some philosophers, historians and political scientists who have taken a leading role in recent controversies. For every one of those in the limelight there are probably hundreds of whom one knows little or nothing, because they do not write books or articles, do not appear on radio or television, do not sign manifestos, may not even be very interested in politics. Such people, it may be argued, cannot be considered true intellectuals, but this is taking a somewhat narrow view. If Kurt Tucholsky and Carl von Ossietzky were intellectuals, so were Freud, Einstein and Max Planck. In short, generalizing on the intelligentsia is like skating on thin ice, an occupation involving constant caveats and reservations.

British and French cultural life is largely concentrated in one city, but this is not so in Germany. In fact, it has never been so except for the relatively short period of Berlin's ascendancy. This dispersal has undoubted benefits but it makes generalization even more difficult. Geographical proximity, to be sure, does not necessarily make for collaboration and friendship. Even in Paris or London intellectual life frequently resembles a big hotel or apartment building in which people lead their own lives quite oblivious of their neighbours. They may nod to each other as they meet in the entrance hall, but on the whole they are not interested in each other's existence. All this applies *a fortiori* to Germany. A recollection comes to mind of a conference in New York in the early 1970s. The late Hannah Arendt hotly contested an observation I had made about German bestsellers in the 1920s and early 1930s. She did not deny that hundreds of thousands of Germans, or even millions, had indeed read these books. She did however emphatically deny that anyone of consequence had read them and that, therefore, they had no impact: 'We did not read these books.' True enough, but when pressed it appeared that 'we' were no more than a handful of people, gifted no doubt, but altogether cut off from what was then the mainstream of German cultural life.

There have been no major changes in this respect. Peter Glotz, then a Berlin senator, commented on German intellectuals who were proud not to have talked for years to anyone outside their own ghetto. During the last decade it has become quite fashionable to live in self-imposed isolation: the inner immigration appears to be considerably more numerous now than before 1945.

It is not disputed that elsewhere, too, Left and Right are not always on speaking terms, that the literary and artistic avant-garde go their own ways, that there are different schools in philosophy or psychology or economics which do not speak the same language and have very disparate interests. But it is doubtful whether there is another country in which the distance between such factions, groups and cliques is as great as it was in the Weimar Republic – or is today.[1] There is no consensus of judgment among British and French literary critics but they will certainly share the same framework. This is not so in Germany. One illustration should suffice: let us compare the hundred or so authors represented in *Deutscher Almanach 1981*, an organ of the extreme Right, including not a few former Nazis, with a book written from a Leninist angle such as *Sozialgeschichte der deutschen Literatur von 1918 bis zur Gegenwart* (1981). Both books admittedly refer to Schiller but not one of the contemporary authors mentioned in the *Almanach* appears in the *Sozialgeschichte*, and vice versa. The *Almanach* mentions no single Jew, no writer of the Left, no liberal. In the *Sozialgeschichte*, on the other hand, there are references to all kinds of people whose relationship to German literature is tenuous, to say the least – the singer Zarah Leander or the banker Kurt von Schroeder. All it has to say about Ricarda Huch, perhaps the greatest woman writer of this century, is that she was thrown out of the German Academy in 1933, and again asked to become honorary president by the East Germans in

[1] When Raymond Aron died in late 1983 *L'Humanité* paid tribute to his greatness and this despite the fact that there had been no more formidable ideological opponent of communism in France than Aron. A gesture of this kind would be unlikely among German intellectuals. An interesting cultural anachronism should be noted in this context: the Association of German Writers has been dominated for years by people close to the West German Communist party which happens to be impeccably pro-Soviet, in contrast to most other European Communist parties which have deviated at one time or another from the lead given by Moscow. The 'Association' does not count for much in political terms and even less as a literary-cultural-moral force, but the phenomenon as such is of interest.

1945. But there is not a single word about why she was a member in the first place. She was neither 'progressive' nor 'anti-communist' and therefore of no interest to the *Sozialgeschichte*. The same is true with regard to many others who do not fit into party political schemes. The *Almanach* is not aware of Lukács and Benjamin, the *Sozialgeschichte* has not heard of Friedrich Gundolf and Max Kommerell. There is one basic difference: the literature of the extreme Right is usually published in small villages in Bavaria or Lower Saxony, and it will not normally be stocked in major bookshops; however, the *Sozialgeschichte* and other such books are available almost everywhere – the book was published, in fact, by S. Fischer, Thomas Mann's old publisher. It is probably used now as a university textbook.[1]

There has been a palpable change in the *Zeitgeist*. The extreme Right has been discredited and leads a shadowy existence. The outsiders of yesteryear on the other hand have become the new establishment. They may not influence the outcome of elections but they certainly help to shape, albeit indirectly, the general intellectual climate. And the general public meanwhile survives oblivious of the writings of the left-wing avant-garde and the heroes of the extreme Right. The sales of their favourites – Konsalik, J. M. Simmel and Marie Louise Fischer – continue to boom even though the histories of literature (including the *Sozialgeschichte* with its special interest in the taste of the toiling masses) fail to mention these names. Which is to say that there are not just two but several cultures in Germany and that while some people and groups are heard much more loudly than others, no one, for better or worse, has a monopoly.

There was a great cultural *Nachholbedarf* in post-war Germany, a feeling of the need to catch up with the rest of the world. But there was no intellectual excitement comparable, say, to the cultural climate of post-war Paris. The country was numbed after the total disaster, the very foundations had to be recreated. The universities, theatres, museums, periodicals, publishing houses had to be made to work again

---

[1] The case of the *Sozialgeschichte* is by no means an isolated example. The editor of a recent massive collection of 'political songs from five centuries' says that 'we have not taken into account the innumerable songs of bourgeois origin. (Annemarie Stern, *Lieder gegen den Tritt*, Oberhausen 1978). The editor of another collection of political poetry covering several centuries (Th. Rothschild) makes it known that it would be against his principles to include poems of whose political tendency he does not approve. It is understandable that these and other authors do not wish to reprint the Horst Wessel song or the poems of Baldur von Schirach, the leader of the Hitler Youth. But it is also true that the great majority of German political poems and songs throughout history were 'patriotic' or 'bourgeois' or 'liberal'; to exclude them is to distort cultural tradition.

before the great intellectual issues could be confronted. Few German writers, artists or academics had played a leading political role in the Third Reich; Hitler did not think highly of intellectuals, their place in his new order was somewhere on the margins of society. But there had been only few who had not made concessions to his regime, and even fewer who had resisted in one way or another. There had been aristocratic victims and working-class martyrs in the anti-Nazi struggle: the number of heroes from among the intellectuals could be counted on the fingers of two hands. A few fell silent after the end of the war, but most carried on, trying to make a fresh start.

Of the new groups which emerged, the *Gruppe 47*, consisting of several dozen writers, poets, critics and playwrights, was the most influential. It was something like a 'mobile academy' (to quote Heinrich Böll). Their interest in politics was not very pronounced, though the great majority would have identified themselves as non-conformist sympathizers with Social Democracy. They thought, as Hans Werner Richter, the founder and chairman of this group wrote many years later, that only socialism could rebuild Germany and that it would take fifty years. They were mistaken on both counts and they were unhappy with the result, which they found wanting. Böll's *Billiard um halb zehn*, *Ansichten eines Clowns*, *Ende einer Dienstfahrt* or *Gruppenbild mit Dame* attack not only ex-Nazis (who have again reached the commanding heights in post-war German politics and the economy) but also the church, the lower middle class, the legal system and, in his later books, the press and the police. Böll was no radical, but in his books one could not see many rays of hope. He depicted a society without love, with many constraints, a society with the stress on careerism, a mixture of a modern Babylon and a modern Sodom. A few good and just people did put in an appearance now and then, but then there were a few just people even in Sodom.

Böll lived to become an elder statesman and a moral arbiter among German writers. His direct political involvement in these early years was minimal and the same is true with regard to another outstanding writer of the period, Wolfgang Köppen, who in a widely read novel described West Germany's new capital as a hothouse (*Das Treibhaus*). Much is to be said in criticism of Bonn, the provincial centre which overnight became the (provisional) capital of a major European nation: it was unexciting, even boring. A hothouse it certainly wasn't. True, Köppen had argued that his satire was poetical, not literal, truth; just as

103

Böll used to claim in later years that the terms he used did not have the same meaning for him as they had for the politicians. But such disclaimers only added to the confusion: either Bonn was a hothouse or it was not, either the new state with all its imperfections contained some promise, some redeeming factors, or it was simply a rehash of the old reactionary order.

Some of the critics of society left the question open, but the more radical among them had no doubt. Martin Walser's *Ehen in Philipps-burg* (1957) painted a picture of a post-war small-town German society which was totally corrupt. There is, in fact, legitimate room for doubt whether it could have possibly been worse under Hitler. Hans Magnus Enzensberger in his early verse and essays felt nothing but nausea *vis-à-vis* his surroundings, the economic miracle with its grossness, its perverse values, the absence of spiritual impulses and general fraudulence. A new adjective ('time-hating') had been invented to do justice to the intensity of Enzensberger's strong feelings.

While most citizens of the *Bundesrepublik* were moderately proud of their achievements during the 1950s, some of the prominent writers were quite unhappy. Adenauer could not care less what these scribblers thought or did, but other political leaders of the majority took them more seriously, partly because their influence through radio and television reached larger audiences than in previous ages. Why did the intellectuals always have to be so negative? If everyone else had to learn the lessons of Weimar, were the intellectuals entitled to ignore them? Chancellor Erhard called them on one occasion *Pinscher*, a term which has considerably more negative connotations in German than in English – a contemptible small dog. Heinrich von Brentano compared Bertolt Brecht with Horst Wessel; 'philistines', 'good for nothings', 'rats', 'blowflies' were some of the epithets used by Christian Democratic leaders. The secretary general of the CDU compared the *Gruppe 47* to the Nazi organization of German writers established under Goebbels. Did it not make and unmake reputations, did it not exercise a virtual dictatorship, maintaining a stranglehold on publishing houses and the means of mass communication?

These accusations contained a grain of truth, but in the final analysis they were about as exaggerated as were Walser's and Enzensberger's writings. The *Gruppe 47* was not actively involved in politics at that time. In later years its members were, in fact, bitterly attacked by their younger and more radical colleagues for their lukewarm and ivory-towerish attitudes, for having written rather than acted, for having been court jesters rather than militants. The first issue of Enzensberger's periodical *Kursbuch* announced that he and his friends were turning away from literature to revolution in the streets and to the 'anatomy of late capitalism'. If the intellectuals of the Left Bank had come out two decades earlier in favour of a committed literature, the German radicals wanted to go even further and to abolish literature altogether except perhaps for documentary plays whose political effect was obvious. Since they did not know much history, they were unaware that their endeavour was by no means original, that literature had been abolished more than once – for instance by the Italian Futurists and the Soviet *Proletkult*, and that the results had been both short-lived and disastrous.

Why did such radicalization occur in the late 1960s? It is a legitimate question because at this very time the Social Democrats joined forces for the first time with the CDU in a 'grand coalition' paving the way for fifteen years of SPD rule. Writers and artists leaning towards the Left should have welcomed this new departure. But this was not at all how they saw it: they thought that the Great Coalition was a horrible mistake, a sell-out. As Karl Jaspers (not a man of the Left but just a concerned citizen) stated at the time: there was a sense of impending disaster, the situation resembled the state of affairs on the eve of Hitler's take-over. Unless Germans could immediately be alerted to the magnitude of the impending disaster and act to prevent it, democracy would be finished. But this, Jaspers went on, was only the beginning: the oligarchy of parties would be transformed into an authoritarian state, the authoritarian state would become more and more totalitarian and would unleash a war. There was not just a lack of a sense of reality in these protests against some wholly innocuous legislation brought in by the new coalition, but a touch of hysteria. A few years earlier Jaspers had recommended (as had Bertrand Russell) the use of the nuclear bomb against the Soviet Union.

Another intellectual aware of the danger was Günter Grass, a moderate at the time. He turned to Willy Brandt, then head of the SPD, beseeching him to desist from his fatal course of action. Böll had given up: 'In 1965 [he wrote] one could still put one's hope on the Social Democrats, in 1967 there was no more hope left.' Brandt, in contrast to Adenauer, held some intellectuals in high esteem. But there were limits to his admiration; had he listened to his writer friends the Social

Democrats might never have come to power. This would not have unduly worried the intellectuals, who believed in the permanence of the conflict between *Geist* and *Macht*, between the spiritual forces and power.

The objection of the intellectuals to the 'system' became sharper during the late 1960s precisely because the economic recovery had been so successful. Prosperity, some had assumed, would make the intellectuals more moderate, but this was an elementary misreading of the intelligentsia in a free society. The greater the prosperity, the greater the need to denounce the negative new friends, the fact that money, power and social standing had become the supreme values, that Germany had become a giant supermarket, that wealth was flaunted ostentatiously.

The economic miracle was followed by the *Fräuleinwunder*, the *Fresswelle* (overeating), the proliferation of expensive models of Mercedes and BMW cars on German roads, the holidays to exotic islands, consumerism in every shape and form. Such a society the intellectuals found abhorrent, hence the lamentations that there had been no real break with Hitlerism; that the same kind of people were still in charge; that German society was still an unfree class society; that the difference between rich and poor was still very large; that Adenauer advocated 'no experiments' whereas the country needed the opposite; that there were no equal chances for young people in education; that other countries had a more developed social welfare system; that Germany had become hopelessly provincial with Bonn as a perfect symbol; that women, homosexuals, foreign workers, gypsies, young people, old people and other marginal groups were exploited and did not get a fair deal; that German policy was pro-American and anti-communist; that Germany should support the just claims of the Third World; that the quality of life had been utterly neglected; that there was unemployment; that the *Bundeswehr* was becoming too powerful. In brief, they opposed what they chose to call 'restauration' and their main slogan was 'We want another republic'. Not all the claims and allegations were wrong, but the overall picture that emerged was grossly distorted, a caricature.

These were the feelings of the more moderate among them. The more radical were sure that the *Bundesrepublik* was already in a pre-fascist stage. It was after all a capitalist state and the lessons of the past, as they understood them, were that capitalist systems were bound to become fascist when under pressure. For the time being fascist terrorism existed only on the periphery, but it was apparently only a question of time before it would take over at the centre. Even Böll, the moderate, said in a speech in 1974 that first the Left had been liquidated (*abgeschossen*), now it was the turn of the Left liberals (of which he was one), next the liberals would be eliminated ('Look only at the editorials in the newspapers'). And eventually the turn of the conservatives too would come. Fascism *ante portas*, for the second time in ten years! But just as no one was executed or sent to a concentration camp at the time of the Great Coalition of 1966, the literary magazines now went on to publish whatever came to their minds, and not one was closed down, no one lost his job. This kind of paranoia was not new in German intellectual life and it is not easy to explain it even with the benefit of hindsight. The critics no doubt felt a special duty. But it is a far cry from fulfilling this duty to fomenting hysteria. They might have genuinely felt that they were facing a mortal danger. This interpretation absolves them as far as their motives are concerned. But it raises disturbing questions about their state of mind, their judgment, their competence to act as advisers, warners and prophets.

Let us return to Böll, a gifted writer, a decent and level-headed man. During the German cultural revolution of the 1960s, when it was not a popular thing to do, he had reminded his friends and colleagues how important American literature had been for them, that they had been liberated in 1945 not only by American arms but also by American literature 'from Saroyan to Salinger and from Hemingway to Steinbeck'. On another occasion, upon receiving the Nobel prize in 1975, he turned against the 'seemingly anti-imperialist attempts to throw poetry and all other art forms on the rubbish heap'. He was one of the few well-known German writers to defend Solzhenitsyn, Sakharov and the other dissidents at a time when this was not at all fashionable in many West German intellectual circles. A courageous man then among the radical chic, but Böll, too, would not overstep the boundaries of the intellectual consensus. The artist, as he saw it, was not a citizen, he did not need the state but only local administration, which would presumably take care of garbage disposal and street lighting. Who would take care of the poor, the weak and the elderly, see to the education of children, the protection of citizens against all kinds of dangers? Was a police force needed? Böll gave no clear answer. Armed forces were certainly not called for: it was not a disgrace (he wrote in

1981), it was an international honour that the number of those who refused to serve in the *Bundeswehr* increased every year. 'Give us Hollanditis, this wonderful disease.' True, Böll thought it would be highly desirable if the Russians would also withdraw their missiles; they, too, constituted a danger. This was further than some of his fellow writers and theologians were willing to go, who saw the danger of militarism only at home. But Böll agreed with the more radical critics that the enemy was largely a figment of the imagination. Thus, not only the missiles had to be destroyed to save the world but also the *Feindbild*, the image of the enemy. This also meant an end to the kind of propaganda about alleged threats with which the West Germans had been fed since the end of the Second World War. Such an attitude was tantamount to 'being in' and to opting out at the same time, being the conscience of the nation but keeping major reservations about the obligations of citizenship.

To understand these attitudes we ought to retrace our steps to the causes of the radicalization which took place in the 1960s. There was, of course, much to criticize in the country of the *Wirtschaftswunder*, nor could anyone in his right mind have demanded that writers must always be constructive in their criticism, acting as befitted elder statesmen. The core of the problem was on the one hand the mistaken assumption on the part of many intellectuals that a critical approach was a synonym for total negation. Such negativism apart, there was the hubris of the intellectuals: they had the newspapers, television and other outlets at their disposal, they could express themselves more forcefully or more elegantly on public affairs than other citizens. But this did not necessarily mean that they were more competent to judge, or that they had anything of relevance to say. They loathed the provincialism, the new *Spiessertum*, of post-war German society, but they were, at the same time, members of this society. Their critique too, was provincial, ignoring the experience of other times and in other countries. In other words, they refused to compare post-war German society with German society before 1945, or prior to 1933 and 1914; they did not compare it with other European societies but with a society such as had never existed in German history, and quite probably could not be found elsewhere.

Mention has been made of the fears of the consequences of the Grand Coalition and of the emergency laws which preoccupied the intellectuals in the late 1960s. Soon it appeared, however, that fascism was not yet to prevail, and within a couple of years everyone had forgotten all about the panic. But the *Radikalenerlass* (adopted by a Social Democratic government and the prime ministers of the *Länder*) caused a great deal of commotion and continues to do so to this day. Underlying this decree was the obvious idea, accepted by every democratic regime in the world, that while every citizen has in principle equal rights, the state is under no constraint to employ in sensitive positions active members of organizations opposed to the democratic order. This principle was never questioned by human rights proponents in West Germany as far as the non-admission or removal of neo-Nazis was concerned. But it became an issue of bitter contention where communists, Maoists, Trotskyites and members of other anti-democratic groups were concerned. The reasoning behind these protests was that while neo-Nazis were indeed enemies of the republic, communists, being anti-fascists, were no more than radical democrats.

The problem faces every democratic society and it has been solved usually in an informal way, which is to say that members of anti-democratic groups were kept out (without any explanation being given) of certain sensitive positions as far as national security is concerned. In Germany this was done by means of bureaucratic decree, which caused iniquities which were never intended. The decree came to cover positions which cannot be considered sensitive by any stretch of the imagination. Furthermore, it soon appeared that a bureaucracy with rigid guidelines was not equipped to differentiate between militant opponents of the democratic order and legitimate critics from well within the democratic spectrum. As the result of trying to solve a sensitive issue in an orderly way, i.e. by bureaucratic decree, the West German government caused more harm than good. It provided ammunition to those of its critics who had claimed all along that the system was unfree, the old autocracy under a new guise. It fuelled the hysteria which was never far from the surface and it did not take too long for the *Radikalenerlass* to be compared with Auschwitz.

The radicalization of the 1960s was accompanied by and intensified the discovery of Marxism in Germany. It is not widely known that in the country of origin of Marx and Engels the theory of 'scientific socialism' had never taken firm root among the intellectuals, except those few who had joined the Communist or Social Democratic parties. In Nazi Germany Marxism was, of course, beyond the pale and thus after the end of the war German intellectuals found themselves even more innocent of Marxism than the French or the British. For more than a decade after the end of the war lectures on Marxist philosophy and economics remained a near monopoly of some Protestant and Catholic theologians, who had independently discovered it and found it of considerable academic interest. Only in the 1960s did Marxism become part of German ideology as far as the intelligentsia was concerned, usually not in the original, orthodox, undiluted version but in various adaptations such as the 'critical' (Frankfurt) School, or the writings of Georg Lukács and Ernst Bloch. It ought to be added in passing that psychoanalysis too was not discovered by German intellectuals for similar reasons until the 1960s. But psychoanalysis had no major political impact, whereas Marxism, assimilated with German thoroughness and often rather uncritically, spread widely, more so than in other Western societies.

Another trend of major importance which affected the new German ideology was the emergence of Third-World liberation movements. Mao's party consolidated its rule and it was, as everyone knew, Marxist-Leninist; Castro and Guevara claimed to be Marxists, as did Ho Chi Minh and most other revolutionary leaders throughout Asia, Africa and Latin America. The struggle against colonialism and imperialism generated a great deal of enthusiasm among the German intelligentsia and also many delusions about the true populist, nationalist and ultimately dictatorial character of these movements. There were thousands of students from Iran in the *Bundesrepublik*; the first major demonstration of the APO in Berlin in 1967 was in fact in protest against the visit of the Shah. These students persuaded their German colleagues that the Shah was a bloodthirsty tyrant and exploiter and that but for him there would be justice and freedom in Iran; that workers, women, students and minorities would be liberated and emancipated once the oppressor and his few lackeys were overthrown. Similar hopes were attached to Vietnam and Cambodia, to North Korea and the various guerrilla and terrorist movements in Latin America.

A little more thought would have shown that it was highly doubtful whether Marxism in any meaningful sense of the term (let alone Western Marxism) could prosper outside Europe, that whilst the national liberation movements were anti-capitalist in inspiration and that while socialist phraseology was *de rigueur* in these circles, they were neither socialist nor democratic and least of all internationalist in inspiration. Even Castro, the most committed of these leaders, had more in common with a charismatic military dictator, a Perón or a Mussolini, than with a revolutionary leader such as had been envisaged by Marx, Engels or Lenin.

Today Iranian students again demonstrate in Germany, but their protests are now directed against their erstwhile allies, the cruel enemies of mankind, fascist killers and usurpers who stole their revolution. All this could have been easily foreseen, but such scepticism would have been considered counter-revolutionary at a time when all national liberation movements were idolized, when pilgrimages were paid to Havana and Hanoi and other such places of ideological inspiration. The countries of exotic socialism seemed all the more attractive because the countries of 'real socialism' – the Soviet Union (and *a fortiori* East Germany) – were of no great interest to romantic intellectuals. There was no revolutionary spontaneity in these regimes, their culture was not proletarian but petty bourgeois. Furthermore, it was now generally accepted that under Stalin certain excesses had been committed which may not have been entirely accidental, even though Western bourgeois media have immeasurably exaggerated these unfortunate stains on the socialist record. Seen in this light it was quite natural that enthusiastic intellectuals should have turned towards revolutionary movements in faraway countries about which little was known, and where everything still seemed possible.

This was how the identification with the Third World came about: hundreds of books and articles were written about it, signatures collected, solidarity demonstrations organized. Some even visited these faraway places but most refrained from doing so, wisely perhaps, because the exposure to realities would have been painful, generating unnecessary doubts. But this shock of recognition belongs to a later period; in the 1960s Third-World enthusiasm led almost by necessity to anti-Americanism. It was not the only source of anti-Americanism but it was certainly a very important one. America had fought the Chinese in Korea, it had tried to suppress the Cuban revolution (this was not, in fact, true, with regard to the rise of Castro, but myth took over early on). America was behind the Shah and the other forces of reaction all over the globe. True, there was anti-Americanism also in Britain and France where it could be found as often on the Right as on the Left. But there it was largely psychological and cultural in character, the resentment of once powerful imperial nations against the upstart uncouth Yankees, who lacked a clear strategy, political and diplomatic

111

experience and, above all, culture. The French furthermore found it difficult to forgive the Americans their part in the liberation of France in 1944; it was in some ways easier to forgive the conquerors from the East than the liberators.

But Germany was different. Anti-Americanism there had never had deep roots except among some circles on the far Right among whom 'Americanization' had been considered, as the Nazis had taught, something exceedingly vulgar – Negroes, jazz, egalitarian mass society. America had played a decisive role in the liberation of Germany; without American help, ranging from the Marshall plan to CARE parcels, German economic recovery would not have taken place. Without NATO and the US divisions in Germany the country would not have preserved its sovereignty and freedom. This, in any case, was how most middle-aged Germans saw it.

But as the 1940s receded into the distant past, a young generation of intellectuals (and some of riper years who should have known better) questioned these assumptions. The Americans, after all, were responsible for the 'restauration', they had prevented a radical break with the past. If they had given economic help the underlying motive was no doubt the desire to retain their hold on the German economy and to prevent a revolution. The so-called Soviet threat was mythical; the Americans, not the Russians, had started the Cold War. As history was rewritten and seen in a new light, it appeared that Germany had committed a cardinal error by sticking too closely to American monopoly capitalism and committing itself to rearmament. By doing so it had helped to perpetuate the division of Germany. But for these fatal Cold-War mistakes Germany would have been prosperous, neutral and socialist, a truly sovereign country, not a mere catspaw in the confrontation between America and the Soviet Union.

This in shortest outline was the new consensus on the Left, and these views gained fairly wide currency among a generation which had only dim recollections (or no memories at all) of the events of the 1940s and 1950s. Anti-Americanism reached a climax around 1980, but it is useful to recall that its origins can be traced back to the period when Kurt Schumacher had attacked Adenauer (without much political success) as the 'chancellor of the Allies'. There had been voices warning against cultural Americanization in the 1950s on the Right as well as on the Left. Martin Walser was one of the first who, in his novel *Halbzeit*, had introduced the advertising agent (trained in America) who embodied the corruption of West German society. Two years earlier Gerd Gaiser, a man of the Right, had published his *Schlussball*, which takes place in a South German industrial city. Behind the brilliant façade, the brittleness and emptiness of the *nouveau-riche* society emerges and it is made clear by more than implication that this was largely the fault of the Americans. They were responsible for the economic miracle and its negative consequences. The country would have been better off without it; if this was the price that had to be paid for prosperity, it was not worth it. Few were talking yet about cultural colonialism but there was uneasiness even then about Coca Cola and chewing-gum culture, and Yankee expressions having besmirched the beautiful German language. There were complaints about disc jockeys and the music they offered, about rubbishy movies and television programmes arriving from the New World.

Some of these complaints were, of course, justified. Not all aspects of the American way of life were admirable and West Germany could well have done without some of them. But no one had ever been forced to drink Coca Cola rather than lemonade or wine, eat a hamburger rather than a German beef steak or *Sauerbraten,* listen to pop music rather than to *Ach wie ist's möglich dann.* Washington would not have broken off relations if fewer American words had entered the German language. It was not America's fault that its popular culture with all the trappings from Smarties and popcorn to pop and John Travolta proved to be so popular, or rather that West Germany (like other European countries) failed to develop alternative attractions.

A general survey of the cultural scene in post-war Germany, with all its conflicting tendencies, is neither possible nor desirable in the present context. It has been said that it is unnecessary to drink the whole ocean in order to taste the quality of sea water, and this is true, *mutatis mutandis*, with regard to the *Zeitgeist*. A few case studies will have to suffice.

The New German Cinema

Of all the aspects of post-war German cultural life, none has attracted as much interest abroad as the German cinema. A recent historical review begins, rightly, with the following sentence: 'The making of the New German Cinema took place to a great extent in the United States. Or to be more precise, in New York.'[1] The reasons for this success are of interest, but not in the context of this study. They have more to do with the post-Vietnam trauma in the US than the intrinsic significance of the New German Film which was probably misunderstood in America. It should be added in fairness that not all leading American critics shared this enthusiasm.

More than writers or artists or academics, the film-makers came to serve as German cultural ambassadors abroad. The German film had had a global reputation in the 1920s and 1930s, and even many movies of the Nazi era were of a high level of technical competence and had considerable entertainment value. Unlike other arts, the movies under Hitler were given a great deal of latitude. The first post-war decades on the other hand were not very inspiring; with a few exceptions the films produced were of the 'Phantom of Soho', 'Our Crazy Aunt in the Pacific' and '*Grün ist die Heide*' variety. But then in the early 1960s the old film industry (UFA) quite literally collapsed, to a certain extent as the result of the growing role of television. The number of movies annually produced in Germany declined from about 115 in 1958 to sixty-one in 1962, so providing the New German Film (NDF) with its opportunity. In a manifesto issued after a meeting of young film-makers in Oberhausen in 1962, the death of the traditional movie and the birth of a new one were announced. Rainer Werner Fassbinder and Werner Herzog were as yet students and Volker Schlöndorff was about to return from his Paris apprenticeship to a country where, he said, no films had been made so far. Nor had Wim Wenders appeared on the scene. After a few years the Oberhausen generation was overtaken by an even younger one, who came to the fore with even more far-reaching claims and demands. As one of them, Werner Schroeter, put it, film was a kind of curative terrorism, exploding all borders and forms. The revolutionaries received the blessing of the ministry of the interior, which gave the money to set up a *Kuratorium* Young German Film. While terrorism has remained a subject of fascination to German film-makers, it is only fair to add that Schroeter's announcement was not to be taken literally; he went on to make a movie about Maria Callas. But on the whole NDF certainly enjoyed almost unlimited freedom in its choice of subjects and their treatment. There were not that many taboos left in the first place, and these they immediately challenged to the

[1] Eric Rentschler, 'American Friends and New German Cinema' in *New German Critique*, Winter 1981–2, p. 7

acclaim of the critics. Fassbinder said in an interview not long before his death that he had been able to get away with a great deal. Anybody else like him would have been put in a mental hospital.

The kind of movie produced by the NDF would begin more often than not in a sleazy bar (or alternatively end there with someone drinking himself to death), or show a man leaving either a prison or a mental hospital. These films usually had a beginning but quite frequently no obvious end; there was a heavy preoccupation with madness as in the films of Syberberg and Herzog, in Rodel's 'Albert' or Wenders' 'The Fear of the Goalie at the Penalty Kick'. 'Society' was the enemy, not just bankers, speculators, the police, the entertainment industry, but the middle class and lower middle class in general, criminal or idiotic or both. The intention was frequently satirical, but since there were no great satirists among the film-makers, the treatment was heavy-handed and one could hardly ever establish with certainty whether a scene or a whole film was meant to be funny or whether it was 'socialist realism'. On occasion even the communists were shown in a bad light, as in Fassbinder's *Mutter Küsters Fahrt zum Himmel* (Mother Küster's Journey to Heaven, 1975) or in Schroeter's *Regno di Napoli* (1978) about the Italian communists.

There is a fascination with murder in these films, but not in the classical whodunnit tradition. It was perhaps inevitable that the Haarmann case should have been disinterred. Haarmann was a mass murderer of the 1920s who had killed several dozen boys. The case underwent up-to-date treatment in Ulli Lommel's *Zärtlichkeit der Wölfe* (Tenderness of the Wolves, 1973) with Haarmann as the good neighbourhood butcher making sausages of his corpses and appearing as a public benefactor at a time when there were still serious meat shortages. The orchestra meanwhile played *Plaisir d'amour* and 'Johnny is the boy for me'. The police contact Haarmann (played by an actor looking like Kojak's younger brother), trying to enlist him as an informer. Everyone seemed to be happy with this film, especially the critics who welcomed it as an expressionist revival and stroke of genius.

More often the central figures in these films were not Haarmanns but petty criminals – young thieves, pimps, prostitutes or alternatively homosexuals and lesbians, as in *Taxi zum Klo* and *The Bitter Tears of Petra von Kant*. It would be too much to say that the public relished these movies – they preferred low-quality American films. But they had a *succès d'estime* among the critics. What did Fassbinder's and Wenders' symbolism mean, it was asked, what was the deeper philosophical import? Since the action was frequently incoherent, it was open to different interpretations and there was always the inclination to read a significance and a message into films which had none, despite the fact that the film-makers seldom made such claims and some dismissed them *expressis verbis*. Herzog, for instance, wrote that there are landscapes without deeper meaning and that, generally speaking, film was not the art of scholars, but of illiterates. When Herzog was asked about his evident lack of interest in more or less 'normal' people and situations, he said that this was undeniable, but what did normal mean? At one time Emperor Wilhelm II had been considered normal and his contemporary Kafka abnormal. There were no telephones in Herzog's movies, nor did his heroes and villains drive cars, and he never produced a real love scene. Herzog is one of the most talented film-makers of his generation but his reply was far from satisfactory. Abnormality is a legitimate subject and extreme situations always attract artists. But they are not all there is to real life; sewers and rubbish dumps are an essential part of the landscape, but there are also other aspects to the urban and rural scene. The Young German Film knew neither real comedy nor real tragedy, only grotesque grimaces at the margins of society, Caligari and Nosferatu rehashed on a lower level of intellectual sophistication. There was the wish to shock the bourgeois – as if the bourgeois did not want to be shocked. Films and books of this kind appear in ages of material saturation; there was probably also an element of bad conscience. The general impression was all too often that of a student farce or melodrama full of shocking ideas and scenes. At first allowance was made for the bad taste and the imperfections with reference to the exuberance of youth. But as film-makers, like Oskar in *The Tin Drum*, failed to grow up, the jokes tended to become stale and the horrors ridiculous and boring.

Film-makers, so critical in their approach to society, should have found the Nazi era an irresistibly fascinating subject, but this has not been the case. The few attempts to confront this period have produced films ranging from the revolting and embarrassing to the insipid (*Lili Marlen* or Syberberg's *Hitler*), trivializing the subject. They turned it into kitsch melodrama, betraying ignorance of the special character of Nazism, or simply became inchoate. One example of this kind of treatment was Ulli Lommel's *Adolf und Marlene* (1977): Hitler falls in love with Marlene Dietrich after seeing one of her films. He sends

Goebbels to London in order to persuade her to come home, but this mission fails and Adolf's own trip to London is no more successful. Lommel's 'Haarmann' film has already been mentioned. He was one of Fassbinder's chief assistants; in this movie he plays Goebbels. Having enjoyed as a boy the performances of Lommel's father, a considerable comic actor, I tried hard to find mitigating circumstances; there were none.

Ideological and artistic confusion abounded. The NDF film-makers sincerely believed that the message of their movies was socialist, democratic and humanist. These claims were not, however, always accepted. A leading American critic (Richard Grenier) has found Herzog's *Men of Destiny* – their willingness to sacrifice human life – both mythomanic and disquietening. Herzog has been interpreted by some of his American admirers as a poet-priest, as one continuing the tradition of the German medieval mystics such as Meister Eckehart, of Jakob Böhme and of Novalis. And Grenier has this to say about Fassbinder:

> I seriously think that Fassbinder would have found much that was congenial to him in the Nazi regime. It was not materialistic. It preached an exalted creed that lifted men out of themselves. It was cruel (there is tremendous unavowed cruelty in Fassbinder's films), but it is consecrated to strength, the power of will. I have no difficulty whatever in reading Fassbinder as a Nazi personality with just a few inversions. He could quite easily be seen as a lost, spiritual Nazi.

More than a few inversions are needed, and the Nazis would have had no use for 'decadents' like him in any case. Nor would the communists: only two of Fassbinder's many films were shown in East Berlin. They needed positive heroes and would have found Fassbinder's negativism and misanthropy (of which *Satansbraten* [Satan's Brew] is an example) unacceptable. Fassbinder's *dégoût de la vie*, to which Richard Grenier has drawn attention, was all-pervasive.

He said he loathed Germany, which was steadily becoming more unfree. Yet with all his sympathies for communism, he felt himself more at home in New York, where he kept a home, and also in Paris. He played with the idea of leaving Germany for good, after there had been attacks on him for, among other reasons, anti-Semitism. This happened following his Frankfurt play *Der Müll* and after it had become known that he wanted to produce a television version of Gustav Freytag's nineteenth-century anti-Semitic novel *Soll und Haben*. He

117

feared that such criticism was an overture to a dictatorship which would 'egalize' all people. Eventually, he said, people would come to look like each other, would be dressed the same way and think alike: strange fears on the part of a progressive film-maker. Fassbinder, one feels, would not have felt at home in a communist country. One suspects that he knew it, but this made him only more angry *vis-à-vis* the country in which he had the misfortune to live. He was far more interested in the *spostati*, those who had been spewed out by society, than class-conscious workers whom he must have found unpromising material. The same seems to be true for the other film-makers. He was a tortured man with many obsessions, whose talent was vitiated by his corrosive misanthropy, a man neither sane nor mad enough to produce a true masterpiece.

Fassbinder showed talent in some of his movies, such as in *Berlin Alexanderplatz* which he did for television, and in *Angst Essen Seele Auf* (Fear Eats the Soul), the story of the young Moroccan worker and his marriage to the elderly cleaning woman, a caricature of the foreign workers' problems in German society with, however, some uncomfortable truths. There is much to admire in Herzog's South American landscapes and there is elegance in Schlöndorff's *Young Törless* and his Proust adaptation. Many actors in the NDF movies perform well. But to the extent that the NDF wanted to create something new, it was a failure; the plots are implausible, they do not convey aesthetically the message of the director and his associates. Far from projecting the problems of society, these movies reflected the little world, the personal complexes and difficulties of the film-makers. They were devoid of compassion and a sense of humour, they had occasional ideas, but lacked force and maturity. They were incapable of sparing a thought for those not on the margins of society. The film-makers would have replied that there is no room for laughter in capitalist society; Fassbinder said there could be no love – only exploitation.

The NDF attracted the attention of some kindred spirits in New York and Paris, but the German public voted with its feet against it. Syberberg complained that a mere hundred and fifty people had seen his Hitler film in Frankfurt in three days; in San Francisco the film was seen by more people in three days than in Frankfurt, Hamburg and Munich taken together. When the NDF was at the height of its fame most cinemas in Germany showed American films (55 per cent in 1980) or, to a lesser extent, French movies, most of them of little artistic or other value. Nor did the New German Cinema ever reach mass audiences abroad. By 1977, when the NDF was discovered in the US, its impetus had been spent; Fassbinder and the others were engaged at the time mainly in the production of literary adaptations for television, such as *Berlin Alexanderplatz*, *The Magic Mountain* and *Felix Krull*. The German movies which did eventually become box-office successes abroad, such as *Christine F* and *Das Boot*, owed little or nothing to the NDF.

If the NDF in its heyday grossed only 10 per cent of the German box-office receipts – and in some years much less: 4 per cent in 1977 – how can one explain that it got off to a flying start and was kept going for so many years? This was almost entirely due to its friends among the critics and to public support, both on the part of the government and of the *Länder*. These subventions helped to finance the making of the movies, they paid the distributors to handle the film and, if the worst came to the worst, the FFA (*Filmförderungsanstalt*) even took care of the exhibitors who otherwise might have shown no interest. True, most of these films were made with a very small budget: *Fear Eats the Soul* with little more than $100,000. Outside Germany the NDF was widely propagated by the Goethe Institutes and other official or semi-official institutions.

The German system of 'cradle to grave' security was noted abroad with irritation and some envy. But it was also criticized by the young West German film-makers for whom it did not go far enough. They argued that it was nauseating that a small clique of overlords should decide 'how much truth ought to be shown on the screen'. The underlying assumption was firstly that the NDF (and only the NDF) was 'showing the truth', and secondly that the film-makers themselves would be the best judges on how to spend public money. It was perhaps only natural that the film-makers would feel compelled to bite the hands feeding them to prove that they were truly independent.

The NDF had only little impact inside Germany; for the committed Left it was too negative, the Right abhorred it in any case, and the general public was bored by it. The foreign avant-garde found some of the new German movies of interest, but not a source of inspiration. It would be difficult to point to American and European film-makers who were influenced by the creation of the NDF.

It is now a thing of the past, though still of interest as a manifestation of the mood of the 1970s. Some saw it as a belated answer to the

Fridericus Rex variety of films of a previous period in German history – patriotic, sweetish and fraudulent. If this was the intention, it missed its aim, for unlike its predecessors it did not attract the public; at most it touched some nerves and even this is not altogether certain. Some of the movies of the Weimar period had been pace-setters, others had provided good entertainment. Quite a few of them are still shown fifty years after the event. It is difficult to imagine that any of the NDF movies will be watched a few decades hence, except perhaps as exhibits to select audiences of historians trying to get a better understanding of the strange convolutions of the *Zeitgeist* in a bygone period.

The NDF grew out of a movement of political and social protest and there is no doubt about the negative attitude towards the society which surrounded it – and financed it. But it never became social and political in character, and this is true even about the politically most committed of the film-makers. They tried to say something about German realities, but for reasons not entirely clear they hardly ever succeeded in making it understood. More often one has the feeling that such an attempt was not even made and that the preoccupation with the self prevailed over all other considerations. Thus in the last resort these movies tell us very little about Germany in the 1970s, only about the people who made them and the critics who applauded them. Seen in a wider context, the New German Film was probably neither better nor worse than avant-garde movies made in other countries at the time. But its ideological and aesthetic pretensions were certainly higher, and it is by these claims that it must be judged.

All this is now history. The New German Cinema no longer exists but its protagonists continue to make movies, good, bad and indifferent. Volker Schlöndorff, in *Swann in Love*, adapted Proust for the cinema, certainly an act of great courage; Wim Wenders received much praise for his *Paris, Texas*. These and other such films were acclaimed because they showed discipline, told a story that was recognizable and were not preoccupied with the changing moods of the producer. To what extent were these specifically German films? This is not easy to say, for *Swann* was also a French movie and most of those who took part in making *Paris, Texas*, were in fact American; the contemporary cinema is to a large degree international in inspiration. These new movies have as much, or as little, in common with the New German Cinema as they have with the old productions of the UFA. Seen in retrospect the New German Cinema was no more than a historical episode which might have been shorter but for the undeserved applause it received.

Marxism and contemporary history

It seems a long way from movies dealing with the private tragedies of Petra von Kant and Maria Braun to discussions about the meaning of recent German history. Both topics, each in its way, help to illuminate the *Zeitgeist* of the 1960s and 1970s. The fierce debates among historians and political scientists focused above all on the character of Nazism and the outbreak of the Cold War. One could have expected, with equal justice, a debate on the Soviet Union, or the role of Marxism in the modern world or the future of Germany. But the issue of fascism seemed crucial, partly because this was the great trauma in recent German history and also because its political significance was obvious. For orthodox Marxists the primacy of economics over politics is a basic tenet of belief. Marxism ought to prove that Hitler and his party had not been free agents, but merely running dogs of monopoly capitalism. It had to show that Hitler's personal role, Nazi ideology and other such aspects were of little consequence, but that the money he received from Emil Kirdorf and other industrialists was all-important. Furthermore, it had to be demonstrated beyond any shadow of a doubt that National Socialism was not a phenomenon *sui generis*, but broadly speaking the same as fascist and reactionary parties elsewhere. Nazism, seen in this light, was more or less the same as capitalism, a right-wing, conservative political party. And lastly it had to be established that certain superficial resemblances between fascist and communist regimes (the 'one leader and one party' syndrome, the central role of the political police and propaganda apparatus, censorship, etc.) were a mere coincidence, and that the attempts to compare, or even equate, these two systems were no more than Cold-War propaganda.

These debates often seemed abstruse to those not directly involved, but they were in fact of considerable symptomatic interest. For political reasons it was essential to show that fascism and capitalism were identical, whereas the resemblances with communist regimes were far-fetched – a calumny. The exercise was of political importance for yet another reason: if it was true that capitalism not fascism was the real enemy, it followed by implication that the fascist era had not ended in 1945 as 'bourgeois' writers maintained, but that the danger continued to exist. Since there had been no Soviet-style revolution in Germany in

1945, the political system was at least potentially fascist and the same was true with regard to all other European countries and above all with regard to America.

This ideological offensive was successful in some respects but failed in others. The orthodox Marxist-Leninist school succeeded in removing the term 'National Socialism' from the political dictionary and replaced it by 'fascism' or 'German fascism'. This may appear an insignificant matter but it was, in fact, half the battle won. For it equated – without the necessity of proof – Nazism with Italian fascism and all kinds of fascisms such as Romanian and Spanish, which, in fact, differed considerably from each other. It was of course quite true that there had been something basically fraudulent in the use of the term 'socialism' by Hitler's party; 'socialism' was fashionable after the First World War, and the Nazis wanted to dissociate themselves from the conservative Right with its limited electoral potential and to appear as a true people's party. But it is equally true that there were in Nazism pronounced radical, populist elements, and if its leaders and supporters were not of proletarian origin, they certainly did not belong to the *haute bourgeoisie* either.

Some of the more enlightened Marxist ideologists pointed to a relatively easy way out of the dilemma. The old definition of the Communist International according to which Nazism had been the praetorian guard of monopoly capitalism, in other words a tool rather than a master, was manifestly wrong. Even if some industrialists and bankers had supported Nazism before 1933, they had given considerably more to the other political parties. Once Hitler had come to power they had very little say in the management of public affairs. True, many of them benefited from the regime. But Hitler would not have dreamt of consulting them as far as the decisive issues of German policy were concerned. In other words, the praetorian guard had made itself independent, it had become the real seat of power. Fritz Thyssen, the great industrialist who had been among the first to give money to Hitler, found himself in a concentration camp, an unfortunate symbol if there ever was one. The more enlightened Marxists of the 1960s, following the example of August Thalheimer, Otto Bauer and Rudolf Hilferding were willing to admit that much. They adopted the Bonapartist model for the interpretation of fascism: there were differences of views and interests between the ruling classes, the bourgeoisie was no longer united and not strong enough to run the country. In this constellation the ruling classes had to abdicate political power while keeping economic power. This was not what had actually happened between 1930 and 1933 but it certainly seemed more plausible. As for events after the fascist take-over, the 'revisionists' could not agree with each other. Some argued that political power was bound to revert back to those who had surrendered it; it was never made quite clear why the fascists should show such nobleness. Others such as Hilferding made a more radical break with Marxist orthodoxy: fascism had subjugated the economy. The relationship between state and economy was therefore not as Marxism had claimed all along.

Marxist-Leninists in the Soviet Union, the GDR and also some in Western Germany realized that such revisions of the doctrine were dangerous for they undermined the whole edifice and had far-reaching repercussions. They insisted therefore that there should be no retreat from the praetorian-guard formula. This had the advantage of consistency even though it involved orthodox Marxism in manifest absurdities: how to explain, for instance, with reference to class interest the murder of millions of Jews?

The issue was not only and not mainly of academic interest; it had a great deal to do with the interpretation of current affairs. For the state in post-war Germany, as in all other 'capitalist' countries, was far more powerful than all the industrialists and bankers taken together and it furthermore owned much of the economy. Since the Social Democrats were the leading force in the land, this led to the question of whether they had become the tools of monopoly capitalism. If so, how to explain the frequent conflicts of interest between the capitalists and the state? Was it a mere smokescreen to mislead the working class? Orthodox Marxists persisted in viewing the West German state as a mere tool of the capitalists, a point of view reflected in the new-old theory of 'state monopoly capitalism' (*Stamokap*). This concept had the advantage of ideological consistency, but how could it be squared with social, economic and political realities? It had a certain short-lived vogue in the 1970s, but has not been heard of since.

The Marxist-Leninist position on fascism was basically untenable, and it might have been wiser to suppress this debate just as others had been suppressed, for it led to absurd conclusions. If every 'capitalist' country was at least partly fascist there was in retrospect not much to choose between Roosevelt and Churchill on the one hand and Hitler on the other, just as in the contemporary world there were no basic differences between say the late Shah or Pinochet on the one hand and the Social Democratic government in Sweden or the Popular Front in France. This was an insult to the political intelligence of the communists, for they showed through their actions that they were perfectly aware of the existence of differences.

The orthodox fascism theory had yet another consequence, which was the trivialization of Nazism. Why get excited about Nazi crimes if other capitalist regimes, if hard pressed, had behaved, or would behave, in the same way? This line of argument led the communists into ideological neighbourhoods they could not possibly enjoy. If all were guilty, victors and vanquished alike, no one was really guilty. Could one not think furthermore of mitigating circumstances for the rise of Nazism such as the fact that Germany and Italy had been 'proletarian nations' after the First World War? This, of course, had been argued by fascists and neo-fascists all along.

The concept of totalitarianism was, not surprisingly, anathema to Leninists. It implied close analogies between 'fascism' and the communist regimes; under both dictatorships all aspects of public life and many aspects of private life were controlled by party and state. The totalitarianism model had to be discredited for obvious reasons and the orthodox Marxists in Germany had more success in achieving this than in providing a plausible theory of fascism. The totalitarianism model which had emerged in the 1950s suffered from the same weakness as did all political-science models: reality was always richer and more complicated than any definition or analogy, however suggestive. As the 'worst excesses' of Stalinism were amended and the 'cult of the individual' dismantled, as the Cold War made room for *détente*, the totalitarianism model seemed anachronistic and was given up by many of its erstwhile advocates. Instead, various theories were advanced which had the merit, seen from the communist point of view, that they obfuscated the differences between dictatorships. Totalitarianism having been discarded, all dictatorships now became 'authoritarian', which is to say that in principle there was no real difference between the modern (totalitarian) dictatorships of the twentieth century on the one hand and old-style paternalistic conservative regimes such as, say, Jordan, Egypt or Morocco, or Paraguay under General Stroessner.

Lastly, Leninist historiography succeeded to a considerable extent in rewriting the historiography of the Cold War. Those who had lived through the post-war period remembered that America had demobilized with record speed after the end of the war, whereas the Russians had attempted to advance as much as they could to the west and south without encountering determined resistance. The milestones in this process were the squeezing out of democratic (and socialist) elements in all East European countries, the Prague coup in 1948, the blockade of Berlin, the rejection of the Marshall plan, the Greek civil war, the attempts by the Soviets to appropriate parts of Turkey and Iran, and ultimately the invasion of Korea.

In all these instances the initiative had come from Moscow. In the late 1960s the belief gained ground that this was a misrepresentation of the true course of events. The Western powers, above all America, mortally afraid of social revolution, had ceased to co-operate with the Russians well before the end of the war. Thus the Russians had become suspicious and in self-defence had established a *cordon sanitaire*. Eastern Europe's fate had been settled in Yalta and, in any case, once communist-style regimes had been established it was unthinkable to expect these countries to retreat to a less progressive social and political order. The Soviet leadership had wanted peace all along, whereas the Western leaders in a systematic campaign of anti-communist incitement had unleashed the Cold War. Even in 1953 Stalin and his successors had been ready to accept a united Germany. It was only owing to the establishment of the aggressive, militaristic North Atlantic Treaty that the division of Germany had been perpetuated.

In this extreme propagandistic form the communist version was not accepted by many serious students of history and politics. But in a watered-down version these views were widespread; perhaps the truth lay somewhere in the middle? The communists were probably not as innocent as they claimed but, having been invaded so often in their history, the Russians craved security above all. If they expanded after 1945 the reason was mainly defensive. Rearmament was a kind of action-reaction spiral, fuelled by misunderstandings and misperceptions (and by ideological cold warriors) on both sides.

In this diluted form, cold-war 'revisionism' became a new consensus for a decade and it is still quite influential today. The political implications need not be spelled out in detail. It is, of course, true that similar views became influential also in the United States and, to a lesser extent, in France, Britain and Italy. But American misperceptions about Europe could be more easily explained, for they concerned a faraway continent. Germany, on the other hand, had been exposed to the full brunt of the Cold War, and European geography had not changed since the 1950s. How to explain that the attempt to forge Hitler's diaries created a storm of indignation whereas the rewriting of European history after 1945 by the 'revisionists' was welcomed or at least received with great respect?

The new interpretation was not rooted in any new and startling discoveries about the events of the 1930s or 1940s. Nor was it based on the greater detachment shown by a new, more objective generation which had not been involved in the passionate struggles of the post-war period. The real cause was far more simple. The history of fascism, the Second World War and its aftermath were rewritten in the light of the Vietnam war, of Iran, Latin America and, last but not least, the Great Coalition in Bonn which Rudi Dutschke had called the 'most abhorrent of all political regimes'. It had to be shown that America, the ruling circles in the *Bundesrepublik*, and the West in general were not only playing a reactionary role at present but that they had done so all along. It came quite naturally to a new generation unencumbered by recollections of the 1930s and 1940s to oppose the Cold War consensus of the generation of the parents. Such negation of yesteryear's conventional political wisdom has always been an intrinsic part of generational revolt.

There still remained some questions: why demonstrate against Uruguay and not against the Soviet occupation of Czechoslovakia, why against San Salvador but not for independent Poland, why the protest against Pershing and Cruise missiles but not the ss-20? Why attack only America and turn a blind eye to the failures of Soviet theory and practice? The reasons were manifold: those on the Left could not very well wage an effective campaign on two fronts at the same time. Furthermore, Soviet-style communism after all used the same arguments and slogans, and even if it had misbehaved there was always the hope that it would reform itself, in contrast to fascism, capitalism and imperialism which were incorrigible. Even a deformed Soviet regime was basically progressive. With all their commitment to 'critical theory' young Marxists in Germany were far more uncritical *vis-à-vis* the Soviet Union than their contemporaries in France or other Western countries. Perhaps there was also the recognition, seldom openly admitted, that it was less risky to protest against governments in faraway countries than against a powerful neighbour. It could be argued, in any case, that protests against democratic governments may have some effect whereas communist rulers were impervious to remonstration. In brief, America was a far more convenient target.

The Left was not particularly enamoured of the Soviet system but it felt that it could do nothing about it, and therefore preferred to look the other way. This, in briefest outline, was the general political context in which the revival of Marxism-Leninism took place among sections of the intelligentsia in the *Bundesrepublik*. There was at first some hope that this would not be a mere rehash of old theories but a new interpretation, critical of the authoritarian anti-democratic elements in Marxism. But the anti-authoritarian elements soon withered away and what remained was old-style Marxism-Leninism. Seen in retrospect it directly affected a relatively small circle of people and by 1980 enthusiasm for the Soviet system and communist policies in general was no higher than it had been in 1960. If so, why bother to discuss it in the first place?

The answer is that while it lost much of its attraction and while the collected works of Marx and Lenin were stored in the cellar, communist theories by no means vanished without a trace. There were undoubtedly more believers in Marxism-Leninism in German universities than in those of the Soviet Union, not to mention Poland or Hungary. The influence of these ideas can perhaps be compared to the impact of Leninism in the Third World. Much of it was rejected, but certain elements, such as the Leninist theory of imperialism, were absorbed and became part of a new Third-World ideology. In a similar way, certain elements of Marxism-Leninism were absorbed into the new German ideology of the 1970s and 1980s – a new view of fascism and the Cold War, opposition to America, a greater willingness to make allowances *vis-à-vis* Soviet and communist policies.

These shifts in attitude were bound to have political consequences: if the military-political threat to Germany was largely mythical, Germany's part in the Western Alliance had to be re-examined. Nor did it any longer seem self-evident that young Germans should be forced to spend some of the best months of their life in the armed forces. Other questions involving German politics and culture had to be rethought. All this might have occurred in any case. But as it happened the ideological fashions of the 1960s and 1970s provided sections of the West German intelligentsia with a quasi-philosophical underpinning, a systematic approach, and a stridency which otherwise might not have appeared.

Intellectuals in the 1970s

In 1968 the death of German literature had been announced by some radical spokesmen, but after a mere six or seven years it appeared that the obituaries had been premature. By the middle 1970s critics noted a 'new subjectivism' and a 'new sensibility' in literature. If for a number of years 'I' and 'me' had almost vanished from novels and short stories, these personal pronouns now reappeared with a vengeance, and 'nostalgia' became fashionable. Someone, alluding to a famous verse by Wilhelm Busch, the great comic writer, headed his report on the literary scene with 'They are singing again'.

One writer who had specialized in industrial reportage now made it known that her relationship with her mother had been disturbed and that she had suffered from great *Angst* all along. A famous poet, who had announced that he was leaving for a long stay in Cuba, was back after a few weeks; he had not particularly liked what he had seen. In his last writings Peter Weiss, one of the leading radicals, retreated from political militancy. Of those who had joined the Communist party, the better known were out again after a few years. Apparently they had not found the climate very congenial. Almost overnight old and half-discarded genres were again very much in demand: autobiographies, travelogues, biographical and historical novels. Romanticism was in – naturalism out. All this is not to suggest that there was a mass exodus from the political scene or that intellectuals admitted gross misjudgment, a collective *pater peccavi*.

Heinrich Böll would agree that in the heat of the polemic he might have exaggerated a little – who had not? – and that, with the benefit of hindsight, he might change an adjective and perhaps even a noun in his political essays. But this did not concern substance. As many open letters and manifestos were published as ever and it was not difficult to find contributors for collections of political essays with apocalyptic titles such as *In this last hour*. The main difference was that the aims and expectations became more modest, and that the attacks were directed less against the government of the day and more against those who had made the planet uninhabitable, against warmongers, nuclear fanatics and their like.

While Willy Brandt had been chancellor not a few intellectuals had believed that a reconciliation between power and spirit (the classic German dichotomy) was possible. Brandt listened to the intellectuals, and it was probably not accidental that two of them (Grass and Siegfried Lenz) accompanied him on his historic trip to Warsaw. Another writer, Dieter Lattmann, even became a member of the *Bundestag*. But Brandt was succeeded by Helmut Schmidt, who had a dimmer view of the competence of intellectuals in foreign affairs and defence, let alone in economics. Intellectuals were no longer flattered on occasions of state, they were not addressed and consulted as the conscience of the nation and so they again began to feel politically homeless. Walter Jens and others discerned a 'growing illiberalism' even while the Social Democrats were in power; the attacks became harsher and louder after the Christian Democrats had taken over in 1982. Politicians were always preoccupied with immediate problems, it was said; they lacked vision and were for ever prevented from acting decisively by dismal *Sachzwänge* – lack of money, lack of freedom of manœuvre, lack of parliamentary majorities. The intellectuals, on the other hand, felt they were called to address themselves to greater issues: to mobilize the public against the growing erosion of freedom at home and the danger of the weapons of mass destruction, and, using a new slogan, to 'maintain the unity of a divided nation'.

These were praiseworthy aims, but what did they mean in practice? Those giving the warning knew that Germany had not become, or was about to become, a dictatorship, and they were also aware of the penalty for crying wolf too often. Nor was it clear how West German writers could decisively contribute to the unity of the nation. They could attend meetings with East German writers arranged by the German PEN club or another such group, where the fight for peace in Europe and in the world would be proclaimed, America would be denounced, and various other concessions would be made to keep the East Germans happy. A few West German writers might even utter mildly dissenting views. But the unity of the nation would hardly benefit from conferences of this kind; most of the books of the Western writers were not even permitted to circulate in East Germany. The same was and is true with regard to West German movies, plays, music and paintings. There was an element of unreality in these gatherings, but the participants seemed not to mind.

They wanted to have political influence but not to accept the constraints of politics. 'One ought to go too far, in order to know how far one can go', Böll had once said in an oft-quoted aside. This was excellent guidance for some occasions but not for others; a mountain climber for instance or a bridge builder would be reluctant to accept Böll's advice about going too far. It made sense only on the assumption that there would always be a safety net in case of a fall, that what the intellectuals did was not really of great importance in the final analysis, that their mistakes were corrigible – by themselves or others. But such an assumption collided with another set of basic tenets – that of the near-infallibility of intellectuals, their role as *magister Germaniae.*

The fact that unlike intellectuals in France they were not recognized as the conscience of the nation was a complaint of long standing; it can be traced back to Heinrich Mann's famous 'Zola' essay published in the First World War. In actual fact intellectuals had played such a role in France only at rare intervals, and never in Britain, the US or in Scandinavia, not to mention such democracies as Canada or Australia, Switzerland or New Zealand. But if the intellectuals were excluded, if they had no share in power, did they not have a right to be irresponsible? Fair enough, but this could not be squared with their claim to be more than court jesters (Walter Jens *dixit*), that they had something of importance to say and that their message mattered. The intellectuals could aim at the role of gadflies or of elder statesmen. A combination of the two did not make sense.

Different people reacted in different ways. Some of the leading radicals of the 1960s, who had earlier come on record with their firm belief that German parliamentary democracy was a mere chimera, now had second thoughts. Walser wrote in 1981 that the West German state was *worthy of support*! Some of the intellectuals of the APO generation withdrew into their private neuroses or, as an unkind critic put it, into their bedrooms. Their attempts to change the world had not gone well, which did not mean that they felt any happier about society. On the other hand, there was the case of Günter Grass, once the chief advocate of 'permanent reform', who became deeply disillusioned and ended up by proclaiming that Germany was not a state capable of living in peace, and calling on German youth not to do their military service.

Radical Protestantism

The most interesting and also the most important new development on the intellectual scene was the growing participation of the churches in German politics. Their record under Hitler had been lamentable. Immediately after the war they had published their *mea culpa*, but there was also a delayed effect. A younger generation of churchmen in the 1970s and 1980s went into politics with a vengeance. If a previous generation of church leaders had been found wanting in the hour of trial, they would show the courage expected from true pastors.

These developments affected both churches, but the Protestants more than the Catholics, who were still mainly preoccupied with internal problems such as the disputes about various reforms, the questions of celibacy and abortion, or the case of Hans Küng, the prominent theologian who had been deprived of the right to teach in view of his heretical views. It is not difficult to see why substantial sections of the Protestant church should move further in the process of radicalization. If the German intelligentsia had been *staatstreu*, loyal to the authorities over and above the call of duty, the Protestant church had been, always with some notable exceptions, the state church *par excellence*, identifying itself thoroughly with the government, frequently reactionary and chauvinistic in outlook. Thus the strong reaction after the end of the Second World War did not come as a complete surprise: it was a reaction against their own past. Early on Protestant leaders such as Martin Niemöller and Gustav Heinemann were in the forefront of the struggle against German rearmament within NATO, and the Church Council (EKD) also dissociated itself from any such endeavour.

During the 1950s and early 1960s the majority of the Church accepted the *Bundeswehr* just as the Social Democrats did. But important sections continued to advocate various 'progressive' causes both on the theological level (such as the 'theology of hope') and even more so in politics. This manifested itself in the church memorandum on *Ostpolitik* (1965), in support for various Third-World liberation movements and, above all, in the backing given to the peace movement. The peace movement became respectable among the German middle class only owing to the help of influential circles within the Protestant church.

There was yet another reason for the greater receptivity of the

Protestants for radical political positions: the Protestant church had become an institution in search of a central message over and above its evangelical mission. There were many nominal Protestants in Germany but few active church-goers, and this was particularly true with regard to the young generation. Protestantism very much wanted again to become a force of relevance in the contemporary world, and while it would be misleading to suggest that for this reason alone it came to take up various militant positions, this consideration, consciously or unconsciously, did play a role. It was not, of course, that protestantism (or catholicism) had suddenly opted for political activism after scrupulously refraining from it for centuries. It had always in one way or another, actively or passively, played a political role; its role had changed from espousing reactionary nationalism to moralistic leftism. This refers to influential sections of protestantism, not the Church as such which, of course, was not monolithic in character.

The issues at stake were bitterly debated inside the Church, and no clear consensus emerged. On one extreme there was the evangelical element which resented the concentration on politics rather than on spreading the gospel. On the other side there was the *Reformbund* which made opposition to nuclear arms (including deterrence!) a religious commandment, a *status confessionis*. How much mainstream German protestantism (the EKD) had changed appeared from its Heidelberg manifesto (1981). On the one hand it argued that defence based on nuclear deterrence was 'still possible' for Christians, on the other hand it said that esteem and understanding ought to be shown both to young Germans joining the *Bundeswehr* and to those refusing to do so. This seemed an even-handed approach but it was, in fact, far from impartial. By implication it appeared that only a refusal was truly Christian whereas those who went to serve were to be tolerated, since they were doing an unpleasant duty.

The more radical Protestant spokesmen demanded that the Sermon on the Mount should be the guiding principle for Christians in this time. The meaning of the Sermon for international politics had been discussed inconclusively by theologians for a long time, but the radical theologians had an answer, simple and uncompromising. As they saw it, it meant unilateral disarmament and pacifism – not perhaps *total* pacifism but at most 'social defence'. 'Social defence' is a concept which was developed by the German *Friedensforscher*, a new academic discipline which came into being with state financial support following the student revolt in the late 1960s. There was a great deal of goodwill and lofty idealism in this field – and an even stronger element of charlatanism. 'Social defence' meant almost anything, from defence by a people's militia to passive resistance. Such ideas had no doubt much to recommend themselves in the case of an invasion of Norway by Sweden, or of Belgium by Holland, but not in most other cases likely to happen in the contemporary world.

Another concept developed by the *Friedensforscher* ought to be mentioned because it had considerable influence on radical Protestant thinking – this was the idea of *Entfeindung*, of getting rid of the image, the very concept, of an enemy. According to this school of thought it was not enough to destroy nuclear weapons: the souls and minds of human beings had to be changed. It had to be explained to them that the image of the enemy was largely (or entirely) a product of their own fears. It was not enough to refrain from making war, one also had to 'think peace'.

Following this train of thought the radical Protestants viewed the arms race as the result of mutual fears; there was 'false consciousness' on both sides, and while individual freedom as preached by the West was important, to keep peace was even more so. Furthermore, a communist system had also much to recommend itself with its emphasis on brotherhood, alien to Western liberalism. Communist systems could therefore with good conscience suppress opposition to their policies. The Church had to take an equidistant position not only between the two power blocs but also between the two ideologies. Real freedom did *not* exist in the West, the freedom of the liberal state was *not* Christian freedom. On the contrary, liberal freedom always contained the seeds of unfreedom and temptation. And in any case Christian freedom could not be defended by force of arms.[1]

Such interpretations were certainly of interest because they showed that the negative attitude towards political freedom and democracy which had been a typical feature of German protestantism before and after the First World War had not really changed that much; it was, in some ways, the old idea of the German *Sonderweg*, a third road between West and East, back in new garb.

But the dilemma facing the radical theologians does not end here. Everyone, after all, wants to prevent a nuclear war: the decisive question is how to do so most effectively. The radical theologians have a

[1] Ulrich Schmidhäuser, *Entfeindung* (Stuttgart 1983), *passim*

right to participate in this debate, but they have no special competence and authority, for the issues at stake are not only moral in character. Granted that the traditional doctrine of the just war had become obsolete in the nuclear age, it was still possible that the answer of the radical theologians was not the right one. Was it not conceivable that by confusing political thought and moral postulates they made war more, rather than less, likely? There is little willingness in these circles to engage in pragmatic discussions of this kind; instead *Angst* is invoked incessantly and also deliberately stirred up. Cardinal de Retz once noted that of all the passions fear weakens judgment the most, a view obviously not shared by passionate people who believe in the curative faculties of fear – *appropinquante mundi termino*, as the medieval monks used to add – as the end of the world approaches.

Church people who chose politics as their vocation were giving a finger to the devil, as Max Weber had pointed out many years before, and no one could be sure whether eventually the devil would not gain possession of the arm, the whole body and even the soul. Events in other parts of the world had shown that radical theology has proceeded from the negation of the doctrine of the just war, to preaching that civil wars were pleasing in the eyes of God. This may be a legitimate point of view, but it can be made with equal ease without reference to God. In such a doctrine there is no need for Christian charity, for love of one's fellow man, and eventually for religion. Bible classes are likely to give way to agit-prop and in the end the differences between religious and non-religious militants are no longer visible to the naked eye. Dorothea Sölle said at the world meeting of the Council of Christian Churches in Canada in 1983 that 'our San Salvador was in militarist West Germany', which was the place where our struggle should proceed – 'this is our Vietnam, our Soweto, our San Salvador, our battlefield for justice and peace'. In contrast she mentioned Nicaragua where 'people could still live as Christians'. Pastor Albertz of Berlin was reminded of a 'super concentration camp' when he saw the barbed wire surrounding a military installation in West Germany. Some thought such sayings extremely shocking, but they were by no means unprecedented: the Red Dean of Canterbury had thought Stalinism the most Christian political system on earth in the 1930s. The Rev. Hewlett Johnson had been a fool, but even if he had been right his decision to transfer most of his activity to the political field would have been dangerous for the Church. Mrs Sölle, Pastor Albertz, the Red Dean and the bishops of the

Deutsche Christen supporting Hitler had a right to say what they believed was the truth. But invoking, directly or indirectly, the authority of the Church (or even God), speaking as religious believers and dignitaries was an act of dubious morality.[1]

The politics of the German intelligentsia is of considerable fascination, but how important is it? Intellectuals have neither elected nor overthrown governments. Paradoxically most German intellectuals believe that they have been quite ineffectual in bringing about significant change in public life whereas their adversaries think them almost all-powerful. Their direct political influence has always been small despite the fact that there are now many more of them than in the past: the number of students alone has quadrupled over the last two decades. Indirectly, through television, newspapers, periodicals and publishing houses and, generally speaking, as disseminators of ideas, as the makers of public opinion, their influence has been out of proportion to their numbers. This is also true with regard to their role in education. There are more communists, Trotskyites, Maoists, sundry New Leftists, not to mention 'Greens' and left-wing Social Democrats in teaching and social work than in all other professions taken together. It is too early to say whether these teachers will have an impact on the political views of the next generation or whether, on the contrary, their creed will be rejected by their anti-authoritarian pupils. Students and university people have certainly gained positions of influence in the Social Democratic party. Georg Leber, a former Socialist minister of defence and a building worker by training, noted with some bitterness in an interview that 'those who have not studied, who do not speak English well, who have learned a craft, who are of working-class origin and who stand with both feet on the ground, find themselves now in the minority in the leading bodies of the party'.

It is too early to know whether the influence of young intellectuals will help or harm the Social Democrats in the long run. If it should emerge that 'intellectual' is no more than a synonym for 'doctrinaire',

[1] Similar trends have been observed, of course, among churches in countries other than Germany. The Rev. Ernest Gordon of Princeton has noted his impression 'that the World Council of Churches has become the last refuge of those denominational bureaucrats who having lost their Christian faith are trying to find a substitute in the pages of Karl Marx's works'. But this does not do justice to the German phenomenon. The radical theologians are not necessarily bureaucrats but true believers, and their radicalism is not that of Karl Marx. Marx was neither pacifist nor 'do gooder', nor 'Third-Worldist'; he had nothing but contempt for sentimental liberals, however radical their slogans; his attitude to Wilberforce is a typical example.

'impractical', and a new language comprehensible only to former students of certain schools of sociology and political science, the appeal of such a party will be limited, to say the least. But the young intellectuals engaged on their long march through the institutions may not make these elementary mistakes. All that can be said with certainty is that the cumulative effect of the media should not be underrated. The impact is indirect: according to opinion polls carried out in 1972 more readers of the *Frankfurter Allgemeine Zeitung* and the *Bildzeitung* voted for the SPD than for the CDU even though these papers were highly critical of the Left. On the other hand, about half of the viewers of the left-wing television news magazine *Panorama* thought that Nazism also had some good points. Investigations have shown that the public turns to the media, and to television in particular, for the confirmation of views already held. But it is also true that massive exposure to certain themes – say that politicians are corrupt or that American leaders are dangerous lunatics – has a long-range effect.

Since, unlike in a totalitarian regime, there is no media monopoly, the impact will be less dramatic – it will be negative rather than positive. The media are not able to build up the image of a certain leader or party. But they will be able to sow doubt, to denigrate by articulating anxieties, by giving expression to the discontent felt by various groups in society. This role can be of considerable importance in a critical situation – or even in creating a crisis by playing on the fears and the dangers never far away from the surface of public opinion. It dramatizes the shortcomings of the state and plays down its achievements, thus reinforcing the innate feeling of insecurity in a people for whom democracy is a relatively new experience. There has been a striking dichotomy in Germany between reality and self-perception, between the achievements of post-war Germany – not only in the economic field – and the lack of confidence which has manifested itself during the last decade. Why should the present system be denigrated in a way its predecessors never were? Is it because the intellectuals cannot love this state or identify with it? Englishmen or Frenchmen will not normally regard their state as an object of love. German expectations, ever since Hegel, have been much higher.

Hence the claims that massive repression is gaining ground, that economic decline is more or less foreordained, that war and ecological disaster are just around the corner. The problem is not, of course, specifically German; the media in all free societies feed on bad news. It is widely assumed that those paid by the state should defend it, excepting only those employed by radio and television, whereas journalists should act as a mixture of ombudsman and public prosecutor.

In some ways all this is a belated reaction to 1933, but there is a difference. Whereas great courage was needed to oppose Hitler in 1933, the penalties for criticizing the Bonn government of the day are not formidable. Once upon a time Germany was the country of Nietzsche and Wagner, the concept of the superman and the idea of a heroic lifestyle, children were taught that even showing weakness was bad. Today heroism is out. Why should the descendants of Siegfried and Hermann the Cheruscan claim that 'today we are only afraid, we have great anxieties and small anxieties, and *Angst* to have *Angst*' – or phobophobia as the psychologists would say. In the main auditorium of the school I attended there was, as I suppose there was in most other German schools, an inscription: Horace's 'It is sweet and honourable to die for one's country.' Underneath was the list of those killed in the First World War. But Horace, who also said, 'Life grants nothing to us mortals without hard work', and *Nil desperandum* (Never despair), is no longer in demand. I remember the cult book of the youth movement around 1932 called *Heldenfibel* (A Hero's Primer) in which, if memory serves me right, all kinds of heroes engaged in desperate struggles were held up for adulation. For years the Germans were told that the community was all and the individual nothing, or next to nothing. Their professors almost succeeded in making a positive hero of Hagen of Tronje, that evil man from the Songs of the Nibelungen who went to his death even though he had seen in detail everything that was coming. Germany was the country in which the ancients' sense of the tragic was perhaps better understood than anywhere else. Strange, how in the span of a generation or two the mood has swung from one extreme to the other. Once they were dying to die, now they want to live for ever. Poor General Haig: his rash *obiter dictum* about certain values being more important than peace at any price appear on the walls of even the smallest German town – effective propaganda for the peace movement, the perfect admission of a warmonger. The explanations have been given a hundred times: two lost world wars, destruction, the nuclear bomb, the division of Germany, the cultural crisis, the identity crisis, the legitimacy crisis. But some of these crises have been going on for a few centuries, and others for at least a few decades, but it is only now that we are told they have reached a critical stage. 'The German *Angst* is anonymous', it is said, 'it is in the air.'[1] People are still singing, but with gnashing teeth; they are dancing as the passengers on the *Titanic* did. Nothing is right any more, everyone feels threatened and taken advantage of.

Germans may talk about emigration, but the queues at the travel agents are for holiday trips to Spain and Italy, to Kenya and Thailand. Once this used to be a country of emigrants, but today there are many more would-be immigrants to this unhappy land. Many would prefer to live, we are told, in a pre-modern small town. But there was as much pessimism and hypochondria in painter Carl Spitzweg's nineteenth-century small town, as contemporary accounts clearly show, and the per capita consumption of Valium is no higher in Germany than in the US or the Soviet Union.

Is the allegedly all-pervasive German *Angst* genuine, or is it a premature *fin-de-siècle* mood, providing an interesting subject for conversation at cocktail parties and literary gatherings? Public opinion polls tell us that Germans have become somewhat less optimistic than they were fifteen or twenty years ago, but still prefer to live in the present rather than in the past. They are now more sceptical with regard to technical progress. But this is also true for other countries. It says little about the depth of such feeling and how easily it may change again. Some fears are subject to wide fluctuations: 50 per cent of all Germans thought a nuclear war likely in the 1950s; this figure declined to 17 per cent in 1979, but shot up again to 50 per cent in 1980–1. Realities hardly changed during this period, only atmospherics did. The fluctuations in other European countries were less dramatic over the same period; other Europeans were less reassured by *détente*, less intimidated by tough talk emanating from Washington and Moscow.

Some Germans love apocalyptic predictions: if Luther predicted the exact date of the Day of Wrath, the practice is again in full swing. Günter Gaus[2] has written that nuclear war is inevitable within the next ten to fifteen years. He was a highly placed, well-informed official of the Bonn government; surely he deserves a respectful hearing? As these lines are written an article in the Berlin alternative newspaper *taz* (12 August 1983) announces that only a few months are left to us; the

[1] Jürgen Leinemann, *Die Angst der Deutschen* (Hamburg 1982)
[2] Günter Gaus, born in 1929, was secretary of state and represented West Germany in East Berlin from 1974 to 1981; he is a well-known essayist and radio personality.

warning seems to be meant quite literally. A textbook recently appeared in Germany under the title *The German House is on Fire*. After a few pages the authors admitted that the choice of the title and the exaggeration in the whole tenor of the book were deliberate and had an educational purpose. True, German society is not on fire; in fact, when compared with the past, or with the present state of other societies, it is in reasonably good shape. But people have to be galvanized into action and this, the authors believe, is possibly only by way of exaggeration: fire or no fire, the tocsin ought to be sounded.

Anxiety is a more interesting topic for novelists and film-makers than courage; brave people are usually dull whereas neurosis is thought to betray (and sometimes does) imagination and sensitivity. But there can be a surfeit of *Weltschmerz* and anxiety, and for all one knows the strong individual hero pursuing his lonely struggle against heavy odds may soon be back with us.

After a short honeymoon with 'power' during the Brandt era many German intellectuals again turned against the state even while the Social Democrats were in power. The opposition of some became more radical after the Christian Democrat take-over. But the trends have been contradictory: among many militants radicalism is no longer as fashionable as it used to be. Green is still (or again) in, but Marxism-Leninism is definitely *passé*. Unmitigated gloom no longer has a monopoly among the avant-garde; some have become guardedly optimistic, others have accepted that fear and insecurity are not a regrettable anomaly that could be put right by a just social order, but are rather part of the human condition.

The 'militancy without risks' approach has also come under fire. Peter Glotz, a man of the Left and at the time senator in charge of cultural affairs in Berlin, has noted that while even the most radical opposition to the state could be legitimate, it was not easy to understand that those negating the legitimacy of the state still wished to do so from the inside: apocalyptic prophecies and total refusal on the one hand, and an equally firm insistence on all the fringe benefits and pension rights due to them. True rebels should be willing to accept certain sacrifices.

Intellectuals are above all critics, and their statements in turn invite criticism. They are likely to be carried away in their enthusiasm and their manifestos must be taken with a pinch of salt; these are not legal documents issued by a high authority in which every word matters.

What applies to a small number of writers or movie-makers of high visibility is not necessarily true for all their colleagues. It is only fair to compare German intellectuals with those in other countries and above all with the record of German intellectuals in the past. They must not be measured by an impossibly high standard in which imagination and sensitivity are combined with prudence and judgment, in which criticism is paired with responsibility, and commitment with detachment. Such a perfect mixture of virtues, while desirable in principle, is unlikely to occur anywhere, least of all in a country with a history as troubled as Germany's.

Seen in historical perspective it is not difficult to understand current attitudes among German intellectuals. Throughout the nineteenth century and up to 1945 too many *Dichter und Denker* were heaping undeserved praise on their rulers or alternatively withdrawing into an aestheticism in which there was no room for engagement in public affairs. In comparison with past attitudes there is much to be said for present-day political involvement. There is radical chic, to be sure, the *Schickeria* of Munich and Hamburg, but there is a seriousness in German intellectual attitudes which contrasts with the flippancy often observed in other countries. If the causes sponsored are sometimes open to question, there is nothing mean about the inspiration and the motives. If there is a hypersensitivity about infringements of freedom and justice, real or imaginary, this is, to repeat once again, to compensate for the sins of commission and omission of previous generations. Seen in this light there has been a radical break with the past; nothing or very little has remained of the old aggressive nationalism among most intellectuals. There was, at least for a while, greater openness towards outside cultural influences in Germany after the war than in any other European country. In some other respects the break is less marked: civility and self-depreciation have not yet become outstanding features in everyday life, there is an extra edge of aggression in personal and public confrontation, a certain dogmatic obstinacy (*Rechthaberei*); to admit error seems to come even less easily to many German intellectuals than to their confrères in other countries. The state and the authorities are frequently regarded as father figures, tyrannical yet all-forgiving. There is unbridled criticism against the authorities but also the expectation that financial support will continue in all circumstances.

Theorizing still has enormous fascination for German intellectuals and this has been a source of strength as well as weakness. In conversation Goethe more than once noted an excessive inclination among his countrymen towards theory and, as a corollary, the tendency to complicate obvious issues.[1]

The German intellectual scene is not a parliament, issues are not decided by bloc votes and party discipline is non-existent. With all this there are interesting differences in the general mood compared, for instance, with neighbouring France. In France the late 1940s and the 1950s were the heyday of pro-Sovietism, anti-Americanism and an uncritical Third-Worldism. Since then the pendulum has swung in the other direction, and the same is true, albeit less pronouncedly, with regard to the United States, Britain and Italy. But *Deutschlands Uhren gehen anders* – there has been a cultural time-lag between West Germany and its neighbours in the West. Many German intellectuals in the 1970s adopted the views which Sartre had pioneered in the late 1940s and which a quarter of a century later had become an embarrassment or a joke in bad taste.

What caused German radicalization to come twenty-five years after most others had been through it? Was it the reaction to the 'Cold War consensus' which prevailed in Germany throughout the 1950s and up to the late 1960s? The German volte-face would be more readily intelligible as the result of some major shocks, but there were no Vietnams and Watergates in West Germany. Perhaps one ought to go further back in the search for reasons and motives, perhaps it was suddenly realized around 1970 that since Nazism had been anti-Soviet and anti-communist (most of the time, in any case) the Soviet Union and communism must be the opponent of fascism.

Since then another decade has passed and there have been more changes on the intellectual scene. Primitive leftism is no longer in, at least as far as the avant-garde is concerned. The interest in revolutionary theory has declined and patriotism has been rediscovered. There has been no return to the *status quo ante*; some of the innovations of the 1970s persist, others have been discarded. The mainstream of the intelligentsia is still 'against' but it is now less clear what it stands for.

It is difficult enough to analyse the mood of an individual, and next to impossible with collective behaviour. Why do groups of people enter a negative phase and put on a mournful countenance? Germans have

---

[1] '*Es ist der Character der Deutschen, dass sie über allem schwer werden*' (in conversation with Heinrich Luden, 1813)

seldom danced with joy in the streets and the general state of the world has not been conducive to such behaviour in any case. Just as Dionysus, the god of wine, enthusiasm, ecstasy and joy never appealed very much to the Homeric heroes, he has never attracted most German intellectuals. They have usually preferred the ambitions and the moral indignation of a Prometheus. Such anger also has its satisfactions, but on the whole it does not make for happiness and harmony; German intellectuals have not been happy in their skins, and the nation has not been too happy with its intellectuals. But were intellectuals ever meant to be happy? This debate has gone on for a long time. A little less of Prometheus on the one hand and a little less negativism on the other would probably be all to the good, but such insights will have to come from the inside.

6 Arminius or Patriotism Rediscovered

The statue of the liberator of Germany is situated in the middle of a forest near the city of Detmold. It stands some 60 yards high from top to bottom. He raises his mighty sword and the inscription above says: 'German Unity my Strength'. It took the sculptors some thirty years to complete this symbol of German nationhood: the statue was unveiled in 1875 in the presence of the German emperor. To this day it attracts pilgrims from near and far. On a weekday last autumn, a day like all others, a few thousand men, women and children came to visit the dark statue of Arminius the Cheruscan. This is a substantial crowd by any standard; I never saw more than a few dozen visitors at Marx's grave in Highgate cemetery even though the grave of George Eliot is a few steps away, and Faraday's not much further.

Who are these people? The view is not exceptional, there are more attractive beauty spots in this part of Germany. Among the crowds there are many young people despite the fact that the story is no longer taught in German schools in any detail as it was a generation or two ago. Much of the story, admittedly, belongs to the realm of mythology. Despite the efforts of historians and archaeologists only a few facts are known about this young man: Arminius was only in his early twenties at the time of the battle of Teutoburg Forest in the year AD 9. Of royal descent, he was a Roman citizen who had participated as an officer in the Pannonian campaign and was knighted for bravery. He then turned against his fellow Romans. Breaking an oath was no small matter in an era in which so much emphasis was put on loyalty and honour. But he was also a German patriot and his great desire was to unite the warring German tribes. He defected and in a guerrilla campaign defeated three Roman legions. About his subsequent career nothing is known except that he lived for another twelve years and was killed by members of his own family.

There is no certainty about the site of the battle: the fighting might have been in this forest, but it could also have been many miles away – there are some seven hundred different versions. For the Romans the whole affair was a minor, if painful, episode in the annals of their empire. The story of Arminius was, in fact, forgotten until Tacitus' works were rediscovered in a monastery not far from this site about the year 1500. Beginning with Luther, the story caught the imagination of German patriots; two dozen operas with Arminius as the hero were produced in the eighteenth century and in the city of New Ulm, Minnesota, a half-size replica of the original was put up by local people in 1897 and presumably still stands. The original statue was hit by shrapnel in the last phase of the war. The rain, the snow and the winds did further damage and in 1952 the sword had to be lowered for repair.

But the crowds continue to arrive. Quite obviously the story of Arminius has some meaning for many Germans to this day. Are they all extreme right-wingers? Hardly: in the last regional elections the neo-Nazis polled just 0.1 per cent of the total, and this in a land which once used to be one of their bulwarks. True, sympathizers of the far Right will not necessarily vote for one specific sect, and the number of votes may not be an accurate yardstick. But the public here does not strike one as a bunch of fanatics; they look, in fact, very much like a fairly typical cross-section of ordinary Germans, neither very affluent nor very poor. There are few high-powered Mercedeses and BMWs in the car park. Unless these people come just because their fathers and grandfathers used to come – which is possible but unlikely – this pilgrimage must have, after all, something to do with the quest for national identity about which so much is talked in these parts these days. '*Heimat*' has been rediscovered with all that it implies, the old folk-songs, dances and customs, the German landscape, above all the German forest, and this at a time when its very existence is endangered.

For many years after the war *Heimat* was synonymous with *kitsch* among intellectuals; folk-songs and local customs were an object of ridicule or alternatively a dangerous relic of the Nazi era. This was the time when many Germans when travelling abroad preferred not to be recognized as such. The nation was discarded during those years and it was assumed that Germany was about to lose its identity in a larger unit – Europe. It was a noble vision but it remained a dream, others did not share this supra-national enthusiasm. And so, inevitably, Germany came into her own again, German values, traditions and of course also German interests. Germany's neighbours have followed such manifestations of national self-assertion with some nervousness, not surprisingly in view of the historical record. But there ought to be no mistake: this is no longer the aggressive, militant nationalism of a great power out to conquer 'our place in the sun', or at least more *Lebensraum*. The dimensions of the political stage have changed and at least some of the lessons of the past have been learned. Even if West Germany were reunited with the East – a most unlikely contingency at present – it would no longer be a global power. The new nationalism manifests itself not in aggression and expansion but, on the contrary, in the desire to withdraw from political entanglements. It shows itself in a new patriotism which is at least as much left-wing in inspiration as rightist, and also among intellectuals in particular in an anti-Americanism of sorts, basically cultural in character.

This new mood is frequently misinterpreted, and it is also true that Germany is measured by much stricter standards than any other European country. Germany was for many years a model member of the European community and of NATO. It behaved more responsibly, its policy was less motivated by a narrow short-sighted self-interest than Britain's or France's. But this integration into the Western world has been unprecedented in German history. It did not come easily and without resistance from Left as much as from Right. As the years passed by German resentment grew; why should the country still be on probation? New generations have come to the fore unwilling to accept that Germany alone among the nations of Europe should always be on her best behaviour. The fact that Europe is a house half finished and likely to remain so in the foreseeable future has been a further source of disillusionment. The public opinion polls show a loss of German confidence in America and in Europe which is about equal.

If de Gaulle and his successors so frequently invoked France's special mission, or if the British stressed their own special place in the world, one didn't need to be a Nazi or a right-wing extremist to believe in a special German *Sonderweg* between West and East. For a long time there has been in Germany an orientation towards the East. Russia, Tsarist and Bolshevik – or rather the elusive 'eternal Russian spirit' – had many admirers in all parts of the German political spectrum, whereas shallow Western 'civilization' (in contradiction to the depth of

German culture) had many detractors. Thomas Mann's essays during the First World War well express this state of mind. Germany was the classical country of various 'national revolutionaries', National Bolsheviks and anti-Western conservatives who had all written *Ex oriente lux* on their banners. It was all a little vague, part of a cultural rather than a political orientation: after all, even the famous 'Rapallo' policy remained a dead letter – the treaty never came into force. But then seventeen years later Hitler and Stalin did sign a pact and the suspicions of Germany's Western neighbours, even if exaggerated, are not altogether incomprehensible.

For more than two decades the two major parties in Germany have firmly supported the Western Alliance. They did not always agree with the strategies of American presidents, but until recently there was a broad consensus: the very existence of the Alliance was not in question. For obvious reasons it had not been easy for the Social Democrats after the end of the war to accept that a German army had become a necessity. The decision to do so was bitterly opposed for years by wide sections of the party which feared that militarization would spell an end to democracy in Germany. It should also be recalled that neutralism was far more popular in Germany than the idea of a Western Alliance. In early post-war polls about 60 per cent expressed their preference for neutrality and even in 1961 when Kennedy was president 42 per cent were in favour of neutrality ('like Switzerland') as against 40 per cent who wanted to remain in the Atlantic partnership. In 1956, 56 per cent said they would welcome it if the Americans withdrew their troops from Europe; this number fell to an all-time low of 11 per cent in 1979, to rise again more recently.

From the early post-war years there were many groups which firmly opposed a 'one-sided orientation' towards the West: leagues for German unity, peace associations, conservative politicians of pre-Hitler vintage, theologians, left-wingers, rightists and others. Their arguments varied: some said that West Germany's participation in NATO made reunification impossible. Nationalists argued that Germany was accepting the role of a junior partner whereas it should have equal rights. From an extreme right-wing position it was maintained that the German heritage was not consonant with Western consumerism and materialism: America (as they saw it) was doomed and by attaching itself to a lost cause the German nation was bound to be drawn into an unnecessary disaster. Some of these critics advocated closer co-operation with the Soviet Union, others advocated collaboration with other European countries. But there was broad agreement in these circles that an alliance with America was bad for Germany.

The neutralists from the right admittedly fought each other even more bitterly than they fought their enemies. Even the two biggest such parties, the SRP of the 1950s and the NPD of the 1960s, never achieved a breakthrough. They combined vehement anti-communism with the demand to improve relations with the Soviet Union. Thus, at the time of the Soviet invasion of Czechoslovakia the NPD suggested that the Soviet action should not be criticized; their attitude in the case of Poland was similar. While these sectarians never united, there were quite a few of them and there was a substantial reservoir of right-wing neutralist feeling.[1] If in the early years half, or almost half, the population preferred a neutral policy to the Alliance, how could the governments of the day and the leadership of the major parties overrule public opinion? They could and they did, because while many Germans would have preferred to stay out of any entangling alliances they knew that this was impossible. Their quarrel was not so much with NATO but with their history, their geopolitical location and their inability to defend their sovereignty without outside help.

The spectre of neo-Nazism

When the Second World War ended it was widely assumed that the eradication of Nazism would be a long and difficult process. The Nazis were thought to have prepared for a protracted guerrilla campaign (by the so-called Werewolves) and also a political underground. Yet not a single Werewolf was ever seen; the plot had been a chimera. Nevertheless the spectre of a Nazi revival has not been put to rest in the last forty years. On the contrary, the underground survival of Nazi groups has not only provided inspiration to thriller writers (from the *Odessa File* to *The Boys from Brazil*), but has been the source of a flood of articles, books and movies under the general title 'Are the Nazis returning?'. On some occasions the question was transformed into a statement. This

[1] The NPD had 28,000 members in 1969, but in 1975 this figure had shrunk to 10,000 and in 1982 it was down to fewer than 6,000. But the weekly *Deutsche Nationalzeitung*, the main organ of the extreme Right, had a circulation of 110,000 in 1983 – much more than the combined circulation of the mouthpiece of the Social Democrats (*Vorwärts*) and the trade unions (*Welt der Arbeit*).

was, in part, the product of an excess of imagination, in part the desire to entertain. For a swastika on the cover of a thriller or a Nazi uniform in a movie were still powerful symbols and exerted a magic influence all over the world.

There was also political calculation: some circles had a vested interest in the survival or revival of Nazism (or neo-Nazism). They had always maintained that the conditions which had produced Nazism still existed; that, in fact, post-war German society was morally so corrupt that it was bound to give birth to another neo-Nazi movement. Since Nazism had been right-wing (so the argument ran), the post-Hitlerian Right was a potential recruit to the new Nazism. With a little effort this argument could be further stretched so as to include the Christian Democrats and even many Social Democrats; for since the Nazis had been anti-communists, did it not follow that all anti-communists were neo-Nazis? These Nazi chasers were not interested in real Nazis but in groups which they defined as 'fascistoid', i.e. potential fascists. What Hermann Goering had said about Jews they applied to these groups – they would decide who was fascistoid. These critics pointed to the persistence of 'authoritarian structures', to the massive use of terror and propaganda in the *Bundesrepublik*, to negative attitudes towards modern art or homosexuality, and to social repression in general.

Exercises of this kind did not need to be taken unduly seriously because of their blatantly propagandist character. But the campaign did have its dangerous implications: it gratuitously gave publicity to a weak enemy who craved such publicity more than anything else, who could not have attracted it in any other way. Directly or indirectly it thus played into the hands of right-wing extremism.[1] The fact that much of this 'anti-fascist' campaign was instigated by communists and their fellow travellers, who claimed that they, and only they, had been the only consistent anti-Nazis from the very beginning, made many people doubt its bona fide character. Since attachment of the communists to the cause of democracy and liberty, or indeed their historical record relative to Nazism, was not entirely above suspicion, this campaign made some believe that a cause so bitterly attacked by the communists could not be all bad, a wrong conclusion but psychologically an

[1] The terms 'neo-Nazism' and 'right-wing extremism' are almost always used these days as synonyms, which they are not. Not all right-wing extremists are neo-Nazis, i.e. stand for a revival of Hitlerism. Obfuscating the differences makes a realistic understanding of the neo-Nazi phenomenon more difficult.

understandable one. Thirdly, and equally importantly, the constant invocation of the neo-Nazi danger involved all the dangers of the 'cry wolf' syndrome: for even if the old Nazis were dying out and the young Nazis were few and far between, the danger of a major neo-Nazi revival, though improbable, could not be ruled out entirely. Constant vigilance was imperative, and through exaggeration and falsification this vigilance was undermined.

Many millions of Germans had belonged to the Nazi party and its various branches. Many more had believed in Hitler and Nazism. The war and the defeat had weakened or destroyed such beliefs, but this is not to say that they all became fervent believers in parliamentary democracy from one day to the next. The Allies dabbled in re-education, though it ought to be clear that they were ill-equipped for an assignment of this sort. It is relatively easy to replace one dictatorship by another. It is infinitely more difficult to make people think and act independently. The Allies engaged in de-Nazification, but the campaign soon ran out of steam. As the German elite in its overwhelming majority had belonged to the party, the Allies soon realized that as far as the middle and lower echelons of the bureaucracy were concerned, it was virtually impossible to run the country altogether without former party members. True, they would not employ leading Nazis, but for those who had not been prominent in politics before 1945 there were no particular handicaps to overcome to make a comeback after 1950. And so the state secretaries, bankers and professors returned, most of them now on their best democratic behaviour. As far as they had been concerned, it had been a giant mistake or a tragic chain of develop-ments, and they had joined to prevent worse crimes. It would have been nearer the truth if they had argued that few had been fanatical Nazis and that most had joined because everyone else did. But this plausible argument was not frequently heard.

To be fair to them, these former Nazis were, on the whole, loyal to the new regime, and did not try to undermine it from within. Whether the conversion was altogether genuine was not even of decisive importance; it was enough to know that no one in public office would dare to speak up for the 'good old days' or tried to justify Hitler. Some thought with regret about what they considered the positive aspects of Nazism, but everyone knew that it was finished.

Not all former Nazis were astute or lucky enough to make a comeback. Some found the new subservience to Western values morally wrong and aesthetically displeasing: how could one abjure one's gods just because the country had been defeated and occupied? It was among these men and women – and there were many hundreds of thousands of them – that Nazi views still found many sympathizers in the early post-war period, even though not much of this feeling surfaced. The old-timers did not arrange mass meetings or provoke street battles, they congregated in unobtrusive places and their views were given expression in internal newsletters of which few outsiders even knew. Most were ready to admit that Hitler may have committed some excesses: it had been a mistake to kill all the Jews, some other way should have been found to get rid of them. Of course the myth of the 'six millions' was a wicked lie: probably there were not more than a few hundred thousand. But it had been an error of judgment in any case, used now to besmirch the good name of the German people. They were willing to point to some other mistakes: on the whole they liked the pre-1939 Hitler better than the strategist of defeat.

They bitterly opposed Allied attempts to put all the blame on the German people, and they tried to show that Hitler had no more wanted the war than the Allies. If some excesses had been committed by the German army, Allied war crimes (such as the bombing of German cities) had been worse. The old faithful saw it as their duty to continue Hitler's fight against the contamination of German politics and culture by alien, sick elements, against the systematic destruction of traditional German values. They were in the forefront of the struggle for discipline and order, for a general amnesty to all 'political prisoners', and bitterly attacked the collaborationists and traitors (such as Adenauer) working for a new Germany so remote from their own ideals.

Such resentment may appear harmless enough in retrospect, the impotent rage of the defeated. But the country was still very poor, the economic miracle had not yet borne fruit, many millions of expellees who had lost everything streamed in from the East – more likely to blame the new order than the old for their plight. If Nazism did not have a real revival in the early 1950s it was mainly because even the most fanatical understood that the clock could not be put back, and that even an attempt to do so would result in total disaster. They had to accept that for the time being they had to lie low: perhaps in the future conditions would be more auspicious for the success of their cause. And so they would meet from time to time and reminisce about the good old days. Their heroes more often than not were military leaders, such as the Luftwaffe ace Colonel Rudel, rather than political figures. As the veterans grew older, they would collect Third Reich memorabilia, rewrite history and publish almanacs in which the months of the year were called *Wonnemond*, *Hartung*, and so on. Politically their influence was nil, for the new system worked and the economy improved. True, the new regime was in no hurry to confront the past; much that was inconvenient was swept under the carpet. Views which resembled Nazi doctrine could be heard from time to time in the 1950s among leaders of legal parties such as the BHE (the expellees), the German party, and even the far Right of the liberals and the CDU. The fact that Brandt and Herbert Wehnert had been emigrants during the Hitler era was used in anti-SPD propaganda; about Erich Ollenhauer, another émigré, it was said that he was a half-Jew. The career of neither suffered, but the very fact that such arguments could be used publicly was a matter of concern.

The neo-Nazis derived little benefit from all this. For while the number of such organizations continued to grow their membership declined, the sects became even smaller and more sectarian. On two occasions in the 1950s and 1960s two major parties emerged to serve as a rallying point, the SRP and the NPD, of which mention has already been made. But even in their heyday, which lasted a mere two to three years, they were never a serious force – unlike, for instance, neo-fascism in Italy. The Italian MSI polled almost 9 per cent of the total in the general election of 1972, while in the elections in Sicily and other southern regions the figure was 17 per cent. The NPD polled between 7 and 8 per cent in Bavaria, Hesse and Lower Saxony, but never overcame the 5 per cent overall hurdle for representation in the *Bundestag*.

After the rapid decline of the NPD (1969–70) it was only a matter of a few years before the old Nazis would have ceased to exist. Even the younger ones among them, those who had been twenty when Hitler came to power, were pensioned off in the 1970s. Nazism had once been the party of youth; no major political initiatives, no great fresh impulses could be expected from these elderly, cautious and disillusioned former party members. The youth groups of the extreme Right were pathetic-ally small, their representatives in the universities (BNS – *Bund nationaler Studenten*) almost non-existent. The attempts to revive the conservative *Korporationen* among the students, including those com-mitted to duelling, were more successful. But even they did not amount

151

to much and, in any case, could not possibly be equated with Nazism; they had, in fact, been banned in the Third Reich.

It could reasonably be assumed that neo-Nazism and the other groups of the extreme Right would wither away and eventually die out with the generation that had been the standard-bearer of Nazism. Such assumptions failed to take into account, however, the fact that in one form or another, extreme right-wing parties exist in every democratic society. For obvious reasons this trend was bound to be relatively weak in Germany, but there was no reason to believe that it would cease to exist altogether. One obvious cause for its persistence was the division of Germany, another the taboo on German nationalism during the first post-war decades. Just as democratic regimes in every European country are attacked from the far Left, they come under fire from the extreme Right by men and women claiming that there is no real freedom, that the democratic leaders are mere puppets who do not forcefully represent the nation's interests, that aliens have too much influence, that the fatherland is in utmost peril and that only true patriots – those of the far Right – can possibly save it from ruin. It would have been a miracle if such views had not found some advocates in post-war Germany.

One specifically German form of right-wing dissent had been the belief that a third road in between (or rather different from) capitalism and communism was needed and that Germany was predestined to lead mankind in this direction. The idea of a national Bolshevism or of a national revolutionary movement has exerted a strong fascination for young Germans since the 1920s. It was not surprising therefore that some of the old ideas were rediscovered in the late 1960s and early 1970s, and reappeared in a somewhat modified form. This 'New Right' had certain features in common with the French *Nouvelle Droite* (GRECE), but in some respects it was quite *sui generis*. It was an attempt to combine incompatible ideas and concepts in which some genuinely believed. For others it was a mere public-relations stunt providing a left-wing, more attractive package for old-fashioned reactionary, or even fascist, ideas. Hitler's movement, after all, had also first appeared in a socialist disguise. Lastly, some suspected Soviet and communist influences behind the neutralist and anti-American slogans which, with varying intensity, were voiced by these circles. In view of the divisions on the New Right one could find proof for every one of these assumptions. Common to virtually all groups of this camp was their

'European orientation'. The most influential periodical on the far Right was called, not by accident, *Nation Europa*. They also advocated a new bio-humanism (more 'bio' than 'human') and a concern with the natural environment in contrast to the strong technological (and technocratic) element in both Marxism and capitalism. They rejected the old-fashioned Nazi race theories in their cruder form but smuggled some of them in through the back door in a more 'scientific' guise. There were marked differences in their ideas about the ideal social order. Some suggested a return to the corporationist and solidarist ideas first mooted in the 1920s. Others advocated a national socialism, not on the Nazi model but following the ideas first developed – they claimed – by Ferdinand Lassalle, a German Jew and a contemporary of Marx. Some even claimed to draw inspiration from the Chinese agricultural communes.

The leaders of this New Right belonged almost without exception to the post-war generation. They had studied with the same teachers who had influenced their left-wing comrades and it is not difficult to point to ideas among the 'New Right' which appeared in the writings of Herbert Marcuse and other gurus of this generation: the rejection of consumerism, the opposition to technocracy, the necessity to fight 'repressive tolerance', the critique of the manipulation of the media, of the American way of life, and, generally speaking, the frequent invocation of an anti-capitalist spirit which superficially sounded quite genuine. The spokesmen of the New Right frequently argued that while their starting-point had been on the old Right, they had more in common with their contemporaries on the Left than with their forefathers on the Right. With their ecological and anti-nuclear enthusiasm, their cultural anti-Americanism and their support for movements of national liberation in many parts of the world, the 'national revolutionaries' tried, in fact, to outflank their left-wing contemporaries. Some regarded Sinn Fein as a model for the German national revolutionaries, others suggested 'political Balkanization' in Germany and Europe as a solution to all outstanding questions.[1]

[1] Fairly typical of the style of the national revolutionaries is the following: 'Germany is occupied, to the left and the right of the Elbe – not only by tanks and Pershing missiles. My newspaper in its fashion supplement proclaims *Grijn is bjutiful*. The neon lights in the suburb proclaim "Sportswear", "Tabac Shop", "Steak Corner" and "Book Center" [all English in original – w.l.]. The language of youth music, as broadcast from almost all radio stations is multinational. The master language is the language of the masters.' Henning Eichberg, 'Balkanisierung für jedermann', in *Wir Selbst*, May–June 1983, a 'journal for national identity and international solidarity'.

While the national Bolshevism of the late 1920s expressed a mood that was fairly widespread at the time, it never became a political force. The same is true for the present-day national revolutionaries. Their inconsistencies are too blatant: truly European patriotism is incompatible with the chauvinist-racialist nonsense which has been part and parcel of the doctrine of the extreme Right in Germany. If their anticapitalist and neutralist slogans are genuine and also their commitment to ecological revolution and participatory democracy, there is no need for a new party – the 'revolutionary Right' could find a new home in one of the existing parties of the Left as some of their precursors did in the 1930s. If, on the other hand, these left-wing professions are mere demagogy, the swindle will come out sooner rather than later.

Such attempts to merge left- and right-wing doctrines may have a certain fascination for intellectuals but the true militants of the extreme Right need more robust fare: a *Führer*, an enemy against whom violence can be directed, and some certainties. Nazism and fascism never tried very hard to conquer the intelligentsia, and consequently neo-Nazism has been more active among soccer crowds, motorcycle gangs and rock groups than among university students.

The number of right-wing extremist groups has continued to rise even in recent years (from sixty-nine in 1975 to seventy-four in 1982, among them twenty-two that were defined as neo-Nazi by the German authorities). But, to repeat once again, these figures reveal more about the fragmentation of the extreme Right than the number of its members which is now more or less static. For the first time some of the neo-Nazi groups have engaged in terrorist operations in recent years, such as the murder of foreign workers in Nuremberg and the attacks against US soldiers near Frankfurt in December 1982. Far-Right paramilitary units have been established on a small scale and weapons collected.

The neo-Nazis have also shown eagerness to adapt themselves to modern forms of organization such as *Bürgerinitiativen*. They have sent out threatening letters to major employers demanding the dismissal of foreign workers. Some of the slogans daubed on the walls of German houses are barely distinguishable from those of the far Left (*Nie wieder Krieg* – Never again war. Smash this state, foreign troops out of Germany!). The periodical of the *Wiking Jugend*, which in one guise or another has been the main youth organization of the far Right for many years, published an article in 1982 to the effect that he who refuses to join the *Bundeswehr* does not object to national defence but merely refuses to serve in the 'international mercenaries' troop called NATO which is guided solely by American imperialist interests' and which wants to make Europe an atomic battlefield. The conscientious objector was therefore merely doing his share to prevent the holocaust prepared against the European peoples. With only slight changes such appeals could have been published by the extreme Left, which has led some observers to look for a hidden hand manipulating the extreme Right. Such penetration of the extreme Right is perfectly possible and has on occasion taken place in the past.[1] But for anti-Western inspiration the extreme Right is in no need of loans from anyone; Nazism always waged war against Western liberal and democratic ideas.

There is one major political issue which neo-Nazism has all to itself and of which it has made the most: the campaign against foreign workers. There is resentment in Germany against the presence of these workers and their families, as there is in France and Britain. It is widely believed that they deprive German families of work and housing, that they have made Germany's streets unsafe. The extreme Right, again as in Britain and France, has tried to exploit these feelings, launching various campaigns against these foreigners. It is not that easy any more to find Jews in contemporary Germany, but there is no such difficulty in meeting Turks. At a time of economic crisis, anti-foreign feeling tends to become exacerbated. But it is still doubtful whether the neo-Nazis will derive lasting benefit from their campaigns against foreigners. They may trigger off some local riots, or score gains at some local elections. But those who join them in Turk-bashing will not usually stick with them at the next elections. The communists have been far more adept with various kinds of popular front tactics, but they too have not benefited much in the final analysis.

Neo-Nazism has been interpreted, just as have the New Left and the Greens, as a manifestation of a cultural crisis or, more specifically, a collective identity crisis, the sad remnants of so many unfulfilled postwar hopes. Some of the blame has been put, not without justification, at the door of the authorities, the political parties and society which did not squarely confront the Nazi period as it should have done in the

[1] While some groups of the extreme Right, especially the more pronouncedly anti-Western and neutralist among them, are no doubt genuine, there is reason to assume that others are financially supported from the East; such subsidies, needless to say, are carefully 'laundered', with Libya or other third countries acting as paymaster. According to German press reports in 1983–4 the Soviet embassy in Bonn showed great interest in these groups, to the extent of employing special experts with excellent background knowledge concerning the nationalist-neutralist scene.

1950s and 1960s. It has been argued that massive indoctrination in a democratic society may be counterproductive. The emergence of Nazi symbols in the Punk-Rock scene seems to provide evidence to this effect. (This refers to the appearance of ss swastikas, rock groups with names like London ss or Nazi Dog, and songs with titles such as *Auschwitz Jerk* and *Blitzkrieg Boy*.) But such occurrences were equally frequent in Britain and should not be seen as a token of deep ideological identification with Nazism, about which little or nothing is known among Rockers and Punks. The main intention is to annoy adults rather than protest against a surfeit of anti-Nazi propaganda. The musings of isolated intellectuals and the exploits of Punk groups are of no great political consequence. What then is the present potential of neo-Nazism in Germany?

Empirical investigations in the early 1980s have shown that no fewer than 15 per cent of all electors in West Germany had a 'complete right-wing extremist world view' (the sinus study). If one adds the number of those not opposed to the democratic order in principle, but fascinated by strong men and in favour of law and order, such a picture could be frightening. But a closer look does not give that much cause for alarm. Such studies teach us more about the use and abuse of public opinion polls than about the true state of affairs. An examination of the scales on which the sinus study was based show that the questions asked are such that many left-wing extremists and perhaps even some critical democrats could easily pass into the right-wing extremist camp or even the 'fascistoid' category.[1]

It is more illuminating (and encouraging) to learn that over the last thirty years the number of Germans who believe in a democratic system has substantially increased and that, on the other hand, the number of those who think that Germany's golden years were before 1945, or that Hitler would have entered history as a great statesman had he not gone to war in 1939, has dramatically declined. A group of distinguished German social scientists discovered in the late 1950s that 30 per cent of Germany's students belonged at least potentially to the extreme Right. But only a few years later German campuses were shaken by a student revolt in which the extreme Right was neither seen nor heard. Had it been a chimera?

[1] This refers, for instance, to law and order questions; to whether the Americans are responsible for Germany's problems; attitudes to the role of the media in society, the nearness of a horrible catastrophe, the belief that 'most Bonn politicians are corrupt', etc.

The presence of hostile feelings towards foreign workers is an indisputable fact of German political life; so is a longing for strong leadership and of attacks, sometimes vicious, against the whole 'system'. Such attitudes exist in most Western countries and they are more deeply rooted than commonly believed. They can be found even in circles which would indignantly deny harbouring such views, which had to be hidden in Germany for a long time and to a certain degree cannot be openly voiced even now without fear of criminal prosecution. For this reason there is need for constant vigilance. But seen in retrospect and taking into account post-war conditions, auspicious in some respects for the spread of revanchism, it is astonishing that there has been so little neo-Nazism rather than so much of it. Can conditions be envisaged in which neo-Nazism might have a major revival in West Germany? Certainly not at the present time: a new fascism, in the form of a dictatorship, brutally aggressive against enemies at home and expansionist in its foreign policy, seems ruled out. Prejudices, resentment, anti-democratic feeling will not disappear in Germany and right-wing extremism in one form or another will persevere. It is possible that the whole spectrum of German politics and the orientation of the major parties may move a few degrees towards the Right or, more correctly, towards national self-assertion. To a certain degree this has already taken place, but to confuse this with a second coming of Nazism is to invite ridicule. Germans are likely to commit all kinds of political mistakes in the years to come, but not the one for which they had to pay so dearly in their recent history.

How to explain the rediscovery in recent years of patriotism, the native land and the old traditions, and how deep does it go? This has manifested itself in debates on Germany's future (one nation or two) and also in a renewed interest in German history such as on the occasion of the recent anniversaries of Prussia and of Luther. After years of self-imposed silence and also perhaps a genuine lack of interest, terms such as 'national interests', 'national aspirations' have returned with a vengeance in left-wing speeches and literature. Figures in German history who had been written off as hopelessly reactionary have been rediscovered and partly rehabilitated in East Germany as much as in the West. There is a new concern with the fate of the German landscape, the old customs (*Brauchtum*), the old architecture and the old songs. The far Right has observed with amazement (and also a bit of concern) the emergence of a new patriotism on the hitherto cosmopolitan left –

Boden ohne Blut (soil without blood) as one observer put it, alluding to the famous Nazi slogan *Blut und Boden*.

Egon Bahr[1] has said that it was wrong to give up the idea of the nation and be surprised that the other Europeans did not follow suit. Hence his conclusion that the nation cannot be suppressed in the long run. Theilhard de Chardin would outgrow nationalism and the nation state, but he was not very successful in persuading even his own compatriots to become more internationalist in approach. One could find even a certain logic in Günter Gaus's demand that the Bonn government should think (and act) more like de Gaulle. Gaus tended to be carried away by his all-embracing German patriotism; he argued that the East Germans were the more authentic Germans because they were poorer and unspoiled. The Gaullist thesis was taken one step further by Rudolf Bahro, an East German Marxist who had defected and become one of the pillars of the Green movement. He came out for a new Europe – Gaullist, Marxist and ecological at the same time, and by necessity anti-American in orientation. Pursuing this aim Bahro was willing to extend his hands to the far Right; 'after all, we are all Germans', as he put it. Bahro's demands were not supported by Bahr and Gaus simply because they had been exposed to the realities of world politics. They favoured the continued existence of the military blocs, both NATO and the Warsaw pact, at least for the time being. At the same time they expressed the hope that as a result of *détente* global tensions would decrease, gradually make the blocs redundant and bring German unity nearer.

A statement such as Egon Bahr's that the nation cannot be ignored or suppressed indefinitely would not be considered controversial or in any way menacing in other parts of Europe. The French and British, the Spanish and even the Italians, have seldom spent sleepless nights in search of national identity. Nationalism has not been a major theme for them simply because it is self-evident: there is no need to engage in self-conscious reflection and ideological justification.

But France and Britain are not divided, they need not engage in a quest for roots and identity. The reasons for the partition are, of course, well known, even though some have argued that it was simply a matter of bad luck, namely, losing the war. The embellishment of the Nazi era

---

[1] Egon Bahr, born in 1922, was ambassador, state secretary and cabinet minister and has been one of the foremost West German negotiators with the East on behalf of the Social Democratic governments.

has not until recently found supporters among respectable German historians; some writers such as David Irving and David Hogan had their admirers but these were not found among the professionals. As time passes slight changes can be detected: *Geschichte der Deutschen*, by Helmuth Diwald, a professor of history at Erlangen, is a case in point. The aim of this book was to confront various 'taboos': that everything in German history had been wrong, that the German past was all sick – claims which had hardly ever been made by any sane observer of the German scene. Diwald took it upon himself to restore national self-respect, and this voice calling in the wilderness had a first printing of 100,000 copies. The treatment of the holocaust in this book became something of a scandal. Diwald said that, while the overall background of this mass slaughter was not yet quite clear, these were the most 'horrible crimes of our history' and that they could not be captured in words. Since the vocabulary was not adequate to express his feelings the author thought that he should not try to do so in the first place: he devoted little more than two pages to Nazi crimes, and almost thirty pages to the atrocities committed by the Allies *after* the war: 'What occurred in the way of crimes of violence and mass murder between the years 1945 and 1949 is scarcely describable or imaginable.'[1]

The issue at stake is not, of course, the Diwald case. Books written by eccentrics or expressing extreme views appear at all times and in every country. More interesting was the reception of this work: his admirers claimed that someone had dared at last to question the taboo of German war guilt. This was so essential because there was no future for the German nation unless it got rid of its guilt complex once and for all. This guilt complex had been fabricated by the victors, assisted by left-wing historians, theologians and philosophers. But these denunciations were unjust, for the extreme Left, starting from very different premises, had reached conclusions which were quite similar. For if Hiroshima was like Auschwitz, and My Lai comparable to Babi Yar, if the leaders of the Western democracies are the Hitlers of today, there is no need to get unduly excited about the record of Nazism.[2]

The revisionist historians from the Right are not neo-Nazis. They only react violently whenever the question of German war guilt is

[1] The section on the holocaust in this book was rewritten in subsequent editions.

[2] James Wald wrote in a review of Diwald's book that it was unfortunate, to say the least, 'that such equations would probably be viewed with favour by many a well-meaning but misguided leftist, as well as by a conservative nationalist of Diwald's ilk'. 'German History Backwards', in *New German Critique*, Fall 1980, p. 169.

brought up. They bitterly resent such *mea-culpitis* – a term which came into being in the 1920s following the debate on the responsibility for the outbreak of the First World War. They find it impossible to accept that the circumstances were not similar. True, public opinion in England and the United States became more hostile *vis-à-vis* Germany in the late 1930s, because Nazism was disliked and Hitler's successive conquests were regarded as a threat. But the idea that Chamberlain and the French governments of the day were warmongers rather than appeasers belongs to the realm of fantasy, and the fact that the US entered the war only after Pearl Harbor and the German declaration of war makes the revisionist assignment even more difficult.

The question of war guilt and of the Nuremberg trials is central for the revisionists of the Right. This is the 'great lie' on which the thesis of the German *Fehlentwicklung* is based (the allegation that German history took a wrong turning). They also resent the negative judgments of foreign observers as well as German liberals and the churches about Bismarck, Prussia and German unity. The revisionists demand an unselfconscious and frank discussion of recent German history which, they are certain, will show that while Hitler wanted a strong Germany he probably did not want war; that while he committed major errors of judgment and even crimes, so did the Allies; that the extent of these crimes has been exaggerated and that the time has come to put them in proper perspective, and to let bygones be bygones. The revisionists are still few in number. But the reception of some of these works has been startling: the works of Diwald's German critics do not have a circulation of 100,000 copies.

The desire to see recent German history in a new and better light is psychologically and politically understandable. But it does not make for honest history and it leads to all kinds of strange aberrations. One further illustration should suffice. A distinguished sociologist developed a new theory of elites, according to which there had been a negative selection in recent German history. Those who had been brave enough to commit themselves politically had been eliminated; only the cowards remained alive. The author, born five years after Hitler came to power, seems to have persuaded himself that great courage was needed in the Third Reich to join the Nazi party.

But there is a new understanding for the Nazi era also on the far Left. Thomas Schmid, an ideologist of the 'autonomous' trend on the German Left, has complained about the 'imperialist de-Nazification of the god-damn Yankees who had prescribed democracy in our country'.[1] Those thinking that this was an elaborate joke in questionable taste soon learned that they were mistaken. For Schmid went on to argue that German horror and German fascination were one and could not be divided. He wanted to 'come closer' to both, and he was not impressed by rebukes of parafascism. He wanted a Left which was also German in character, hard, relentless in its struggle, capable of pressing the foe to the wall, a Left that did not get stuck in superficial common sense but went on to 'mysterious and unfathomable depths'. For this, too, was part of German political culture.[2] Schmid complained that at international meetings every other country was represented as almost perfect – only the Germans had still to apologize for their very existence. Such subservience was unacceptable, a view that is certainly shared by many young Germans. Thomas Schmid is not the elected spokesman of the German Left, and some of his colleagues were frightened by his excessive language. But it is also true that he expressed what others were thinking but had not dared to enunciate.

Schmid was born after the Second World War; another writer of the Left, Gerd Fuchs, is old enough to remember the last days of the war. His father had been a leading Nazi in the village and Fuchs quotes (with approval) the feelings of shock his mother suffered listening shortly after the war to the horrible things Thomas Mann had to say about German crimes. He writes angrily about the informers (against the Nazis) and the collaborators with the Americans among the local population. Fuchs argues that the Americans 'bought' Germany with their Marshall plan, their Vespas (*sic*), radio stations and the Cold War, and in a 'gangster-like way' divided Germany. He is exceedingly bitter about the lack of backbone on the part of his fellow citizens who accepted without even grumbling the right of the stronger.

Reading these personal recollections one is led to believe that Fuchs's ideological home is on the far Right but this is not so. For he also relates how he came to accept the 'economic interpretation of fascism' (meaning the Leninist version), and how, again, the Americans had criminally and systematically sabotaged any honest and genuine confrontation with fascism in Germany. This interpretation, as has

---

[1] *Rotbuch 83*, 'Über den Mangel an politischer Kultur in Deutschland', p. 112

[2] The preoccupation with 'political culture' has become a popular pastime in some German intellectual circles; countless books have been written on the subject. The phenomenon is not unfamiliar – there are few cookbooks in Italy and few sex manuals in France: competence in these fields is taken for granted.

been mentioned, lifts much of the responsibility for what happened before 1945 from the generation of Fuchs's father and puts it on 'objective circumstances' and/or the wicked essence of capitalism.

To provide yet another example: at a conference in Italy some years ago I made the acquaintance of a well-known German poetess who made no secret of the fact that she had little but contempt for the governments of the Western democracies but thought of North Korea, which she had just visited as a shining example of socialism, of humanism and democracy. A few weeks later I happened to read some of her poems published during the Nazi era; they were not, alas, permeated with the same militant anti-fascist spirit.

It may be wrong to make too much of such cases; the last of this generation are now disappearing from the scene. There were similar cases in Italy after 1945; critics of 'liberal democracy' from the right have found a common language with the anti-democrats of the Right.

Nazism is out of fashion and will have no second coming in the foreseeable future. There are more attractive mixtures of nationalism and socialism such as the national revolutionary trend of which mention has already been made, the 'Left people of the Right'. The West German communists have disinterred their 1930 programme for the 'national liberation' of the German people, and Lieutenant Scheringer, the much publicized *Reichswehr* officer who converted from Nazism to communism in 1931, became active again in post-war communist politics as a national symbol. General Remer, the Nazi officer whose action in support of Hitler was of decisive importance in putting down the anti-Nazi coup of 20 July 1944, came out with a passionate appeal in favour of a German–Soviet alliance forty years later. Rudolf Bahro has compared the intrusion of the Western lifestyle in Germany to the impact of the Spanish *conquistadores* on the poor *Indios*. Other German Marxists have reached the conclusion that the Allies' de-Nazification was the cultural counterpart of the integration of West Germany into the capitalist world market. The National Revolutionaries stand for an 'independent united and socialist Germany, committed to revolutionary change in the ecological field and to basis (participatory) democracy. It is for solidarity with the struggle of all oppressed peoples for freedom and independence against all kinds of chauvinism and imperialism.'[1] It would be wrong to dismiss these and similar

---

[1] *Wir selbst*, editorial statement. See also the writings of Henning Eichberg, *Nationale Identität*, n.d. *Wir selbst* is the German for Sinn Fein; there have been sympathies among the extreme German Right for the IRA since the 1920s.

statements as mere demagogy.

What are the basic differences between such doctrines and Soviet communism? The revolutionary nationalists point to their great emphasis on the revitalization of local dialects, songs, regionalism in general and, of course, a specific 'German socialism'. But these are not fundamental differences; after a short cosmopolitan interval the Soviet system became strongly nationalist and has remained so ever since. The national revolutionaries argue that for the first time in German history nationalism is not aggressive in character, is not directed against neighbouring peoples; on the contrary, the love of peace is linked with the desire for self-determination.

Given Germany's diminished power, how could it be differently? Though advocating neutrality, the outlook of the national revolutionaries is hardly neutral: the West is the main enemy. Criticism of Soviet policy is seldom, if ever, found in their speeches and articles, partly because there is a greater kinship with the East, but also because such attacks would be risky. Unlike the West, the Soviets may not receive them in good spirit.

Anti-Americanism

The more one studies the literature of the national revolutionaries, or talks to its exponents, the stronger the feeling of *déjà vu*. Most of their ideas have been borrowed from the Left-people-of-the-Right sects of the Weimar Republic. And there is every reason to assume that the outcome will be the same again, which is to say: precisely nothing. The far Left has rediscovered the nation, and some of the extreme Right look to the East as an ally in their struggle. But there is no future for a 'third force' in Germany. Not much more importance should be attributed to theories of the national revolutionaries than to the slogans daubed on the walls of German cities such as 'Kill Reagan' or 'Out with Reagan, destroy the state' (*Reagan verjagen, BRD zerschlagen*). There is a lunatic fringe in every country and it is a mistake to take the display of their slogans as a yardstick for their real strength.

Anti-Americanism in its less extreme forms is a different proposition: it bears repeating that it has proponents on the Right as well as the Left. It was a young German left-wing critic (Wolfgang Pohrt) who pointed out that the German Right had every reason to feel bitter about the

United States. It had been America, above all, which had prevented a German victory in two world wars. After the Second World War America became for many, probably most, Germans the promised land; the strong anti-Americanism of the APO in the late 1960s was a reaction against the admiration of all things American in the 1950s. It was a case of lost illusions for it appeared that America was neither all-powerful nor always right. Herzog's movie *Stroszek*, the story of the poor unskilled worker from Germany who tries his luck in Plainfield, Wisconsin, and fails miserably expressed this new mood, and there were many other examples such as articles in the popular press, television shows and even popular histories of America in a new critical, even hostile, spirit. If the tone had been deferential only yesterday, it now became arrogant and condescending, the kind of attitude which used to come naturally to British and French critics of America. In Wolfgang Koeppen's novels of the 1950s the American GIS were still good-humoured and harmless if a little primitive. In the late 1960s US soldiers became a target of hate and contempt. Herzog and Hannes Wader spoke up for cultural decolonization and Piwitt, a journalist earlier known as a scourge of the extreme Right, now thundered about the need for 'cultural decolonization'; some announced their willingness to put a wreath at the statue of Arminius. Piwitt also complained about this 'Yankee language which with "fighting" and "dope", with "power" and "message" dominates us even when we offer resistance'. How to defend oneself against the 'daily colonialism'?

Commenting on such manifestations of anti-Americanism, Wolfgang Pohrt wrote that whatever the consequences of American cultural imperialism in other parts of the globe, in Germany it had fathered not barbarism but civilization:

Every new branch of the McDonald Hamburger chain is in this country a new island of hospitality and *Esskultur*. . . . The great political crimes committed by Germany do not release us from the obligation to attack the smaller crimes of America. But every protest against US policy is reactionary in this country, if it forgets to mention one little fact: no one would be alive on this planet if Germany had been militarily as strong as the United States. . . . The nationalist demagogy which should strengthen, as it were, the peace movement, deprives it in truth of its moral and political legitimation. And thus one has to suspect that it was not the neutron bomb which made the German Left lose its reason, but that it had lost it well before. One cannot get rid of the bad suspicion that it is not really the stationing of missiles which is at stake as far as the peace movement is concerned. It was merely the spark which triggered off the explosive mixture which existed well before – the whispering about Blood-and-Soil and *Heimat*, the mother cult and the longing for vegetarianism, nature and *Heidekraut* [Scotch heather], a mixture of whining and brutality.[1]

Pohrt is the most powerful younger essayist on the German Left; as with every good pamphleteer there is an element of exaggeration in his writings. But there is an even greater element of truth and no one recently has said more clearly and uncompromisingly that one can never be quite certain these days in Germany whether those attacking bourgeois society and the 'system' really mean the injustices and the oppressions, or whether they protest against the freedom provided by the system; whether they abominate the United States as exploiters and oppressors in the Third World, or as the liberators of Europe from the concentration-camp regime of the Nazis.

Anti-Americanism among certain circles of the young generation became so intense that Willy Brandt and Egon Bahr thought it necessary to call to order the young comrades who were overdoing it. Brandt said that one should never forget what the Americans had done for Germany during the war and after. Even if the younger comrades regarded him as a sentimental old fool because of his past involvement in Berlin, they had to remember from time to time that even now Germany was largely dependent on US support. But this was precisely a thought which those who were addressed did not wish to entertain.

This anti-Americanism was not unconnected with the economic situation. For years after the war Europe had been desperately poor and America had been the rich relation who provided vital help. By the 1970s America was suffering from serious economic difficulties whereas the per capita income in some European countries had caught up or even overtaken it. Europe had more progressive social services, its crime rate was lower, it suffered from fewer public scandals, and there were other reasons to feel superior to America. The new self-assurance found expression in a new literature half attacking and half pitying it. The fact that with all this Western Europe still depended on America for maintaining its freedom and sovereignty provided additional impetus. For no one likes to be dependent, and the protector becomes an obvious target for the resentment that dependence generates.

All that has been noted so far is correct, but it does not amount to the

[1] Wolfgang Pohrt, 'Ein Volk, ein Reich, ein Frieden' in *Endstation* (Berlin 1982), pp. 75–6

full picture. For despite the lamentations of intellectuals and some others about imperialist cultural penetration and the need for cultural decolonization, there is still the enormous fascination exercised by American culture on almost every level of sophistication. There is no such interest in the Soviet way of life or East European culture. Germany had been historically a cultural bridge between West and East, the study of Russia and Eastern Europe had been more developed in Germany than in any other country. Since the Second World War there has been a basic change. Very few German tourists visit the Soviet Union; if Russian literature is translated it is seldom read and the few Soviet movies play to empty cinemas. The impression emerges that many Germans want to know as little as possible about the Soviet Union, its political system, culture, way of life. This may be considered flattering from a Western point of view but it makes it so much easier for some Germans not to face realities but to think in world political abstractions. Or, to put it more crudely, an ostrich-like policy makes it considerably easier to assume that there is not that much to choose between West and East, that there is constant – if slow – change for the better in the Soviet Union and that, in any case, Russia has a very strong army and should not be given offence. It makes it easier not to see and hear evil, not to protest against Afghanistan and Poland and to concentrate one's attention on Nicaragua, Grenada, San Salvador and other such outrages. This kind of tunnel vision is frequently presented with a great deal of conviction, charges of hypocrisy are angrily rejected. The partial blindness towards the East and the negative attitude towards America are the result of a complex psychological process, not a deliberate decision: 'Since we cannot afford to criticize the Russians we ought to concentrate on the crimes of American imperialism.' Rationalization, no doubt, does take place on an unconscious level: the desire to suppress uncomfortable realities in politics as in private life takes many forms; there is no need to go over reasonably familiar ground.

The anti-Americanism of the Left has been attacked from within its own ranks as a 'socialism of fools' not so much because the critics are blind admirers of the American way of life but because they understand that the new Gaullism of the Left owes more to Charles de Gaulle and perhaps even Franz Josef Strauss than to Marx and Engels. They know that the anti-American *Kulturkritik* could easily be traced back to traditional German feelings of superiority to Western civilization such as voiced, for instance, by Thomas Mann in his *Reflections of an Unpolitical Man* during the First World War. In other words, while such cultural criticism may well be anti-bourgeois, it is not necessarily proletarian or left-wing in inspiration.

Hence also the scepticism about the reawakened enthusiasm for the unity of the nation. This ranges from Martin Walser's: 'We have to keep open the wound called Germany . . . they may print new maps but they cannot reconstruct my historical consciousness', to the firm promise given by Willy Brandt's son Peter: 'German unity will most assuredly come.' The suspicions are derived from two sources: the opening to the Right is displeasing and, more importantly, there are misgivings in view of the difficulties Germany has had in the past trying to establish a normal relationship towards nation and nationalism, free of excess and self-consciousness.

Heimat

The new patriotism is closely connected with the re-emergence of *Heimat*, which originally meant little more than the parental home. But gradually its meaning widened and it had a first blossoming in the mid nineteenth century, a turning towards the past, part of a general anti-urban mood. *Heimat* was not, perhaps could not be, clearly defined. It meant, on the one hand, feeling at ease, at home, a place in which one could relax because there were no dangers. But it also meant the preservation of local traditions, such as a dialect, nature or monuments. *Heimat* was more than a symbol; it meant security and an emotional experience, familiar images, noises and smells, associations with family, one's youth, friendship and love. Then, even before the First World War, there developed a *Heimat* industry: novels naïvely extolling and embellishing its virtues and, in later years, *Heimat* films and hit songs which were immensely successful. Since many people had moved to a big town and thus lost their *Heimat* (for it was not at all clear whether a big city could ever be *Heimat*) all kinds of ersatz *Heimat* came into being to counter the effects of uprooting and alienation: little allotments on the fringe of town, weekend houses for the rich and camping sites or trailers for the less affluent.

But *Heimat* was not only fields and trees at sunset, it was also human beings, the need for contact. Hence the sprouting of the *Vereine*, voluntary associations to pursue ideals or activities of common interest, but also to spend one's time profitably and enjoyably, to find a home away from home, in short a second *Heimat*.

The fact that Nazism had promoted *Heimat* made it suspect for many years after the war; the very term was seldom used and the phenomenon ignored. Until recently one would have looked in vain for studies on *Heimat* in the publications of German sociologists. But whatever abuse had been made of it in the past, *Heimat* obviously corresponded with some deep longings. It was no mere nostalgia and it received fresh impetus as the result of the rapid modernization and urbanization after the Second World War which involved, of necessity, further uprooting of millions of people.

Heimat had never been out of fashion as far as the general public was concerned; it was rediscovered by the intellectuals only in the 1970s.

This may have been connected with the move of some intellectuals out of the big cities into the countryside or the far suburbs. There is no denying that the open country, the fields and forests have much to recommend them, and that great enjoyment can be found walking a lonely path far from the noise and the contaminated air of the big cities, watching the birds in the skies and ears of corn and grass bowing like waves in the wind. Life in small towns and villages also had other compensations: it was less hectic and anonymous, people knew each other, the schools were frequently superior to those in the big city, and people even took culture more seriously, perhaps because there was no *embarras de richesse*.

The small towns were bypassed by history, the philistine narrow-minded character of the *Kleinstädter* became a subject of anger, ridicule or at best pity among many of the educated. Then, in the 1970s, the advantages of backwardness were discovered: the inner composure, proximity to nature, closer family ties and friendships. There was romanticizing in this new mood, but having been exposed for so long to the growing drawbacks of big city life many did not mind this. They were even ready for a little kitsch; it was probably no coincidence that the *Gartenlaube* began to appear again in the wake of this nostalgia wave, the very same journal which once had been the essence of all that had seemed reprehensible and comic about small-town philistinism. The same happy ending stories were reprinted ('The secret of the silent bells') and the same old drawings: in the garden, in the shade of a chestnut tree a young lady is seen knitting, seemingly oblivious of the young man, tall but tongue-tied, obviously in two minds about whether this was the right moment to confess his love. It was a touching reaction after two decades of breaking all conventions and the total demystification of sex. Life in the small cities and the village which had been 'fascistoid' almost by definition became acceptable again, indeed almost enviable. A small town could (perhaps) be *Heimat*, the grey concrete boxes of the big city would always remain alien. The less fortunate who could not leave the big cities tried at least to make the best of it by the infusion of a new spirit: the emphasis on neighbourhood activities, street fêtes – a little awkwardly perhaps but full of goodwill.[1]

These new trends are in some ways natural and sometimes quite charming. Intellectuals rationalized them in post-Marxist terms: the need for *Heimat* was forward-looking, not reactionary. Even the new interest in Prussia was quite understandable, for not everything had been negative in the Prussian tradition. The rediscovery of a simpler life and a world which had been ignored or forgotten was part of a general trend found in many European countries, even the Soviet Union. The wish to preserve its traditions and customs had been, for instance, behind Norway's decision not to join the Common Market, and it could be found in one form or another in many other places. The new patriotism, as it ought to be called for want of a better term, is inward-looking rather than aggressive, it may be reactionary in the original sense of this term. But then the belief in infinite progress has waned.

How deep does it all go? The evidence is contradictory: everything considered, anti-Americanism is a marginal phenomenon in West Germany, less common than in Britain, France or Sweden. In West Germany 73 per cent of the population felt overall favourably inclined towards America in 1982, in comparison with 63 per cent in Italy, 55 per cent in France and only 46 per cent in Britain. When asked in 1954 whether good relations with America were more important than with the Soviet Union, 62 per cent opted for America as against 10 per cent for the Soviet Union. In 1981 the figure had risen to 65 per cent; the same proportion felt spontaneous sympathy towards America and only 17 per cent had contrary feelings. In 1957 only 37 per cent had said that they liked Americans. But at the same time 45 per cent of all Germans

[1] The *Vereine* too have had a revival. On a random weekday in a small town in Germany last summer, I counted in the columns of the local newspapers the announcement of seventy-eight voluntary associations meeting that evening, covering between them almost every field of human endeavour. Their political activity is considerable on the local level – the choirs, the voluntary fire brigades, the pigeon breeders and all.

under the age of thirty prefer neutrality to the 40 per cent who opt for an alliance with the United States. This is the generation which no longer remembers Nazism, the war and the early post-war period, neither the blockade of Berlin nor the CARE parcels, for whom the Cold War and threats to Germany's sovereign existence are relics from the distant past, of no meaning in present conditions.

In recent years there have been long and heated debates about the future of German nationhood – whether two nations have come into being because the partition has lasted so long, whether a *West* German national consciousness can be combined with the dream of national reunification, whether the two Germanies are cultural nations (*Kulturnationen*) but not nations in the traditional, political sense. The fact that so much heat had been generated on both the Right and the Left concerning this issue makes it appear as if the majority of Germans, old and young, regard this as the most important of all issues. Opinion polls however do not bear this out. Reunification once figured very highly on the scale of German priorities: for 47 per cent it was the most important political task facing West Germany as recently as 1965. Ten years later only 1 per cent still think so. In the early 1970s only 25 per cent of Germans felt that they would remain one people in one nation. The majority believes that they will grow apart like Germans and Austrians. Significantly, the younger generation is even less interested in German reunification: of those over sixty questioned in 1976, 77 per cent said they wished for German reunification very much indeed; of those under thirty, 52 per cent said it was not so important. The trend is unmistakable, it is less clear how far it will progress in the near future, and whether and to what extent it is reversible.

How proud are Germans of their nation? About as much as other Europeans according to the polls, but less than the Americans.[1] Very slowly the new state, its appurtenances and symbols have been accepted by the majority of the population. The attitude to the national flag – that 'mere piece of cloth' – is typical. There was a surfeit of flags in the Nazi era and it is not surprising that sales resistance developed after the war. Asked in 1951 whether they felt joyful when seeing the black-red-and-gold flag of the Republic only 23 per cent answered 'Yes, indeed' whereas 54 per cent replied 'No'. It reminded me of a scene I had witnessed as a boy, a year or two before Hitler had come to power. On a

---

[1] The figures may be misleading because 'extremely proud' in American usage is used more freely than 'unconditional pride' in Europe.

Sunday afternoon my parents had taken me for an excursion on a steamer. As usual the national flag was hoisted on the aft deck but suddenly several swimmers jumped on board, tore the flag off and demonstratively used it to wipe their behinds – to the great amusement of the public. Even the twelve-year-old boy understood that a state in which the public applauded such scenes and no one dared to stand up for its honour was not likely to last.

In 1977 the same black-red-and-gold flag of the Republic received for the first time in the history of the FRG the approval of Germans. But a majority of those under thirty still did not know the opening words of their national anthem. The identification with the country and the nation is lower among young people than among their elders, and lowest of all among young people with a higher education.

In 1945 few people in their right mind would have worried about the prospect of a decline in German patriotism and the lack of willingness to defend the homeland. In modern European history German national-ism has so frequently meant striving for hegemony, the ambition to impose its will on others in Europe. Perhaps, as some have argued, an undivided German nation has been too large for Europe. But such are the paradoxes of history: the decline of national pride also has its danger for it means that there seems to be no good reason to stand up for the democratic order which has emerged since the war. Thus, paradoxic-ally, not a few observers of the German scene have begun to worry about a possible loss of backbone; however critical young Frenchmen or Italians may be of their country and its institutions, only very few of them refuse to serve in its army, no French and Italian intellectuals have encouraged them in such action. All this on the one side of the ledger, and on the other the resurgence of a new kind of patriotism, a new emphasis on the national interest of the German people. No excessive importance should be attributed to the writings of essayists represent-ing no one but themselves and small groups of like-minded people, to orators carried away by their own eloquence, by the specific occasion or by their audience. Even the demonstrations by highly committed and motivated minorities should be seen in the proper context. While the demonstrations for peace, for neutralism, against NATO and American policies have been the biggest in Europe, it is also true that a larger percentage of the young generation participated in such meetings in Denmark, Holland and Belgium.

But if Denmark decides to opt out of world politics is one thing; if

Germany does is another matter. Denmark may get a free ride as far as Western defence is concerned, Germany cannot. Why has Germany moved in a direction different from the other major European countries? Much of it has to do with history and the well-known fact that the swings of the pendulum always go to greater extremes in this country than elsewhere. The results of public opinion polls are of interest, but one ought not to be hypnotized by them. They cannot predict substantial changes which may occur suddenly. A great deal of critical acumen has gone into finding out whether the views of the young generation have been shaped more by a feeling of fear, by the group dynamics of school and university, by deferred adolescence (the fact that young people now remain for a considerably longer time removed from real life and do not have to accept responsibilities), or whether perhaps the new 'telecracy' is of decisive importance – the fact that many key positions in radio, television and the cinema (the new culture industry) have passed into the hands of missionaries of 1968 vintage. Perhaps it has been a mixture of all these factors. Such studies are of interest but they do not explain the 'Falklands factor', the fact that Mrs Thatcher, not an expert in social psychology or the theory of communication, received the backing of the great majority of her compatriots for the defence of an unimportant island 9,000 miles distant. True, many Germans found the British reaction difficult to understand, it seemed almost atavistic. But such atavisms happen to occur almost anywhere, suddenly, and with considerable force.

Seen in retrospect Germans since the Second World War have behaved with remarkable maturity, showing greater restraint than almost anybody expected at the time. They have acted reasonably and responsibly and it does not really matter that much whether such behaviour was a marriage of convenience and prudence rather than an affair of the heart. Almost four decades have passed since the end of the war, new generations have grown up which no longer feel the need to behave as if Germany was still on probation. If France and Britain frequently put their own national interests first why should Germany not do so with equal justification? Why should they not have the right to behave a little irresponsibly from time to time? It is a legitimate question and in some ways such a reaction is natural and inevitable. Since the movement towards European political unity has come to a halt, the various nationalisms are bound to reassert themselves. But legitimate or not, this development entails certain dangers. Britain and

France with all their nationalist escapades in recent decades have not, on the whole, exceeded certain boundaries. They bear much responsibility for the lack of progress on the road towards greater European unity, but they have kept, on the whole, to the ground rules of Western defence. Neither Britain nor France is a divided country; but if West Germany should put reunification high on its political agenda this could have far-reaching repercussions.

A united Germany to be sure would not be a new superpower, a mortal threat to its neighbours; it would have global power status only in the realm of athletics and swimming – in other respects such risks are non-existent. The real danger is that any advance on the road towards German reunification is possible only on the basis of political concessions *vis-à-vis* the Soviet Union. This, of course, is not unknown to the protagonists of German unity in Bonn, and most of them argue that their goal will not be achieved in the near future and that their main concern now is not to set up any further obstacles, not to close any doors which may make it more difficult at some future date to achieve an aim which is, after all, part of the West German constitution. The road to German unity leads through Moscow; it is equally true that the Soviet leadership has no desire whatsoever to engage in experiments of this kind in the foreseeable future. But it may be enough to dangle some vague promises in front of some Germans to keep illusions alive in West Germany: decades have passed since Rapallo (which was never signed or followed up) and the allegedly missed opportunities to reunite Germany in 1952–3 (which belong to the realm of mythology). But these memories have been sufficient to provide inspiration for the advocates of an Eastern orientation to this day.

True, German unity despite the ritual invocations on various parts of the political spectrum does not figure very highly among the priorities of the present generation of Germans. But it is also true that unresolved national issues – and what could be more painful than the partition of a nation? – tend to re-emerge as major issues after lying dormant for many years. There are frequent examples in history, and it is clearly premature to write off the cause of German reunification as a major issue. Nor is German unity the only cause of a possible resurgence of 'Germany firstism'; the new nationalism, to repeat once again, is not militaristic, aggressive, or expansive in character but a passive count-me-out attitude, a resentment against too close an integration with the West – cultural, as much as political and military. Paradoxically it expresses itself at one and the same time in a certain lack of national pride and scruples about whether it is right to serve in the *Bundeswehr* – and on the other hand in the desire to establish closer relations with East Germany and to maintain friendly relations with East Germany's chief protector.

The era of a German *Sonderweg* pursued through military means is past and will not recur. But the Pied Piper can appear in many disguises and he can play more than one tune; a *Sonderweg* can also be followed by means other than war and this dream has not vanished: why make Germany the main battlefield of the future if it could attain safety through neutrality between West and East? It is a delusion, but those familiar with the attraction which myths have exerted in the history of nations – and German history is as good an example as any – will not dismiss the possibility that a myth of this kind may attract even more followers than it has at present. I feel confident that the re-emergence of German patriotism will continue but that either the instinct of self-preservation or a guardian angel will keep the Germans from committing yet another fateful error in their history. There is reasonable ground for optimism, but there are no certainties.

7 The State of the Economy or After the Ball is Over

Once upon a time when Germany was a great power it used to be said that foreign policy was fate (*Schicksal*); when the great-power ambitions had disappeared it was claimed that the economy had become *Schicksal*. There was always a considerable element of exaggeration in categorical statements such as *Volk ohne Raum* or 'Export or Die'. It is equally unreasonable to argue, as some have done, that, but for its economic success, West Germany would have disintegrated, that the economic miracle is the major cohesive factor as far as German society is concerned and that the country will not survive a major economic setback. There is no particular reason to waste much time and space on such prophecies of doom: nations are not corporations with limited liability to be merged, reconstructed or dissolved if they show a loss for a number of years in succession.

The West German economy faces serious problems; there will be considerable difficulties in the years ahead. So does everyone else; which among the member states of the United Nations would not be willing to exchange its own economic problems with those facing Germany?

But this is of little comfort to the Germans, who have a tendency to worry about the state and the future of their economy. To understand the background of these fears we have to retrace our steps to the days of the famous 'miracle'.

In 1948 German industrial production was half what it had been before the war. During the subsequent two decades the German economy grew more quickly than at any other period in history, faster than any other European country at the time. Per capita income trebled, the output of the German car industry, of electrical and chemical products and mechanical engineering soared. Productivity increased, exports expanded as never before and the balance of payments was one of the wonders of the world: Germany became the country of the *Wirtschaftswunder*, even though this term was abhorred by the experts. The explanations for the miracle have been adduced many times: the availability of a solid industrial base, even if half-destroyed, the presence of skilled labour, American aid, German and world demand which had been suppressed for a decade.

All this is true, but the miracle was still not foreordained. If for one reason or other it had not occurred, it would have been equally easy to find good reasons for a post-war German depression. In fact, most experts had predicted such a depression in 1944–5, for there had been one after the First World War and it seemed safe enough to go by past experience. In the final analysis one has to look for psychological and political reasons as much as for economic factors to explain the great post-war upsurge. All that matters in the present context is that the 'miracle' did take place, whatever the underlying causes.

During the early 1970s the stormy growth came to an end: if the GNP had grown 8 per cent (on average) during the 1950s, the rise was only 5 per cent during the next decade and it fell to 3 per cent in the 1970s. There were periods of stagnation and even decline such as between 1974 and 1976, and 1981 and 1982. In 1975 the number of unemployed exceeded one million for the first time since the beginning of the 'miracle' and there was a substantial increase in the number of bankruptcies. True, this mainly concerned small and medium-sized enterprises; the big ones when in trouble merged or were taken over. But exports continued and the low German inflation rate was still the envy of her neighbours.

But Germans, like most other people, had become accustomed to steady growth, and tended to compare their achievements not with the state of the Polish economy. The idea that miracles do not last for ever caused first disquiet and later dark visions of disaster. The hyper-inflation of the early 1920s and the great depression of 1929–33 were still very much remembered, as were, of course, the bitter post-war years. The shocks to which Germany had been exposed in the twentieth century had a more traumatic effect than in any other West or Central European country: elsewhere the crises have been less abrupt or severe. Many Germans have tended ever since to react more nervously than others to an economic downturn.

The 1970s brought a slowing-down process but per capita income again rose substantially between 1970 and 1980, a phenomenon without precedent before 1914, let alone in the Weimar Republic. However, the public was no longer aware of the fact that, seen in historical perspective, economic growth is not the rule, and stagnation not the exception. Hence the unease and nervousness: the perception mattered more than the economic indicators.

Some of the reasons for the slowing down in the 1970s were global in character, others specifically German. The post-war reconstruction phase had come to a natural end by the early 1960s largely because the immediate internal demand was satisfied. Later on turbulence was caused in the international financial system as a result of inflationary pressure in many parts of the world and also the oil shock. The use of new technology created unemployment which was not seasonal but structural in character. Far Eastern competition became a major threat for some German industries. It would have been yet another miracle, infinitely greater than that of the 1950s, if in the midst of a world-wide recession West Germany alone had remained an island of prosperity.

In the post-war period West Germany became more dependent on exports than ever before, more dependent, in fact, than any other major industrial country. Some 40 per cent of the output of the German machine-tool industry is sold abroad and about one third of the production of the electrical and chemical industries. In these circumstances it was a great achievement that in such a period German exports continued on a fairly high level.

But there were also some internal German causes for the slowing of the economy to which we ought to turn next. Of the total available income, 21 per cent had been invested in 1960, but less than 10 per cent in 1980. Indebtedness had grown, and at the same time German industry had not shown sufficient flexibility and awareness of new technological developments: it was not that individual Germans had gone on a reckless, ruinous buying spree. But German society had entered commitments which it found more and more difficult to honour for they coincided with a weaker performance of the economy.

A glance at the record of Germany's biggest corporations points to the problems facing the German economy. When the lists of these giants were first published in the 1950s, they were headed by Krupp and a few other firms of world renown. Of these, quite a few were still family owned and they were concentrated in coalmining and iron and steel production. In 1983 Krupp had fallen back to eighteenth place, having survived owing to state intervention in 1967 when it had been on the verge of bankruptcy. Some of these major heavy industry corporations still figure today fairly high in the list: among them are Thyssen, Ruhrkohle with its headquarters in Essen, Gute Hoffnungshütte in Oberhausen and Mannesmann in Düsseldorf. But all have experienced trouble in recent years as the result of the decline of coal and steel. Almost all have had to ask for state help, and most have diversified their activities. Mannesmann went into engineering, Flick acquired a good part of Daimler-Benz and major interests in the paper industry, Thyssen went into trading.

The list of the biggest corporations is now headed by one that did not even exist twenty-five years ago, VEBA, based on the company managing the property of the Prussian state. Subsequently it acquired interests in energy, the chemical industries, transport and trading, with the government as the biggest shareholder. VEBA is not the biggest employer: Siemens, second in the list, employs four times as many people (320,000).

Siemens is the biggest German electrical corporation and, together with Philips, the greatest of its kind in Europe. It is a rich corporation by German standards: its critics maintain however that it has been moving too cautiously of late. The founders of the German electrical industry in the last century were true pioneers, their successors have been more reluctant to take risks. In some respects they have been falling behind the leaders in the field of high technology, microchips and data processing.[1] Siemens' traditional rivals, AEG and Telefunken, fared worse; their merger (and subsequent split) has not brought about so far a dramatic improvement. Formerly in Berlin, they now have their headquarters in Frankfurt. Bosch, based in Stuttgart, has overtaken this ailing giant in recent years.

The leaders of the car industry all figure among the biggest corporations. Volkswagen (Wolfsburg), for many years second on the list, has now fallen behind Daimler-Benz, producer of Mercedes Benz and other well-known cars and trucks. Daimler-Benz is now the most profitable big German company whereas Volkswagen, after its

---

[1] The pessimism which had prevailed in the early 1980s in the electric and electronic industry gave way in 1984 to a more optimistic mood following a new upturn mainly in the field of new information and communication technology.

phenomenal success in the 1950s and 1960s, went through a lengthy period of setbacks as demand for its traditional products shrank. No model as popular as the 'Beetle' was produced in time to replace it. Furthermore, the company suffered as the result of production costs which were about 30 per cent higher than in Japan. The lessons of the crisis were learned: the company invested heavily in robots and some of its plants are now the most modern in the world. But vw has still not quite recovered, to a certain extent the result of the failure of some of its operations outside Germany.

Opel in Frankfurt and (German) Ford in Cologne also suffered substantial losses in the 1970s but their chances too have improved following rationalization and the discontinuation of unprofitable lines. In 1973 dire predictions were made concerning the uncertain future facing Munich-based BMW. But over the last decade it has been doing well, catering for a more specialized clientele and therefore less vulnerable to competition. Innovation in the car industry involved saving energy through the construction of new engines, the use of better tyres and, generally speaking, making cars lighter. This made the recovery of the country's biggest exporter possible: despite automation, the car industry in 1984 employs more people than ten years ago – 800,000 compared with 740,000.

The chemical trust IG Farben had been before the Second World War the biggest German corporation by far. The Western Allies in a fit of trust-busting decided to split it up into three components, Bayer-Leverkusen, Höchst and BASF in Ludwigshafen. Today all three are considerably larger than the old IG Farben: after the British ICI, they are the leaders in Europe. BASF was initially the smallest, but eventually caught up with its rivals. All three produce a great variety of chemical and other products from fertilizers to aspirin, cosmetics and tapes for recording. More than 50 per cent of their production is sold abroad and many of their plants are also located outside Germany. The sales of pharmaceuticals and cosmetics have done well irrespective of prosperity or recession. Most of the products of these three corporations are, however, not for the consumption of the general public but for other industries, and this sector is more vulnerable to the effects of a business downturn. Agro-chemical products have also been affected partly as the result of dumping from Eastern-bloc countries. The chemical industry, too, has been criticized for showing excessive caution; it has gone for 'safe products' and shied away from risky innovations.

The German textile industry is relatively small by world standards and like textile plants elsewhere in Europe, it went through a long period of retrenchment. More recently it has shown signs of recovery as the result of drastic rationalization. The number of those employed has been halved, but exports have almost doubled. Up to 40 per cent of its output is now exported. To a considerable extent the textile industry has moved from its traditional locations in North (and East) Germany to the South.

Building fared badly between 1979 and 1983: more jobs were lost in this than in any other branch of the economy. Underground and road building were affected even more than the rest and there were many bankruptcies. It is estimated that another 300–400,000 jobs may be lost by 1990.

Two more groups of corporations ought to be mentioned in this context: the oil companies such as Deutsche BP, Deutsche Shell, Mobil Oil, Deutsche Texaco are no major employers; the whole industry employs only some 30,000 people. Mobil Oil, for instance, has about 2,500 men and women on its payroll in contrast to the 56,000 employed by the Salzgitter steelworks and wharfs corporation. Yet the total turnover of Mobil Oil is higher than that of Salzgitter. As in other countries, the oil companies have been able to hold their own in recent years.

The record of the big banks has been a major factor of stability and the biggest of them, the Deutsche Bank, has been doing very well indeed. True, even in the 1950s it was bigger than its rivals the Dresdener and the Commerzbank. But since then, led by Hermann Abs, and more recently by Wilfried Guth and Wilhelm Christians, it has experienced spectacular growth: its turnover is now as big as that of the five biggest industrial corporations taken together. It is so influential that it is sometimes mistakenly thought to be the state bank of West Germany. It is not only the biggest savings bank but also the greatest source of credits and the most important gold merchant. It finances about one quarter of Germany's foreign trade and has more than five million customers. The Deutsche Bank is represented on the board of many leading industrial and trade corporations and its influence, direct or indirect, on the German economy is greater than that of any other firm or group of firms.

Only twenty-five years ago, around 1960, shipbuilding seemed one of the most promising of all German industries, the pioneer of the miracle, but during the last decade it has suffered the saddest decline of all. More than a third of those employed have lost their jobs and, in view of a shrinking market and the competition from Japan and South Korea, a substantial recovery seems to be virtually ruled out. Shipbuilding has been concentrated, for obvious reasons, in northern Germany, in Hamburg, Bremen and Emden. Since the loss of jobs on such a massive scale was unacceptable from a political point of view, strong financial support was given over many years by public funds to an industry without much future. True, even larger state subsidies were given in countries such as Italy or France. These subsidies had a negative effect; they endangered the survival of the smaller firms which did not get subsidies and could no longer compete against their bigger rivals. The situation was further aggravated by mistaken projections concerning future demand. German wharfs continued to build big container ships and supertankers even though it should have been clear since the middle 1970s that demand was satiated, and that in this specific field Germany could not compete with the Far East. Instead there should have been a concentration on highly specialized ships, or on the construction of supply ships for oil drilling platforms or on ferries.

Nor were the shipping companies doing well. The two largest were Hapag, based in Hamburg, and Norddeutscher Lloyd of Bremen; old companies, held in the highest esteem, their ships plied all oceans and their names were known in every harbour. But sea transport in the post-war years underwent a great deal of innovation and the two giants were not sufficiently adaptable to new demands and conditions. Their merger in 1970 seemed to offer new hope; the new and bigger company tried its luck in all kinds of new ventures such as charter flights, but it lacked experience and the experiment did not succeed. For years the company showed no profits, and it was only in 1983/4 that an upturn took place.

The list of invalids among the leading corporations is substantial. It includes the second largest employer of all, the national railway company (the post office being the largest), which has consistently shown deficits for many years. Mention has been made of AEG, founded in Berlin by Walther Rathenau's father one hundred years ago, of some of the big steel-producing corporations, such as Klöckner and Arbed Saarstahl, of Agfa-Gevaert, Magirus and MBB. Even Grundig has to be listed here: established after the war, it was for many years a

181

success story *par excellence*.

Such failures, however, ought to be seen in perspective: even at the best of times some companies succeed and others fail. Recent success stories in addition to Daimler-Benz include BMW, German IBM, Deutsche Babcock (which constructs industrial plants), and some relative newcomers such as Nixdorf in Paderborn. Nixdorf was founded in 1952 by a student of physics and mathematics who had received a loan of some $10,000, and is now a force to reckon with in the computer field with some 15,000 employees in thirty-one countries. This newcomer understood (as Clive Sinclair did in the UK) better than the major established firms the advantages in this field of decentralization: hence the concentration on mini- and micro-computers. There have been other new rising stars: some have done well as a result of their operations abroad rather than inside Germany.

The industrial migration from north to south which had begun during the fat years gathered speed during the lean ones. Hamburg, with its sixty-three wet docks handling 60 per cent of the country's exports, used to be Germany's richest and most expensive city; in recent years, however, its economic situation has deteriorated, and the *mercatores imperii*, the imperial merchants of Bremen, once so self-confident, were doing even worse. In both cases the main reason was the crisis in the shipbuilding industry, the shipping lines and the various trades connected with them.

Nordrhein-Westfalen is the most populous of the German *Länder*. Economically it was once so much stronger than the rest that many feared its hegemony: it provided, to give but one example, half of Germany's exports. But following the decline of mining and the steel industry this *Land* has become the problem-child of West Germany – and the one most in need of economic support. Its unemployment rate is higher than that of most other *Länder*: hundreds of thousands of jobs have been lost and the old factories have not been replaced by new growth industries.

In contrast to the northern regions, Bavaria has shown higher than average growth, its share in exports has risen, and the unemployment rate is lower. True, there are inequalities within Bavaria. While Munich (Germany's answer to Silicone Valley), where one-third of Bavarian industry is concentrated, continues to prosper, other main cities such as Nuremberg and Würzburg have not fared equally well. But the overall picture is certainly more encouraging and observers have argued that this may be connected with basic differences in industrial structure. The average South German industrial enterprise is smaller than in the north, and has proved to be more adaptable when facing changing economic conditions. Some minor disasters occurred in Baden-Württemberg among the precision-tool makers, the watchmakers and the optical industry. But local industry in the south-west has shown flexibility with regard to specialization and technical innovation. The unemployment rate in the *Musterländle* is less than half that of Bremen or the Saar.

There has been bitter controversy about ways and means to help the branches of the German economy which suffered more than others. But for some exceptional cases state subsidies have been a failure. Over the last fifteen years the steel industry has been the biggest recipient; billions of dollars have been paid to Hoesch, Klöckner, Salzgitter and other giants, yet the decline has continued. Altogether the German iron and steel industry employed 420,000 people in 1960; 340,000 in 1974 and only 239,000 in 1983. By and large the German steel industry is as efficient as any in Europe, but existing production exceeds demand; instead of looking for a radical solution, West European governments have engaged in a race to support industries which, in the long run, face diminishing demand. About forty billion taxpayers' dollars were paid to steel in Western Europe between 1975 and 1983 – above all in Britain and Italy (some $12 billion each), but also in France ($7 billion) and Belgium ($5 billion). German subventions per ton of steel were smaller but the consequences equally negative. The European governments have agreed to reduce their steel-producing capacity by some 26 million tons by the end of 1985. But this is still not enough and there is reason to believe that subsidies will continue to be paid after that date.

These policies have been criticized for a number of good reasons: state aid could have been helpful if it had been spent on the modernization of the industry rather than for lowering prices on the world market, selling steel frequently at a loss. Such practices merely postponed the inevitable, they did nothing to avert it. State assistance has usually been given to the bigger and older corporations: they were better known and had more political clout in Bonn or with local governments. There is reluctance to help newer and smaller firms despite the fact that their long-term prospects may be better. Furthermore, it is usually cheaper in the short run to aid the old industrial plants rather than help establish modern, up-to-date ones, and bureaucracies and parliaments are always inclined to prefer the less expensive solution. The authorities in Bonn were under pressure to protect the German steel industry against unfair foreign competition, they had to prevent the loss of so many jobs. But the strategies chosen failed. It should have been clear almost from the beginning that the problem was not specifically German and that it could be solved only in close agreement with the other Western industrial nations.

There are no obvious solutions in this case and in other instances which would have given quick results. Detailed studies of the recession of the early 1930s have shown that irrespective of how much money was spent at the height of the crisis, only a relatively small number of jobs would have been created. The artificial stimulation of demand is possible only within narrow limits; it may succeed at a propitious moment and with specific aims, but it cannot provide a cure for ailing industries in an age of rapid technological innovation and changing demand.

Facing a major storm, industrialists are inclined to look for a larger protective roof, usually through fusion and merger. Other reasons also strengthened the trend towards concentration in German industry. In the 1950s there were some nineteen major car producers. One went bankrupt (Borgward); others, such as Audi, joined bigger existing companies. Today only seven are left. The three biggest chemical corporations control 50 per cent of the output in their field, the leading eight electrical firms produce 70 per cent of the total volume. Some of the giants are further interconnected in various common enterprises at home and abroad. Altogether the part of the fifty biggest industrial corporations in total industrial output has more than doubled during the last thirty years. It was 25 per cent in 1950 and is now above 55 per cent.

The trend was most pronounced in mining, mineral oil and the car industry. Sometimes the reason was lack of capital, in other cases the rising costs of research and development, in yet others the threat of foreign competition and the inability to find a more effective division of labour – or a combination of all these factors.[1] Some of the mergers affected very well-known firms – the fusion of AEG and Telefunken, of Hapag and Norddeutscher Lloyd have been mentioned. Krupp and

[1] But a similar trend could also be detected in small business. The number of groceries fell in twenty-five years from 131,000 to 73,000. The number of petrol stations was reduced to half in a mere twelve years (1969–81).

Thyssen negotiated for years; eventually the talks broke down because the state refused to contribute the funds which had been demanded by the companies to make their merger a going concern. Mergers and take-overs took place in almost every branch of the economy; of the three biggest German removal companies, Schenker found support in the *Bundesbahn*, Rhenus-WTAB joined VEBA and Lonrho, British firms bought Kühne and Nagel. A Swiss firm took over Pelikan, known to every German schoolboy or girl and to every office worker as the main producer of pencils, ballpoints and all kinds of other office equipment. Mannesmann acquired a decisive portion of the Kienzle shares; one of the best-known take-overs concerned Karstadt, the department store chain, which bought Neckermann, one of the leading mail-order houses. Agfa-Gevaert became part of Bayer; Dynamit Nobel part of Flick; Blaupunkt is part of Bosch and Triumph-Adler belongs to VW. Foreign firms and governments (Iran under the Shah, Saudi Arabia and Kuwait) also entered the German market and bought shares in leading German firms. Swiss Ciba-Geigy added Hoffman's *Stärke* to its empire; Grundig looked for support in France and the Netherlands; the German cellulose industry found partners in Sweden. True, the trend towards concentration was not limited to the capitalist economy, it could also be observed in the economies of the Soviet bloc. But while the mergers solved some problems, they provided no solution for others and, in some cases, they had a negative effect.

The forecasts for West Germany's economic future range from deep pessimism to optimistic predictions about steady growth and a more or less untroubled transition to a post-industrial economy – retaining the position as the third largest economy in the world. Past experience has shown that economic developments depend as much (or more) on social, political and psychological factors as on purely economic developments, which makes truly scientific forecasting *a priori* impossible. The experts agree on certain basic trends, such as the fact that accelerated growth has come to an end and that, like other industrial countries, Germany will achieve relatively slow growth in the years to come.

German economic forecasts since the Second World War have erred more often than not on the side of pessimism. Germany's recovery since 1948 was staggering in comparison with that of its eastern neighbours and impressive even in comparison with the rest of Western Europe. Yet even while the stormy growth was under way there were plenty of dire prophecies.[1] Mention has been made of the 'relative pauperization' of regions of Northern Germany, to borrow a term from nineteenth-century political economy. These are no longer the leading and richest regions in the country, but foreign visitors to North German cities, even the 'poorest' of them, will still find a great deal of affluence, more than in the past, more than in most other countries of Europe. And they will return with the clear impression that they had been wrongly informed. The figures were probably right, but they were provided out of context. Combined with the German proclivity to concentrate on the dark clouds on the horizon rather than the blue skies, the impressions are bound to be in stark contrast with the expectations of misery and poverty.

The crucial issue facing Germany in the years to come is its ability to compete on world markets. At first sight the prospects seem excellent: even during the recession of the late 1970s, when Japanese and American exports shrank, German exports continued to rise. In 1982 Germany exported goods and services estimated at 33 per cent of the GNP compared with 17 per cent in the case of Japan, and 12 per cent for the United States. Despite all its problems the German automobile industry sold about 60 per cent of all its cars and trucks abroad. But this was partly due to the devaluation of the DM. A closer look shows a decline on the part of high technology products in German exports. By and large, Germany has not tried as hard as some of its rivals to modernize its plants; the growth of Japanese productivity has been higher. Even leading German export branches, such as the machine-tool industry, have come under pressure and the same is true with regard to electrical and chemical corporations.

The causes of the relative German weakness in some aspects of electronics and biotechnology have been the subject of much heart-searching. German universities are at least as well equipped to conduct basic research as American and Japanese, but microchips were pioneered in California, not in Munich. Some have pointed to the fact that the American electronics industry received a great boost as a result of defence purchases. But this hardly explains the success of the electronics industry in Japan. Others have pointed to a decline in the

---

[1] There is the story of the German industrialist who persuaded himself in the early 1960s that his country was facing an unprecedented crisis, was about to be taken over by the Bolsheviks or undergo some other such calamity. He transferred his capital to Switzerland and bought gold at $35 an ounce. He did well, but for the wrong reasons.

general level of German science; once it was leading the world, now the Nobel prizes go to MIT and Caltech, and papers by German authors are not that widely quoted in professional literature. But the Japanese have not been in the forefront of theoretical science either.

Yet other observers have drawn attention to a certain conservatism in German industry, excessive caution, lack of communication within major enterprises between research and development and the decision-takers. The case of Konrad Zuse, one of the pioneers of electronics, is sometimes quoted: his team engaged in important creative work in West Germany in the early post-war period.[1] Then it became part of Siemens, the leader in the field – and was not heard of again.

German industry has been excellent in producing all kinds of special machinery, but it faces price wars in many fields and its marketing effort is not always very strong. German industry is exposed to changing fashions in world demand, yet the emphasis still remains on traditional products. True, the uncertainties affecting the steel industry and consumer electronics are not specific German problems, but other countries, to repeat once again, depend less on export. Germany employed in 1983 four thousand robots, as many as Britain, France, Italy and Benelux taken together. But Japan, its main competitor, had almost four times as many. High wages, high social costs, and relatively low growth taken together constitute a serious handicap. Hence the exodus over the last fifteen years of some German corporations overseas – to other European countries, to Latin America and South-East Asia.

Such a trend may easily be reversed. As a leading industrialist once put it, one single technological development may reduce the part of wages in the cost of the finished product, and thus change the whole picture. Tax rebates and subsidies in foreign countries are a constant temptation but there are other benefits, not always quantifiable for those preferring to stay at home. In the end only some of those playing with the idea of transferring their operations to foreign parts have actually done so, and some of the emigrants have come back. Hence the apparent paradox that despite the negative prognoses and despite an anti-industrial mood among sections of the young generation, Germany

[1] Konrad Zuse, a Berlin engineer, built in 1938 a machine scheduled to mechanize mathematical operations which eventually became a digital calculator, similar in purpose but different in execution from the early British and US computers of Turing, Aiken and others. Zuse's calculations were used in the engineering of V/2 rockets. He was also a pioneer in the art of computer programming which he called *Plankalkül* (Andrew Hodges, *Alan Turing: The Enigma*, New York 1983, p. 299).

still (or again) has higher standing as an industrial location than most other countries in the world. The low rate of inflation of about 4 per cent is an additional inducement.

Most experts agree that some branches of the economy will do well and others rather badly, that the overall record will be one of small growth and that the *Bundesrepublik* will have to cope with major social problems. But this is also true with regard to every other country; the decisive question is how these challenges will be faced. The differences of opinion between government and opposition are smaller in Germany even now than in France or in England, where a victory of the opposition would almost immediately make nonsense of all long-range economic forecastings. Even the left Social Democrats do not claim to have panaceas for coping with unemployment, shrinking resources and greater competition on the world's markets. Even the German communists are willing to admit that it would be pointless to increase the output of steel at a time of rapidly shrinking world demand. There is greater willingness among German unions to collaborate with industry and the state. While such readiness does not by itself provide solutions, it contributes to a better social climate and creates the preconditions for problem-solving.

German anxieties have been mentioned as one of the factors which may have a negative effect on future economic developments. Fears have also been expressed with regard to a decline in work ethos. Germany has been traditionally a country of high work motivation. The image of the workaholic was part and parcel of the stereotypes of Germany; 'Made in Germany' was a stamp of excellence which could be trusted and a 'job well done' seemed to be the slogan of the entire nation. Whether all Germans actually loved their work all the time is a moot point. No public opinion polls were carried out in the early phase of industrialization; one suspects that work enthusiasm was strictly limited then, what with long hours, bad conditions and low wages.

Attitudes subsequently changed: of those asked in the 1950s whether they found their jobs either always or mostly interesting, 80 per cent answered 'yes', and a follow-up inquiry in 1979 showed similar results. But social scientists still claim to have detected a change in motivation: whereas only 33 per cent preferred the hours of leisure to the time at work in the 1950s, their number has risen to almost half three decades later. In the United States half of the workers said they gave their best at work, in Germany only one quarter. Commenting on the statement: 'I am doing at work what is demanded of me. But I do not see any reason for any special exertion. Work is not that important as far as I am concerned', 40 per cent of Germans agreed, but only 30 per cent of those questioned in Britain and 24 per cent in America.

According to these findings most Germans have, furthermore, reached the conclusion that as far as monetary reward is concerned, great exertion is not worth while, for working hard and well brings no commensurate reward: the desire to work longer hours (and earn more money) has also declined. Such trends are unlikely to be cured by more industrial democracy; the decline came at the very time German workers received greater opportunities to influence policy at their place of work ('co-determination'). One should look for explanations elsewhere. Some refer to a general hedonistic mood generated by the media. But this fails to explain the fact that among those working independently there is increasing interest and that, on the other hand, there seems to be a similar decline in the Japanese work ethic. The most substantial decline is among unskilled manual workers and untrained clerical employees in both countries.

Inquiries of this kind point to a change of mood, but neither its reasons nor its extent are entirely clear. There are inexplicable contradictions: only 30 per cent of Germans still regard technology as a blessing (in comparison with almost three-quarters in 1966). But at the same time 70 per cent favour further economic growth. German listlessness may be explained – as elsewhere – against the background of greater prosperity and generational change. National characteristics are subject to change. In Tacitus' days Germans did not have the reputation of a nation of work fanatics: the Roman historian referred to lazy Germans resting on bearskins. When were their descendants converted to hard work and industry?

Thus, it may be wrong to draw far-reaching conclusions from these opinion polls: the fact that the British frequently scored higher in this context than the Germans gives rise to suspicion. Yardsticks differ very much from country to country and comparisons are problematic: discipline, industry, exertion, sacrifice do not mean the same everywhere.

Even if correct, the significance of such findings should not be exaggerated for they indicate nothing about the future. The changes in work ethics took place during a period of full employment and economic prosperity. Now, only a few years later, everyone agrees that the working week ought to be shortened. The issue at stake is no longer overtime, but a shortage of jobs for those needing them. Those eager to have more spare time, or to be pensioned off at an earlier age, are only too welcome.

Germany, like other industrial countries, faces structural unemployment; workers have become redundant and, even in the industries which continue to grow and prosper, there are few new openings. Of the hundred largest German corporations, sixty-six reduced their labour force in 1982; this included all the ten largest employers with the sole exception of the post office. Even the German railways have published a plan to make 70,000 out of 300,000 employees redundant.

A few figures explain the magnitude of the problem. In 1965 the number of employed reached an all-time high of 26.7 million. Hundreds of thousands of foreign workers streamed into Germany and were warmly welcomed by employers; the number of women (including married women) entering the labour market continued to grow. Demographic trends also contributed to building up pressure on the labour market: some 620,000 babies are now born in Germany each year. But twenty years ago there had been a baby boom with about a million births annually. These are the graduates of 1982 and 1984, knocking now on the doors of employers.

Up to 1973 big and small enterprises competed in attracting workers by offering high wages and extra benefits. By the end of the decade more and more people were chasing fewer and fewer jobs. The authors of an important study published in 1977 reached the conclusion that if a growth rate of 4 per cent could be maintained up to the late 1980s, unemployment would gradually be reduced and full employment could be achieved again by the end of the decade. (It is thought that the number of jobs actually declines if growth is below 3 per cent per annum.) But since 1977 there were further years of no growth, resulting in yet another million unemployed. The target of full employment seems now attainable only on the basis of a 5–7 per cent growth, which is clearly out of the question. Yet another possibility was considered by the authors of the 1977 study: nil economic growth. In this case they predicted that unemployment by the end of the 1980s would be 6.5 million, as much as at the height of the depression in 1932. The situation may be further aggravated by high unemployment rates in other European countries. Since the doors of Germany have to remain open – as do those of its neighbours – it is possible that there may be a further influx of foreign workers, albeit at a reduced rate.

These figures point to serious problems facing the *Bundesrepublik* in the years ahead. True, the figures may be somewhat exaggerated. Not all those registered as unemployed are in fact looking for a job. Some receive unemployment benefits but for one reason or other have no wish to work. Yet others – more frequently women than men – register as unemployed because they did work at one stage, ceased doing so, but want to preserve their right to an old-age pension which only those receive who have been holding a job for fifteen years. These two categories probably cover some 10–15 per cent of those now registered as unemployed.

No mention has been made so far of the 'second economy' which, though less substantial in West Germany than in other countries, is still a factor of some importance. According to reliable estimates up to 300,000 foreign building workers are employed illegally in West Germany during the season – tens of thousands of Austrians and up to 50,000 British. In this working army of the evening and night there are not a few Germans, working alone or in small groups; most professions are represented from hairdressing to plumbing. But even if these categories are deducted, the total number of unemployed is still high, and may increase further.

Many employers believe that German labour costs are too high, but even those who want to lower wages agree that this cannot be done too drastically and that a high rate of unemployment will endanger both political stability and the economy – by lowering domestic consumption. At the other extreme, left-wing politicians and militant trade union leaders accept the proposals for a reduction of the working week with some enthusiasm; the demand for a thirty-five-hour week has been, after all, part of the Social Democratic programme for many years. But they insist that fewer hours of work should result in no loss of income. Such demands are unrealistic at a time of recession. When pressed, the militants are willing therefore to accept some linkage between wages, working hours and productivity.

Trade union officials represent the interests of the employed, but who speaks for those who have lost their jobs? There is the danger of two working classes emerging, those with jobs and the unemployed; solidarity between these groups cannot always be taken for granted. The overall case for a reduction of the working week is irrefutable. A variety of approaches may be needed, part-time labour, job sharing, state support for a shorter working week, the abolition (or reduction) of overtime, the introduction of an earlier statutory pensionable age, say at fifty-eight. It is thought that employment might be found for up to two million people using these and other strategies. But the complications should not be ignored or underrated. Just as economic growth does not automatically create new jobs, a voluntary (or involuntary) shortening of the working week will not always lead to new openings. Older employees may not be replaced because their jobs have become redundant, unskilled workers (and about half of the unemployed have no full training!) cannot possibly replace highly skilled workers. The redistribution of work may be possible in some branches of the economy, but not in others.

There is no panacea for unemployment, but job sharing is still the single most important approach to solve a painful social ill. The problem of job loss has not been explained so far in an entirely satisfactory way, nor has it been addressed by the politicians. In Germany, as elsewhere, it has not yet been fully accepted that this is not a temporary emergency but that lasting changes are taking place: job loss may occur as the result of industrial decline but it happens also for very different reasons. To a large extent it is the result of the growth of productivity which has doubled overall in agriculture as well as in industry; thirty-four German workers were needed in 1961 to produce an output valued at 1 million DM. Twenty years later this output was achieved by seventeen people. The number of those employed in industry will not fall as drastically as in agriculture, but it will certainly continue to decline, and the service sector of the economy will not be able to absorb all those who have lost their employment in industry.

Full employment was achieved in most West European countries in the 1960s, and the achievement of this goal was widely regarded as irreversible. Twenty years later there is scepticism about full employment as a societal goal, and it comes from the enemies of the work ethic on the Left as much as from the Right.

The microchip revolution offers great promise for the future but it does not help with the redistribution of work. This cannot be left to the market but involves active state planning and intervention, at a time when this has more enemies than ever. Regional imbalance, to give but one example, quite obviously makes state intervention imperative. Yet, at the same time, the problems of redistributing work demand a great deal of flexibility and an innovative spirit seldom found in a huge bureaucratic machine. The redistribution of work will proceed smoothly only if there is social peace and active co-operation on the part of management and labour. Yet the strains and dislocations of mass unemployment are likely to cause a social climate in which such co-operation is difficult to attain.

Seen in a wider context, the decisive issue is whether a country produces enough for its needs: the redistribution of labour need not be more than a transient technical problem. But the transition is also made difficult by recollections of a not-so-distant past: the great fear that the depression of 1929–32 may recur. It is forgotten that Germany is now infinitely wealthier than fifty years ago; that, in contrast to the great economic crisis, industrial production has not shrunk by a third or more; that unemployment today no longer means disaster for those affected – starvation, the loss of home and of medical services.

Germany's economic achievements in the post-war period, like those of other countries, were possible because there was relative social peace which, in turn, was the outcome of the emergence of generous and far-reaching systems of public welfare. Will the nations of Europe be able to pay for welfare on a rising scale in the years to come?

The cost could be covered without difficulty while the economy prospered, but in recent years some costs have continued to rise while the economy has more or less stagnated. When the West German welfare system was first introduced, its annual cost was slightly more than two billion dollars. By the late 1970s this had risen to $125 billion, slightly less than 30 per cent of the West German GNP, and in 1982 it had reached 33 per cent: one out of four Germans receives a pension. The payments are linked to the cost-of-living index, and the number of those receiving assistance continues to grow in view of the increasing longevity of the population: the German state debt has more than quintupled between 1970 and 1984.

The redistribution of wealth by taxation is practised in every country and is part of modern social policy. But if carried beyond a certain limit investments decline, taxpayers become less honest, the incentive to work decreases. Extreme cases of abuse of the system are given wide publicity but may not be that frequent. More serious is the growing feeling that everyone is entitled to make the most of all the state services offered, including, for instance, the right to six weeks' full pay in the case of sickness. German physicians are paid for every prescription and test they order for their patients. Consequently the consumption of pills in the West German health service has increased ninefold in fifteen years. It is virtually certain that the state of health of the nation has not improved in the same ratio.

According to East German doctrine, West Germany is a capitalist country based on the exploitation of the masses. But old age pensions are more than three times higher in West Germany than in the GDR; invalidity pensions twice as high, widows' and orphans' pensions more than twice as high. Altogether some 26 per cent of West German public expenditure is spent on social security and statutory welfare benefits in comparison to only 14 per cent in the GDR. If West Germany were to reduce its social security spending to the per capita level of East Germany, its financial problems would be less acute. But such cuts are quite unthinkable even though West Germany, like all other West European governments including those headed by socialist parties, had to reduce social welfare spending in the 1980s. France under Mitterrand changed the rules according to which workers could draw unemployment benefits; Italy introduced stricter guidelines for welfare benefits; Sweden made cuts in welfare benefits and public spending; and Holland cut social welfare benefits and civil service wages across the board by 3 per cent in 1983.

These measures were taken to stop the further increase of welfare costs and also to stamp out obvious abuses. (In the Netherlands, one worker out of six is officially registered as disabled and in Germany too there was a dramatic increase in the number of disabled during the 1960s and 1970s.) The steps taken by the West German government in 1983 were less far-reaching than those adopted by other EEC governments: the reduction of child allowances, the length of maternity leave and the addition of small charges to the premium paid by pensioners for health insurance.

Some critics have suggested a radical dismantling of the German welfare state, but such demands are not politically feasible, and furthermore ignore its role as an economic stabilizer, not just a political and social one. Investment in education and health is not unproductive, and the stabilization of popular demand is of economic importance. Even the sharpest critics of the welfare state in Germany and elsewhere have been unable, when in power, to carry out substantial reforms. The welfare state is here to stay unless a situation arises in which the state and the local authorities are no longer able to cover its costs. Between the early 1960s and the early 1980s the cost of the German health service has risen tenfold, far in excess of the rise in the GNP. It has been estimated that if the trend continues, this one item in the budget of the welfare state will exceed the total GNP thirty to forty years hence. State and local authorities finance the rapidly growing expenditure by means of loans. Sooner or later such loans will dry up. But it is also true that during the last two years welfare state spending has no longer risen. In this instance as in others the inclination towards worst-case predictions should be resisted.

German economic performance has been indifferent in recent years. But statements of this kind make sense only if compared with other periods in the past or with other countries at present: indifferent compared with whom? The difficulties besetting Germany affect all other Western industrial countries and, in different ways, also the communist bloc. Unemployment in Germany has risen from 3.4 per cent in 1980 to 9.3 per cent in 1984 – an alarming increase. But the rate of increase has been similar in France, higher in Britain, Italy, Belgium, Holland and Canada. The increase in wages and earnings has been less (2.7 per cent) than in virtually all other countries. The same is true with regard to consumer prices, which rose over the last two decades fivefold in France, sixfold in the United Kingdom, more than threefold in the United States, but only 2.5 times in Germany. German exports have done better than those of any other country, including Japan.

True, the German overall industrial performance has been weaker during the last ten years than that of Japan and the United States, but is still somewhere in the middle of the industrial growth league, and the same refers to productivity.

None of the problems facing Germany is insurmountable and the effort needed is not half as great as the one which was made after the Second World War. It was obvious in 1948 that, but for an all-out effort, the country would not recover, that most Germans would never eat well, live in well-heated and spacious apartments and, generally speaking, enjoy more than the essential amenities of life. Today it is more difficult to get the country moving again precisely because it has become accustomed to a fairly high living standard. Everyone has a car, and many have a second one; holidays abroad have become the rule rather than the exception. There are no immediate threats now, but a widespread belief that somehow the state will take care of everyone. This belief is shared by sections of the young generation with their firm views about the negative effects of soulless work, and the horrors of consumerism.

The economic difficulties facing Germany are to a considerable extent psychological in character; it is a question of lowering excessively high expectations. Need, the German proverb says, is the mother of inventiveness; it also helps to concentrate the mind. Expectations will eventually be lowered, public and private budgets will be trimmed. Just as an intake of calories above a certain level does not necessarily make for better health, an excess of luxuries does not make for happiness. Even if the country had to return to the standard of living of 1970 – a worst-case assumption – this does not warrant invoking visions of the apocalypse. The cures for the present difficulties belong largely to the realm of common sense, which, unfortunately, is not as common as commonly believed. True, there remain certain vulnerabilities such as the great dependence of the German economy on exports.

If there is to be a deep, lasting, world-wide recession West Germany will certainly not survive as an island of prosperity. But this is unlikely; meanwhile the main danger is fear and over-anxiety inhibiting investment and economic activity in general. Fortunately, most of those constantly invoking Armageddon do not really act as if they believed that the end of the world was around the corner.

8 Facing the Future

One morning not long ago I had the opportunity to view the Ruhr region (or the *Revier* as it is locally known) from the top floor of the Essen municipal building, the tallest in all Germany. It was not a particularly bright day yet one could see far towards Gelsenkirchen, Herne and Bochum and beyond. Only fifteen years earlier impenetrable smoke from steel mills and coalmines barred the view. Essen – this had been heavy industry, Krupp, the German edition of Blake's satanic mills. Today in all of Essen only one coalmine is operating and this will be closed in a year or two; the biggest taxpayer to the city is not Krupp but Coca Cola, whose headquarters are in a suburb. The water in the Ruhr river is clear, fish are caught and even eaten. Who would have anticipated these changes in 1960? But the joy of the ecologists is the sorrow of the local leaders, for the economic basis of this giant conurbation of five million has been eroded. These are tough and industrious people, one of them told me: they'll think of something and they will muddle through. I have no reason to disbelieve him but there will be difficult years ahead, and in some ways the problems facing the *Revier* will confront the country in general.

To engage in prediction is a thankless task; the notion that within a mere dozen years Germany would be united (and an empire!) would have appeared fanciful in 1860. No one assumed in 1913 that within six years Germany would be considerably smaller, headed by a president rather than a monarch. Hitler in 1927 was down and out, and no one in his right mind thought that he would be chancellor within a mere six years. Neither believers nor opponents of Nazism imagined in early 1940 the ruins the Führer would leave after his suicide.

Historians continue to debate to this day whether there was a German

Sonderweg, whether, in other words, historical developments in Germany proceeded on lines different from the rest of Western and Central Europe – and if so, why? If it is difficult to interpret the past, why engage in reflections about the future? Yet it is safer today to point out probabilities than in the past, not because the tools of prediction have improved, but because there is more continuity. Of the four examples of rapid and radical change adduced, three occurred as the result of war, or wars, and the fourth, Hitler's rise to power, happened in circumstances altogether different from those now prevailing.

Armed conflict in Europe can be ruled out in the foreseeable future and political change in Germany, as in other countries, is proceeding at a slower rate. Seen in the perspective of almost four decades, Western Germany has done far better in every respect than could be expected. Its democratic institutions have functioned well, there has been political stability and economic prosperity. With all their self-doubts, most Germans have not been oblivious of these facts. Walking the streets of any German town, talking to Germans whatever their social background and age, no one will reach the conclusion that contemporary Germany is a poor and unfree country. The feeling that 'we are again somebody in the world' returned as early as the 1950s, and not without some justification. For even if Germany is no longer a global power or the leading cultural centre it has again become a key country in Europe, fairly prosperous, reasonably stable and democratically governed. But there is still no real self-confidence, satisfaction is mixed with feelings of insecurity: perhaps the recovery was only temporary, perhaps the democratic institutions are not deeply rooted and will not survive a major storm? Perhaps economic prosperity is the only cohesive force holding together post-war German society? And if this is the case, how will the Germans react now that the 'miracle' has given way to a period of stagnation, or at best of slow progress?

One of the main problems facing contemporary Germany is lack of true self-confidence. Various explanations have been adduced to explain this: the delayed shock of the total defeat in the Second World War, the negative influence of the media, the traditional German craving for perfection, and the corresponding belief that the alternative to absolute success is absolute failure. Whatever the reasons (and there may well be a combination of these and other factors), insecurity is an important fact of life in contemporary Germany.

The manifestations of acute anxiety and the cultivation of fear, which have appeared in recent years in some sections of the German people, have caused consternation among Germany's neighbours and allies. How deep do they go? It would be wrong to take them too seriously; pervasive fear – like any mood – is unlikely to persist for long. Wide sections of the population were not affected, and by and large Germany is no more prone to a violent attack of collective hysteria than other European countries. But once the fears recede into the background fresh doubts arise among Germany's allies as a result of the invocations of German unity and some hardly veiled neutralist longings.

The intellectual elite, the articulators and trend-setters, have played a prominent part in all this: not the intelligentsia *per se*, and even less the young generation as a whole, but those modelling styles and fashions. There has been among them an oscillation between extremes and a remoteness from reality (and indeed common sense), the like of which cannot easily be found elsewhere. The violent swings in history between Left and Right, between chauvinism and absolute denial of patriotism, between poses of heroism and fear are an almost unique phenomenon, as has been the tendency towards exaggeration and overreaction. Conformist when resistance involved considerable risks (such as in Wilhelminian Germany and, *a fortiori*, in the Third Reich), there has been a trend towards hypercriticism and negativism among the intelligentsia when dissent involved no danger – as in the Weimar Republic and again since the 1960s.

There were always exceptions and silent majorities. But the voices most loudly heard in the universities or the literary circles during critical periods have been the more extreme ones. Today, with the wider reach of the mass media, their impact is greater than in the past. How much idealism have they generated and how much confusion and what dubious causes have they sponsored! The genius of peoples is in different fields: Russia has produced some of the greatest writers but no world-class painter; the British with all their accomplishments can point to few composers of the first order; many treatises of great value on political theory have been written in Germany, but this has not made for a happy relationship between German intellectuals and political practice – they have always found it difficult to find their place in the world of political reality.

The political parties

The political parties on the other hand have not been unlucky with their leadership during the post-war decades. The general level of competence shown compared not unfavourably with other European countries, and continuity was provided which the country badly needed. Konrad Adenauer became chancellor by one vote – his own – and he went on governing for fourteen years. A vote of 'constructive no-confidence' was launched in 1972 by the Christian Democrats (for the first time in the history of the *Bundesrepublik*) against the ruling Social Democrats. It was defeated by one vote – and the Social Democrats remained in power for ten more years.

German domestic politics, like those of other democratic countries, move in cycles. The Adenauer regime provided stability for seventeen years, but by 1966 the Christian Democrats had run out of steam, of ideas and also of leading personalities. The door was opened first to the Great Coalition (from late 1966 to 1969) and then to thirteen years of Social Democratic government. Even before the end of this period, the Social Democrats showed signs of tiredness and disunity; Helmut Schmidt's difficulties had as much to do with his own party as with the CDU. The circumstances of the 1982 change came as a surprise, but not the overthrow of the government and the subsequent electoral defeat of the SPD. If the law of cycles still applies, the Christian Democrats should be in for a fairly long time to come. But the laws of politics are not those of natural science; individuals sometimes play a decisive role, and also the cohesion (or the lack thereof) among the leadership of the parties.

There are other question marks: the Social Democrats never attained an absolute majority, and the Christian Democrats only once – in 1957. They have always depended on coalition partners, the Liberals (FDP) which, at one time, gravitated to the Centre-Right, later to the Left, and now collaborate again with the Christian Democrats. But the FDP has become progressively weaker, and with the emergence of the Greens the constellation has become more complicated. Some of the Greens have agreed, after unspeakable agonies, to collaborate with the Social Democrats on a regional basis. If they again overcome the 5 per cent hurdle in a future election (which is not certain), and if the Liberals should fail to do so (which is possible), the Greens could tip the political scales. This remains, however, a remote possibility; more likely the

Greens will split between those willing to play the parliamentary game and the others who will, as in the past, see their main assignment in extra-parliamentary activities.

It is also possible that in a truly critical situation, caused by domestic crisis or foreign threats, another Grand Coalition may temporarily emerge. The Greens seemed at one time the wave of the future, the great hope of the young generation. But they have remained a generational movement of protest against the established order without any workable solutions to the major social and economic questions facing Germany. The lack of organization, the absence of elementary party discipline, and the cumbersome process of decision-taking, make it virtually impossible for them to become an effective political force.

Much has been said of *Staats-* and *Parteiverdrossenheit*, the discontent with the state and the existing parties. Such attitudes always exist in democratic societies, sometimes to a greater and sometimes to a lesser extent. They become a threat only if the grumblings turn into a mass movement, as happened in the Weimar Republic. Germans tend to be grumblers, but the aversion to the parliamentary regime is no greater in Germany than in other European countries. With the exception of the Greens, radical groups have not been doing well in post-war German politics, and the Greens, too, are no more than a transitory phenomenon. The experience of the Third Reich will continue to act as a deterrent against any massive resurgence of right-wing extremism, and the realities of East Germany make it difficult to generate mass enthusiasm for Soviet-style communism. Would the present system survive a major political-economic crisis, such as the Weimar Republic faced and as a result of which it perished? History, notwithstanding widespread popular belief, never repeats itself. The difficulties that will face Germany in the next decade or two will be different in character. Even in 1932 a military dictatorship was no serious alternative; in the 1980s such a possibility need not even be discussed. Parliamentary democracy has come to Germany to stay, irrespective of the magnitude of the problems and threats ahead.

There is social and political conflict in Germany, as in other countries; there has been polarization which makes the intercourse between political leaders of different parties less relaxed than, for instance, in Britain and America. But the climate is now infinitely better than it was in the Weimar Republic and there is a greater measure of agreement than commonly assumed. Some parliamentarians may demand the nationalization of certain ailing industries, as an emergency measure, but no one in his or her right mind expects that either wholesale nationalization of industries, trade and banks, or alternatively, massive de-nationalization, will provide a cure for the economy. Everyone agrees that drastic action ought to be taken with regard to unemployment, but no one claims to have a panacea on how to deal with it. No one suggests dismantling the welfare state, the only question is how to keep the expense manageable. There are heated discussions but the differences of opinion are, in fact, relatively small. All parties are perplexed. *Nachdenken* (to ponder) and *Denkpause* (an interval for rethinking the issue) are now among the most frequently used (and abused) terms in the German political language. No one expresses wild enthusiasm about the present political and socio-economic system, but few pretend to have a plausible alternative and those claiming they do, are not taken very seriously.[1]

The strength and the weakness of the CDU is the fact that it is a coalition of many groups, from north and south, Catholic and Protestant, conservatives such as Alfred Dregger and liberals like Kurt Biedenkopf, big industrialist and small artisan – not to mention the Bavarian CSU. It is the natural majority party because of its wide appeal; it could lose, however, its hold in 1987 or in the election after that, if it mismanages affairs of state too obviously, if its leaders do not stick together, if there are too many crises and scandals, if the chancellor does not at least inspire confidence, if the Bavarian CSU strays too far from the centre of German politics. The main danger facing the CDU is that the social consensus on which it is based may break up at a time of economic crisis when the struggle for social priorities becomes more intense.

On the municipal level, stagnation and even deterioration are tolerated to a certain extent by the electors. Bremen has been doing economically worse than any other major German city, but its mayor and his party (the Social Democrats) have been returned all the same with considerable majorities, partly in view of his personal popularity but also because the voters of Bremen recognized that the local *malaise* was caused, at least in part, by circumstances beyond the mayor's

---

[1] Coalitions on the municipal level between Social Democrats and Christian Democrats are by no means uncommon: Cologne is one example, Kiel, Augsburg, Hameln and Oldenburg were or are others. In these places, the mayor belongs to one of the big parties, his deputy or, in North Germany the town clerk, to the other. Essen, the metropolis of the Ruhr, has been dominated by the Social Democrats, but the city treasurer was for many years a very capable member of the CDU.

control and that a change in personalities (or even parties) would not necessarily lead to a change in the situation.

Such allowances are not, however, made as far as the central government in Bonn is concerned. The main danger to the ruling party is still the wear and tear accruing from years of governing the country, and the desire of the public to give others a chance. It is doubtful whether the number of CDU voters would significantly decline if it dispensed with a party programme. People 'know' what the Christian Democrats stand for; a party which fights for change needs a detailed ideological platform, but the CDU is more or less in favour of the status quo. It has never been known as the party of youth: the Social Democrats and the Greens have been doing better in the under-twenty-five age-group. There are few Christian Democrats in the various student parliaments. The CDU has not made a great effort to have a larger impact in the universities; it is doubtful whether such an effort would have been very successful in any case. Given the demographic trends, the electoral importance of the young generation is declining in Germany. But, on the other hand, the party has tried hard not to create the impression that it is hostile to the young or neglects ordinary people – *den kleinen Mann*.[1]

The basic problems facing the Social Democrats in the years to come are not dissimilar to those confronting the CDU – to accommodate various interest groups and, at the same time, not to move too far from the Centre. The pull towards the Left is strong now in the SPD, but what does 'Left' mean these days? Like the CDU, the SPD has traditionally been a coalition between a pragmatic, a reformist (or 'revisionist') and a Marxist-revolutionary wing. Under Schmidt's

[1] The leadership of the CDU is predominantly lower middle class by origin: Helmut Kohl's father was a small municipal employee, Strauss's a butcher, Rainer Barzel's and Karl Carsten's fathers were teachers (so was Helmut Schmidt's), Gerhard Stoltenberg's father was a parson, Manfred Wörner's a self-made businessman, starting from very small beginnings. Norbert Blüm, minister of labour under Kohl, worked as a toolmaker in the Opel plant at Rüsselsheim. Among the previous generation of CDU leaders – men such as Heinrich Lübke, Richard Stücklen or Heinrich Krone – the incidence of working-class background was quite frequent. A substantial part of the CDU leadership is of middle- and upper-middle-class background. This refers to Friedrich Zimmermann, for instance, to Alfred Dregger, to Biedenkopf and Leisler Kiep; their fathers were senior business executives or well-to-do merchants. But the Social Democrats have more *Herren von* . . . in their leadership than the CDU. Generally speaking there are no significant differences as far as the social background of the leadership is concerned, between the CDU and the post-Brandt and Wehner SPD. Hans Jochen Vogel's father was a professor in Göttingen, Horst Ehmke's father was a surgeon who owned a private clinic. The FDP is more 'bourgeois' than the two major parties.

chancellorship there was not much scope for a left-wing policy. But once the party had passed into the opposition this drift became quite strong, manifesting itself, above all, in the rejection of the old defence policy. Also new was the willingness to co-operate on a regional basis with the Greens.

How revolutionary, how Marxist, are Hans Ulrich Klose, Peter von Oertzen, Peter Conradi, Lafontaine and the other leading represent-atives of the new left-wing? The short answer is – not very. They do not dream of general strikes, let alone armed uprisings. Oscar Lafontaine has been mayor of Saarbrücken for years, but the dictatorship of the proletariat has not been established in that city. To a considerable extent the differences between them and their 'right-wing' comrades are of style and rhetoric rather than of substance. The critique of NATO and US foreign policy, as voiced by Bahr and Gaus, Lafontaine and Erhard Eppler, owes more to Prussian nostalgia, the Gaullist model or South-West German pietism than to Karl Liebknecht, Rosa Luxemburg and the German revolutionary tradition. Neutralist leanings by no means coincide with a radical orientation in domestic policies. Opposition to stationing the missiles has been quite popular, but this alone does not make for credible alternatives in defence and foreign policy. The SPD has to find a programme that satisfies the radical comrades who want no part in NATO, but is sufficiently moderate not to frighten away those potential voters who prefer belonging to a strong defensive alliance to splendid isolation. While in opposition the party may find formulae vague enough to satisfy opposing viewpoints, but if it should return to power one day it will have to come down on one side or the other.

The dilemma facing the party in its relationship with the Greens (and the 'new social forces' in general) is even more acute because decisions, in this respect, cannot be postponed. Their lifestyle, morality, attitude to work and other traditional values are anathema to the average working-class supporter of the Social Democrats and also, of course, to traditional lower-middle-class elements. The SPD does not want to antagonize the alternative students, teachers, social workers, nor does it want to offend the sensibilities of its traditional working-class sup-porters. It has to be various things to different groups of people and there is always the danger of losing the one or the other by excessive concessions. Sometimes these problems may be soluble simply because each local organization is different. A local branch in a university town differs markedly from the party organization in a heavily industrialized city. But frequently a choice will be inevitable, and the party will have to opt for one element or the other.[1]

Seen in retrospect, the Social Democrats succeeded in the 1960s in broadening their appeal as a people's party, breaking out of the 'working-class ghetto'. Since then the proportion of manual workers in the population has declined, and the number of those who think of themselves as 'proletarian' has even more rapidly decreased. More workers vote for the SPD than for the CDU, but the difference is not very great. According to some recent polls, 46 per cent of manual workers give their vote to the Social Democrats and 44 per cent to the CDU. The two parties have about the same percentage of salaried employees. The number of workers among Socialist party officials, even on the lower echelons and on the local level, has dwindled; they have been replaced by younger militants with higher education usually of a non-working-class background. The SPD bureaucracy is now overwhelmingly middle class by origin. The key words used in CDU and SPD propaganda are the same, freedom – solidarity – justice (albeit in a different order), and the social composition of the parties is also very similar.

The greater radicalism of social democracy in recent years is rooted not in working-class militancy but in the cultural and political orientation of certain layers of the new middle class for which the CDU is the enemy *par excellence*. These middle-class radicals, including the Greens, are important allies for the Social Democrats, partly in view of their strong foothold in the media and in education. The cultural – ideological dividing line in German politics runs between different sections of the new middle class; geographical factors, religious attachment and generational formation are now more important than social conflict. Willy Brandt and others feel concern about keeping in touch with the young generation, its feelings and demands. However, the Social Democrats are facing not a monolithic young generation, but young people with very different lifestyles and often conflicting

[1] Electoral returns in 1983–4 have shown that the Greens are strongest in university towns such as Tübingen, where they polled up to 20 per cent. They are weak in working-class areas and predominantly agricultural regions. Their lack of clear political profile does not bode well for the long-term future, but is a source of strength at the present time: it is not a political party in the traditional sense but a catch-all movement for various single-issue groups, a coalition of sectarians and, generally speaking, those in firm opposition to the existing political and social order without necessarily having clear ideas on how to bring about change.

orientation. Furthermore, the outlook of these generations tends to change quickly. The generation of 1984 differs from the class of 1970, and the generation of the 1990s is bound to be different again. By the time the party leadership has adjusted itself to one young generation, this will have been upstaged by the next one. Nor is it possible to find a common denominator for those among the young willing to live and work within 'the system' and those who have already opted out.

The new divisions in German politics create problems of a new sort for the two big parties, but more so for the SPD than for the CDU, which cannot hope anyway to attract significant numbers of people from the alternative scene. The 'scene' is potentially important for the SPD, but these allies are not reliable; in some ways the Social Democrats are not radical enough for them, and for specific working-class concerns they have no great interest. Seen in this light, the left-wing of the SPD is radical in some respects, but not in others. It stands for change, but its orientation is not at all that of the Left of previous ages. Members of the SPD standing committee dealing with ideological principles reached the sensible conclusion that there are indeed wide divergencies of opinion but that the traditional terms 'Left' and 'Right' are no longer of much help in defining them. All the same, these labels will persist for a long time to come.

Being in opposition at a time of crisis has undoubted advantages. The Bonn government will have to face many difficult problems in the years to come and there will be no dramatic successes as in the Adenauer era. At best it will be a period of consolidation and rather modest achievements. If the Social Democrats refrain from too much in-fighting and if they restrain the wild men and women in their midst, they are likely to do well in 1987, or the elections thereafter, simply by capitalizing on the mistakes and failures of the CDU rather than by pointing to any plausible alternatives of their own.

The parties are not the only actors on the political scene: the trade unions are bound to play an important role in the years to come with the sharpening of social problems. About four German workers and employees in ten are organized. There has been no significant change in this respect since the Second World War, notwithstanding a slight decline in the total number of organized workers. Almost all Social Democratic members of the *Bundestag* belong to a union, as do about three-quarters of the Christian Democrats. But the direct impact of the unions on CDU policy is small, and relations between the unions and the

SPD have not always been smooth, which is perhaps not surprising since there are considerable differences of views and interests between various unions. The great event in German labour policy is the annual tariff round in which demands for wage increases are thrashed out. These annual rounds, usually bitterly fought, have prevented labour stoppages and strikes and given German workers a higher income than workers in Britain and France. German workers have also more paid holidays than others (six weeks, not to mention thirteen to sixteen legal holidays), many get a thirteenth or a fourteenth monthly salary. But for the last three years they have had to accept a decline in real earnings and a younger, more militant leadership is pressing for a harder line on the part of the unions. Structural unemployment with the threat of a further loss of jobs contributes to a worsening of the social climate. In 1983–4 the reduction of the working week to thirty-five hours without any reduction in income became the key demand of the major unions. But short of a substantial recovery in the economy there is no chance that industrialists or the state, the major employer, will be able to accept this or similar demands.

If there are divergencies of interest between the unions, the same is true, of course, with regard to industries – and even within most industries. Those doing well are ready to pay a price for social peace, those ailing and depending on state subsidies will not be able to do so. Declaring a strike in such circumstances is a prescription for disaster, as the steel workers discovered in 1979–80. Nor will the demand by the unions that the state should take over declining industries have the desired result. For however much the government may want to help, it cannot artificially stimulate demand for products not needed, nor can it stop the introduction of newer machinery. The unions have a legitimate case fighting for the interests of their members, acting as a pressure group on the parties and government. But greater militancy cannot hide the fact that their position has weakened for reasons over which neither they nor the government have much control.

The influence of the churches and of education on public opinion is unlikely to be ignored, whereas the role of the media, while obvious, is still frequently underrated. The main function of television is, of course, to entertain, but its importance as a source of information is no less significant. Of those asked in 1980 about their sources of information on world events, 49 per cent mentioned television in first place, more than newspapers and radio taken together. More surprisingly, the credibility of television was also rated far higher (53 per cent) than that of radio (17) or the newspapers (12). The list of journalists and political commentators in whose opinions the public is interested includes only television journalists.[1] In a past age the long columns and learned editorials of leading German newspapers were closely studied and widely discussed inside Germany and abroad; they were aimed, needless to say, at an elite audience. Today's television comments are short and snappy, they aim at a mass audience and there is insufficient time to go into any detail as far as facts, arguments and reasoning are concerned. Messrs Nowotny, Löwenthal and Luek are bound to remain quite unknown to those outside the radius of the German television stations, but their influence at home – which is all that matters – is very substantial indeed.[2]

Television programmes in democratic countries tend to concentrate on shortcomings and failures, and since the government of the day, not the opposition, is 'making news', its record is subjected to harsher scrutiny than that of the opposition. There are, needless to say, limits to TV hostility. The television stations are financed by the *Länder*, who have a decisive say in the appointment of the director of the service; it is unlikely that a *Land* ruled by Christian Democrats will tolerate unbridled systematic and partisan attacks. Thus a certain balance has been established. If the *ZDF Magazin* – the programme featuring political comment on the second channel of German television – expresses a pro-CDU bias, 'Panorama', 'Monitor' and other such features are inclined towards the SDP. However, by and large the Social Democrats come out better in the contest for the minds of German television audiences. Television commentators will seldom be caught singing the praises of any politician, and this includes also Willy Brandt and Hans Jochen Vogel, but there will be some extra sharpness (or venom) in their criticism of Christian Democrat politicians.

There are more sympathizers with the Left in the German telecracy than with the Right, and this is reflected not only (and not mainly) in

[1] The list was headed – by an enormous margin – by Friedrich Nowotny, author of a weekly programme from Bonn. After him figured Gerhard Löwenthal, Ernst Dieter Luek, Werner Höfer and Franz Alt.

[2] Franz Alt's book in support of the German peace movement sold more than 600,000 copies in hard cover within a few months. It contained virtually nothing that had not been said many times before by other writers. But the very fact that Alt was the author attracted great numbers of people, greater, in fact, than the writings of Böll, Grass, all their colleagues and the theologians. Few people outside Germany will ever hear of him and his book will not be translated into foreign languages. But this does not affect in the slightest his influence inside the *Bundesrepublik*.

straight political broadcasts, but in other programmes as well, such as social and cultural reportage, plays, and even children's programmes. It would be unrealistic, almost inhuman, to expect TV writers and producers to engage in acts of self-negation – their opinion will almost always show through. The situation in other countries such as the US, Britain, Italy and Scandinavia is similar; TV programmes – as distinct from the press – are more often than not to the 'Left' of their audience: not systematic indoctrination but a persistent, discreet (or sometimes not so discreet) bias.

How much influence do these programmes have? Less than would be expected, more probably in the foreign political field than on home affairs. The average viewer has no independent means of information about the situation in far-away countries and is therefore more likely to accept uncritically the opinions of others. On domestic affairs and developments he or she is bound to have greater knowledge and experience. If the views expressed on television are persistently in sharp contrast to their own judgment viewers will not be overawed by the authority of TV, but the credibility of the medium will be affected.

Germany between East and West

The domestic affairs of West Germany are of absorbing interest to the experts, but to few others outside the country. The non-specialists care about internal German developments only to the extent that they affect foreign policy. If, nevertheless, at the present time outside interest in internal German affairs is greater than it would normally be, this reflects not intellectual curiosity on the part of Americans and Frenchmen about the views and actions of the Greens, the exploits of Franz Josef Strauss, the political theology of German protestantism or the plans of German social democracy on how to cope with unemployment. It reflects concern on the part of Germany's allies that the very country which for many years was considered a model of stability has become wayward and unpredictable, that its resolve has weakened, that once again in its history it is about to engage in a long march on a *Sonderweg*. Within a very short time the best pupil in the class of Western defence has become the sick man of Europe. This on the one hand, and on the other the renewed interest of the Soviet bloc in the

German situation; could Germany be the weakest link in the 'imperial-ist chain', the link which, if broken, could bring about the downfall of the whole system?[1]

What is the origin of these Western fears and to what extent are they – and Soviet hopes – rooted in a reality of sorts? It is, of course, no secret that strong currents in German public opinion have been increasingly critical of the policy of absolute loyalty (*Nibelungentreue*) towards the Alliance over more than a decade. The national consensus on defence, which once existed, has given way to sharply divergent views. True, Social Democratic spokesmen have maintained that they object only to certain NATO strategies – such as the stationing of Pershing and Cruise missiles in Europe – and that their general support for NATO, let alone for the *Bundeswehr*, has not been affected in the least. If this were true, Allied worries about a weakening in Germany's resolve would not just be misplaced, they would be slanderous. Disputes about strategies are normal among allies, every alliance rests on compromises between diverging viewpoints within a given framework.

But does the common basis still exist? When asked whether a strong *Bundeswehr* was important, a majority (56 per cent) of SPD voters answered that this was not the case, or that they had no answer to this question.[2] The deep concern about the preservation of peace can easily be understood; but how to explain that the peace movement turned its wrath almost entirely against the US? Demonstrations against the Soviet nuclear build-up were symbolic, such as the unfurling of a banner for two minutes in Moscow and East Berlin. The peace movement blames US policy more than the Russians, the menace of US missiles seems greater than that of the Soviet ss-20. More important still, they see no real threat facing Germany – except the threat of a mad arms race triggered off by the strategy of the Atlantic Alliance dominated by bellicose Americans who believe that nuclear war is winnable.

According to a study undertaken in 1983 by the SINUS Institute, a majority of Germans think that there is nothing to chose between the United States and the Soviet Union where interference in the affairs

[1] This is by no means a novel idea; it was very popular in Soviet writing in the late 1920s. *Pravda* (1 February 1930) wrote on Germany as 'the weakest link' and the 'direct and immediate threat of a break in the imperialist chain'.

[2] The majority of FDP voters in favour of a strong *Bundeswehr* (61 per cent) was not overwhelming and in the CDU there was also a sizeable group of dissenters from this proposition (28 per cent).

of other countries is concerned and also in some other respects.[1]

On the basis of such moods the alliance with America must appear perfectly senseless if not altogether damaging. Yet Germans are no more consistent than other people: a great majority (78 per cent) believes that NATO is a vital necessity, and only 9 per cent favour leaving it.

How far have anti-American sentiments spread within the SPD and other circles, and what are their origins? The previous generation of leaders and rank-and-file who had lived through the war and the Cold War regarded the Soviet Union as the main threat to German freedom and America as Germany's good and great friend. Those who grew to maturity in the late 1960s and after remember neither the blockade of Berlin nor the Marshall plan. As they see it, Germany has always been divided, and while the Soviet political system is not particularly attractive, it does not seem very dangerous either. There is no 'Soviet aggression' except perhaps in faraway countries (such as Afghanistan), about which little is known and which do not matter. And has America not behaved even worse in such places as Vietnam? If the Soviet Union has greatly changed for the better since Stalin's days, America has deteriorated since Kennedy. And even if there is perhaps a minute threat of Soviet pressure on a disarmed Western Europe, such a danger is of almost no consequence in comparison with the total ruin that would be caused by a nuclear war.

The shift in mood has been largely the result of generational change, but not entirely so. Leaders such as Brandt and Bahr witnessed the Cold War in the 1950s from a very close angle indeed. But they too have been persuaded, or persuaded themselves, that fundamental changes have taken place in the East, that Soviet policy is not remotely as dangerous as many American and other Western observers think. Soviet strategy (as they see it) is dictated mainly by the traumatic memories of the past – the fact that Russia has been invaded so often. It is defensive rather than offensive: since the Soviet leaders have such difficulty in keeping Eastern Europe in line, there is no desire to expand their sphere of influence any further. The sanest Western (and German) strategy, in

[1] *Die Neue Gesellschaft*, 1, 1984, pp. 46–52. Was this deterioration in the American image perhaps the result of Reagan's Republican administration? The commentators say it began well before; according to them it had to do with economic conflicts of interests and the trend towards more independence in national and European policies. Seen in a longer perspective it is not certain whether there has been any significant change in the image of America as far as the population at large is concerned, but there certainly has been such a change among the opinion-makers.

these circumstances, is to reassure the Russians that there is no reason for fear and generally speaking, engage in a dialogue aimed at removing tensions between the blocs.

The older generation of Social Democratic leaders in Germany feels uncomfortable with the foreign policy of the Republicans – and with their conservative policies at home. But Brandt, Bahr and the others have vivid recollections of the 1940s and 1950s. Unlike the younger generation in their party, they were hardly affected by the ideological fashions of the late 1960s. They cannot possibly accept the exaggerations of the radicals. They even know that the constant invocation of Reagan's 'pathological' (or paranoic) anti-communism is misplaced; the Republicans have been, after all, very eager to maintain normal (and better) relations with China, Yugoslavia and Romania. The issue at stake is clearly not anti-communism *per se*, but the belief of consecutive US administrations in the need to contain the Soviet Union. Unfortunately, containing the Soviet Union cannot be combined with *détente* (as the Soviet leaders interpret it), nor is it in the interests of German unity, as Bahr, Gaus and their friends see it. There was not the slightest doubt with regard to the profoundly democratic belief of a Kurt Schumacher, the first leader of the SPD after the war. How deeply rooted are the democratic convictions of the Social Democratic leaders who are critical of the direction of the Atlantic Alliance?

They will react with indignation to the very posing of this question, and it is, of course, perfectly true that their attachment to democratic ideals is second to none. But the present state of the world is highly precarious; there are nuclear bombs, there is the danger of war, and in these circumstances the cause of peace must, by necessity, take first place. For in the case of general ruin and destruction, the inevitable consequence of a war, it does not matter any longer whether a country is free or not. Seen in this light (as Egon Bahr and some others have pointed out), emphasizing freedom and human rights is tantamount to 'ideology'; worse, it is Cold War propaganda. However justified in principle the Polish demands for more freedom may be, it is imperative that they should subordinate their aspirations to peace. And why only the Poles? If the Soviet Union cannot feel secure unless it is stronger than all potential enemies taken together, concessions must be made to allay these fears in order to promote world peace.

Yet another consideration has contributed to the change in the attitude among some Germans towards the Soviet Union: the desire to bring German reunification nearer, or at least to prevent any further deepening of the division. The road to German reunification leads through Moscow; the Western Alliance can offer West Germany protection but it cannot help to bring German unity any nearer. Hence the conclusion drawn by some Germans that membership of the Western Alliance contradicts Germany's long-term national interests.

But if Germany were to leave NATO, would this be sufficient inducement for the Soviet leaders to accept reunification? Not unless the united Germany were *gleichgeschaltet* on the East German pattern, as South Vietnam was after the end of the war in South-East Asia. For a united democratic Germany could offer no guarantee against 'backsliding' towards the West at some future stage. Germany would still have a substantial army by European standards, on which the Russians could not count.

One might envisage other solutions, such as a neutral German confederation in which the political and social system of East Germany would be maintained, but this could be considered only as an interim solution. Even iron-clad guarantees for keeping Germany neutralized, if such could be provided, might not cause great enthusiasm in Moscow. Germany is much bigger than Finland or Austria and thus more difficult to control. Whatever the merits of a German decision to leave NATO, it would not bring German unity nearer, and this has been accepted even by those politicians for whom this priority ranks very high. They know that reunification is not near and that meanwhile it is more advantageous, from their point of view, to operate from within a Western alliance, acting as a 'moderating influence' and hoping that ultimately there will be *Wandel durch Annäherung*, change as the result of *rapprochement*, to quote Egon Bahr's formula of the early 1960s.

Seen in retrospect, there has been *Wandel* over the last twenty years, but more of it in West Germany than in the East. The East German authorities have behaved on the whole with caution and moderation towards West Germany; the unbridled attacks of the 1960s have ceased. A limited *rapprochement* is certainly desirable from the East German point of view because it entails substantial financial support, West German help for East Germany with the EEC and other useful assistance. Furthermore, a special relationship with West Germany may be desirable from East Berlin's point of view, at a time when most other East European countries are stressing their special national traditions and interests one way or another. If West Germany has difficulties coming to terms with its history and identity, so has the GDR.

But all this is tolerable only within limits and under strict control; if it should appear that the relations between the two Germanies have undesirable political effects inside East Germany, there will be an immediate and, if necessary, radical reversal of policy. During 1984 the East German leaders were willing to risk, up to a point, even the displeasure of the Soviet Politburo who favoured a harsher line *vis-à-vis* West Germany in contrast to East Berlin's *détente* policy. Since, at one stage or another, virtually every East European country has refused to give total support to Soviet foreign policy, such dissociation within accepted limits is not a portent of momentous change in Central Europe, such as German reunification.

As the proponents of German reunification see it, political circumstances may change at some distant future date, even if the prospects at present are faint or non-existent. They will find some understanding, though no great enthusiasm, among their Western partners. But what price will have to be paid? If it is recognizing Germany's 'special interest in the preservation of peace', as some Social Democratic leaders tend to stress, there should be no disagreement. For there is no such special German interest; everyone shares it. If it involves friendly speeches and some economic assistance for East Germany, Germany's allies will hardly mind. But if West German leaders give priority to the links with the GDR, if it means appeasement rather than the preservation of peace, the Western Alliance will hardly survive.

For this reason, West German leaders with all their insistence on their special relationship with East Germany will be careful not to overstep certain boundaries in pursuit of their goal. The mutual dangling of promises between the two Germanies will continue in all likelihood, there will be too much of it to lose hope, too little to make a significant change in the present state of affairs. Those who believe that reunification is inevitable argue that once the division of Europe is overcome the division of Germany will also come to an end. True, the partition of Germany was an unnatural act, a wound that will not heal in the foreseeable future. But it was not accidental and there is no known cure now. Those who pretend that they have a cure delude themselves and others, for something much more far-reaching than bloc-free Europe is needed to bring about the reunification of Germany. Unless a neutral Europe is also united and strong it will not be the master of its own destiny but be exposed to outside pressures, even if neutral according to the canons of international law. To expect the East German leaders to agree to German unity except on their own terms is to assume that they are willing to sacrifice the achievements of 'real socialism' (not to mention their own careers) to the ideal of German unity, an unlikely proposition even if there were no Brezhnev doctrine. To expect West Germans to give up their free political order for the sake of unity is equally unrealistic – a few may be willing to pay this price but most will not.

Some have argued that seemingly impossible obstacles will disappear in the course of time: the East Germans have rediscovered their national traditions including Prussia and Luther, the new generation succeeding the *Altkommunisten* in East Berlin is more pragmatic, surer of itself, less constrained by outworn ideological beliefs. There is a grain of truth in these arguments, inasmuch as certain changes in mentality have indeed taken place and more, no doubt, are bound to come. The East Germans have rediscovered Stein, Karl August Hardenberg, General Gneisenau and other outstanding Prussians but not political democracy. Freedom may return as a result of an evolutionary process but only over a long period. In the meantime the two Germanies are likely to grow apart, as Britain and America did, or Germany and Austria, despite all the efforts to keep the idea of unity alive. It is a powerful idea, but too many political realities would have to change to make the dream come true in the foreseeable future.

To what extent are contemporary German politics motivated by fear? The Soviet Union has been accused of playing on European (and particularly West German) fears for obvious political purposes. But if there has been intimidation, it has been by implication rather than direct means. The Soviet Union is not strong enough at present to impose its will on Western Europe. It must, at one and the same time, project an image of being very strong and very peaceful. Too much bluster would almost certainly be counterproductive; Soviet strategy has to be carefully attuned to the mood of the country concerned. So far there have been no direct, specific Soviet threats, but such pressure cannot be ruled out in the future.

Upon what is the optimism based, which some Social Democratic leaders voice, with regard to Soviet intentions? Is it the product of intimate knowledge and mature judgment, or is it rooted in wishful thinking?[1] Has the physical proximity to the Soviet Union helped Brandt, Bahr and Gaus and their younger comrades to gain greater detachment; or has it, on the contrary, beclouded their judgment, imposing restrictions not only on their public utterances but also their private thoughts?

Their views, as far as can be ascertained, rest on certain indisputable assumptions: that the character of the Soviet Union has indeed changed since Stalin's days and is continuing to change. There has been an erosion of communist ideology, but the basic political structures created under Lenin and Stalin still exist and will not vanish in the near future. They will ultimately give way to something different, but not in this decade, probably not in this century. Nor has the fundamental belief disappeared that 'in our time one does not count with the weak, one counts only with the strong'.[2] There can be no two views about the essentially conservative character of Soviet policy. But such conservatism does not preclude the expansion of the Soviet sphere of interest when it does not confront resistance. Soviet policy in Europe has been moderate and cautious because of NATO. It has been less cautious and moderate in other parts of the world.

The differences between the American and some German assessments of Soviet politics are not differences in principle, but reflect a different focus. American leaders may or may not lack the wisdom and the experience of German (or British or French) statesmen, but in contrast to West Germany, the US is a global power with world-wide interests. It must consider the global picture and cannot afford to conduct a parochial policy, *Kirchturmspolitik* to use the apt German term. It may be quite natural for European party leaders to argue that, even if *détente* in other parts of the world has broken down, this should not affect the situation in Europe. This, however, is not a policy which a global power can take as its guideline; Germany and the United States have different political horizons. But unless an intellectual and psychological effort is made by the junior partner in an alliance to consider the wider responsibility and commitments of the senior partner, the alliance is bound to come to grief. For it is not unreasonable on the part of the Americans to expect their allies to share some of the

---

[1] Such views, needless to say, are also found in other countries, among George Kennan's friends in the United States and among the leaders of the British Labour party. But the situation is still not comparable, for the new leaders of British Labour are not foreign policy experts, whereas Brandt, Bahr and their colleagues have had direct contact with Soviet leaders for many years.

[2] Stalin, *Sochineniya*, vol. 13, pp. 299 *et seq.* For a more detailed discussion on Soviet policy, see Walter Laqueur, *America, Europe and the Soviet Union* (New Brunswick 1983), *passim*.

responsibilities in other parts of the world in exchange for the protection offered in Europe.

The more persistent advocacy of para-Gaullist (or semi-neutralist) policies in Germany has come mainly from political parties – or to be precise from certain sections in these parties – which are not in power now, which are unlikely to return to power soon, and which, if in power, would almost certainly behave with greater restraint than in opposition. A Social Democratic chancellor, a foreign or defence minister, will not be too eager to cut himself off from the Alliance. It is useful to recall, from time to time, that other NATO countries have frequently behaved less loyally than West Germany; France and Greece are partly in NATO, partly out; Denmark has openly dissociated itself from commonly agreed strategies; Holland and Belgium have shown reluctance to live up to their obligations.

But Germany is neither Greece nor Denmark; if it acted in a similar way, the consequences would be far-reaching. Some Germans find it difficult to accept that Sweden and Austria can be neutral, that a German chancellor, unlike Olof Palme of Sweden, cannot go cocking a snook at the Americans, that some NATO members get away with mainly nominal membership, and that Germany is always judged more harshly when it wishes to assert its national interests. Such unfairness does exist, but it is not the fault of the Americans. It is the result of inescapable and unalterable historical and geographical facts. Sweden and Austria have been neutral not because of their intrinsic strength or because international relations are governed by high morality. They could stay neutral because there exists a balance of power in Europe which makes it possible for some small countries to get a free ride. Were this balance to disappear, their domestic freedom of action would be severely restricted and their foreign policy would be dictated from outside. One should perhaps envy the Swedes of this world, for on top of getting a free ride, they can also strike a high moral posture. The bigger countries are in a less fortunate position.

Seen in a neutralist perspective, it is Germany's tragedy that it is situated in the heart of Europe and not in a distant part of the globe, where it could pursue almost any kind of policy without detrimental effect to itself or to others.

Three foreign political strategies will be open, broadly speaking, to German leaders in the years to come. One is to stay in the Alliance in the hope that Washington and the other Western capitals will conduct a policy both firm and moderate and show understanding for the special German interests. Some German fears can be accommodated by raising the nuclear threshold. But it is more doubtful whether any American president, however flexible, will find an alternative to deterrence in the near future, which means that criticism of NATO and the demand to leave the Alliance will persist in some circles in Germany.

A second possible strategy is the establishment of a European Defence Community with or without American support. Some Europeans have doubted for a long time whether any American president would be willing to sacrifice Detroit for Hamburg; de Gaulle's contention that, in the last resort, the defence of Europe had to be undertaken by Europeans was not devoid of logic. The idea of a European Defence Community was hotly debated in the early 1950s but ceased to be a real alternative when the French National Assembly defeated it in 1954. Since then there has been increased support for concepts of this kind in various countries. Some have thought of establishing a strong European group within NATO in such a way that Europe's political weight would be equal to that of the United States. Others prefer a European Defence Community outside NATO; this involves major complications since a French or British nuclear guarantee would hardly be more convincing than one given by America.

The special status of Germany in such an alliance would also cause many problems. But it is not impossible that these difficulties could be overcome in the long run; the crucial question is whether those concerned are willing to make a substantial defence effort in a European framework, or whether their European enthusiasm is merely a pretext for inaction. Certain preconditions have to be fulfilled before a European Defence Community is established, and this refers to closer political and economic co-operation between the countries of Europe. However, the impetus towards closer collaboration has faded, there has been a retreat from the ideal of European unity. It is perhaps significant that Germany's European hopes have declined as much as the faith in American leadership. There is widespread belief in Europe that Washington may not welcome closer European integration, but this belongs to the realm of mythology. A majority of Americans would be only too happy about any arrangement which would reduce the American commitment in Europe in men, material and money alike.

The obstacles to a European Defence Community are not in

Washington but in Europe. The idea of basing the defence of Western Europe to a much larger extent on conventional weapons is admirable, but such weapons are by no means cheap. Parliamentarians are always under pressure to reduce defence spending and there are many other priorities. A European defence organization may be an excellent solution in the long run. But the political will to build such a community does not exist at present. It may emerge one day in a different political constellation, perhaps as the result of a growing rift with the United States, or the growth of neo-isolationism in America, or greater Soviet pressure on Europe, or a combination of these and other factors.

The third alternative is the neutralization of Germany. This is, at present, the least likely possibility but it cannot be ruled out altogether. Those advocating a neutral Germany have never made it clear how they envisage this to come about. Neutrality is not achieved by a unilateral declaration; to have any meaning, it has to be recognized by third parties. Neutralists usually argue that their basic aim is to overcome the division of Europe into blocs. But they also know that if Germany were to leave its alliance tomorrow, or the day after, East Germany, Poland and Czechoslovakia would not reciprocate. Some neutralists believe that the balance of power, deterrence and 'Finlandization' are meaningless concepts. They should therefore be eager to take the plunge quite irrespective of Soviet willingness to reciprocate. For neutrality would make them safe from nuclear war without any danger of being subjected to pressure, direct and indirect, of gradually being absorbed into the sphere of influence of the powerful neighbour to the East.[1]

But the neutralists seem to lack the courage of their convictions; perhaps they have certain doubts about their own assumptions concerning the likelihood of remaining independent in a world of power politics. Most neutralists, except perhaps the most radical among them, prefer therefore to remain in the Western Alliance for the time being. While staying under the NATO umbrella, they will be reluctant to pull their weight as far as the defence of the continent is concerned. Their main political concern will be not to cause offence to the Soviet leaders so as to induce them gradually to do away with the partition of Europe.

[1] Some German critics of NATO such as Gaus, Lafontaine and others have recommended a Gaullist solution for Germany or, at the very least, 'more Gaullism'. It is a moot point in the first place whether Gaullism is a viable policy in present-day Europe. But even if such a policy were feasible, it ought to be recalled that Gaullism presupposes considerable military power – including a *force de frappe*. The German advocates of Gaullism are unwilling to accept these implications.

In the meantime, American patience is wearing thin. American leaders are ready to negotiate a reduction of tensions in Europe. But there is not much tension in Europe in the first place, except perhaps as the result of resistance to Soviet rule in East European countries, such as Poland. The Soviet leaders will not make this the subject of negotiation. US foreign-policy-makers believe in negotiations on the basis of roughly equal strength; their critics in Western Europe, such as a majority of German Social Democrats, maintain that the Americans tend to exaggerate Soviet military power and that, in any case, it is not necessary that the West should match the Soviet build-up. The debates on Soviet military strength have gone on for a long time, but only America has the technical means of verification. The Pentagon will not be impressed by European assessments which, by necessity, are based either on speculation or on information which originally emanated from the United States and was suitably 'reinterpreted' by European wishful thinkers.

The reasons for the US disenchantment with Europe are known; they are partly rooted in misunderstandings about the function of NATO. The Alliance is still widely interpreted as a political pact in Washington (which it was not meant to be) rather than a defence treaty. There are the complaints, by no means unjustified, that it is unreasonable to expect Europeans to adjust every four years to changing foreign political orientations in Washington. US policy makers may accept greater European political assertiveness within NATO if this is matched by greater European willingness to strengthen NATO. They will not in the long run put up with foot-dragging coupled with the wish to have a greater say in running the Alliance. There has been a growing inclination on the part of the European governments towards selective co-operation with the United States to reduce defence spending, not to support American initiatives, but not to submit realistic alternatives either.

At the same time the movement towards European unity has run out of steam, except perhaps in joining forces from time to time in opposing certain American initiatives. One sometimes wishes that the critics of America in Europe would get together and decide to do something about European and German independence rather than extol in abstract terms the virtues of Gaullism, national or European, in their speeches and articles. Perhaps America, the new menace, could act as a catalyst for a fresh impetus to European unity? For such an initiative we shall have to wait a long time; the critics of America are in no hurry to break the shackles of their dependence and prefer to bemoan their sad destiny. This rift is leading to increasing conflict between the senior partner in the Alliance and the others, and it may even bring about its disintegration. The process may be checked by a threatening Soviet policy in Europe, which would cause the European governments to draw closer into the American orbit. The Europeanization of the defence of Europe is costly, risky and will not be undertaken except in an emergency. Perhaps NATO will be transformed into a looser – and by necessity, less secure – alliance. Some of its European critics favour this process but hope that it will take a long time, and that meanwhile the centrifugal trends in Eastern Europe will leave their mark. They hope that the disintegration of NATO will give a fresh impetus to the disruptive forces in the Warsaw Pact. For once the threat which caused the establishment of the Warsaw Pact has disappeared, it will have lost its *raison d'être* and the Soviet leaders will find it difficult to justify its existence.

Such mirror imaging, the belief in a symmetry between developments in Western and Eastern Europe, is unreal; Soviet rule in Eastern Europe does not rest on legitimacy, but on power. Neutralism in Europe may get its opportunity at some future date, not as the result of a decision to leave the Alliance, but because America may lose patience with its reluctant allies. If this should come to pass, it will at long last be *Hic Rapallo, hic salta*, and the rest of the world will watch with fascination on what part of the body the jumpers will land.

Weak countries have coexisted with powerful ones since time immemorial even without the benefit of a balance of power. Some of the weaker ones were occupied and became part of larger empires. Others, such as ancient Rome's *clientelae*, acknowledged the hegemony of the imperial power and took upon themselves all kinds of obligations, but kept a certain degree of independence as far as their internal affairs were concerned. There is no predicting with any degree of accuracy how West Germany and the other European countries would fare if America were to withdraw her forces from Europe. It is the kind of risk which few individuals would take in their private life.

It will probably never come to this test, which in some ways is a matter of regret. From America's point of view and also that of the Alliance, a clear decision on Europe's part is desirable: either overwhelming support or an equally clear rejection. But this, unfortunately, is unlikely; there is not one 'Europe' but a dozen divided countries.

Of late the tide has been running against US–European co-operation. There is a self-correcting mechanism; once there is a real danger of a breakdown the pendulum will swing back and support for such co-operation will again become stronger and more vociferous – at least for a while. But the doubts and the indecision in Europe will not disappear, and this is the burden which America will continue to bear until such time as the majority of Americans and Europeans are persuaded that a threat of Soviet hegemony no longer exists – or that Soviet power has become so overwhelming that it is senseless to resist it any longer.

Germany – twenty years ahead

What kind of country will Germany be twenty or thirty years hence? Amidst the ruins of 1945, the general feeling was that never again would the country rise, and the pessimism only deepened following partition. The recovery was almost a miracle, it succeeded beyond the wildest dreams of the optimists. But the ruins of 1945 are now forgotten and present fears are looming large. The population of Germany is shrinking; it ranges now eleventh or twelfth in the world and will be overtaken by many other countries within the next thirty to forty years, if present demographic trends continue.

Germany can no longer dominate Europe, nor does it nurse such ambitions. But the state of Germany is still a matter of immediate concern for Europe and thus for the world; not of paramount importance, as in the days of the emperor and of Hitler; how close it came to victory in the two world wars! For some Germans this may be a cause of regret – most prefer the calm and relative obscurity which has come after decades of over-exposure to world history.

Throughout history nations have risen to great power and import-ance and then suffered an eclipse: Britain's decline since the 1940s has been more palpable than Germany's. It is no secret that the most powerful countries are not necessarily the most civilized and the happiest ones. Germany's great contribution to world civilization came when, as a military power, it did not exist. Sweden and Switzerland were once leading military powers of the first rank; it is unlikely that many citizens of these countries still shed bitter tears about the glory of

Gustavus Adolphus and the battle of Morgarten. Germany is a bigger country to be sure, but its experiences as a world power have not been happy. The desire to live perilously and to do great deeds is no longer there: let the *Weltgeist* pick someone else for its major assignments.

Germans have spent more time than any other nation pondering their identity and their destiny. Such preoccupations point to a deep philosophical bent in their mental make-up but also to insecurity. Happier people live in the present, are less weighed down by the past, or concerned about the future. What special missions are there to be undertaken in the last quarter of the twentieth century? To make peace between the two power blocs, to be a pioneer on the road to a new civilization?

To a considerable extent, Germany has come to terms with its existence, its new place in the world, more so than could be expected. Almost every year since the end of the Second World War some over-anxious outside observers have announced the impending resurgence of neo-Nazism, or some such calamity. But the 'Boys from Brazil' have not returned to power in Bonn, the fears were unfounded and this spectre should have been exorcized. Germany's foreign political ambitions have shrunk or disappeared, but the discontent about its internal state of affairs has not gone away. Is it a case of aggression turned inward? The country has certainly become richer, but is it any happier? There is still, or again, a palpable restlessness, a specific German unease disregarding reality and nurturing illusions about the perfectibility of institutions. Political leaders, parties, the constitution, the law, the police – everything has been measured and found wanting. Few would apply the same perfectionist standards of competence, altruism and morality towards their personal life. There are complaints about the lack of freedom and justice in public life, and not all of them are unwarranted. There is the ambition to have more freedom than anyone else. Having shown excessive admiration for, and even blind faith in, authority, there is now the wish in some circles to do away with all authority. But the virtues needed for success in the democratic master class are not easily or quickly acquired. Consensus politics, compromises, tolerance in general were not the outstanding features of German politics before 1945. They take a long time to grow roots.

The experience of the Weimar Republic showed that a democracy will not last unless there are enough democrats to support it. Germans traditionally wish to have a close relationship with their state, they want not just to identify with it, but to love it; few Frenchmen or British will insist on such intimate terms. The Weimar Republic was not beloved, not even respected. Today, there is less open hostility but constant complaints that a fetish is made of the constitution, that the authorities are not doing enough for the people, that there is a lack of warmth and kindness in society, that the state is a monster against which the helpless citizen has to be protected. There may be some truth in all of this, but it is only part of the picture. The need for active co-operation on the part of the citizens to make the democratic system work is not always understood. Those who complain about the lack of warmth in society and the arrogance of the authorities are not always a model of kindness and humility in their relations with each other.

There is a negative trend in German public life which is dangerous and may, in certain conditions, undermine the democratic system. This is the all-or-nothing syndrome: since the system is not perfect, it is worthless. These may be no more than the growing pains of a young democracy. No one can deny the progress that has been made. Most Christian Democrats, however dim their views of the aims of the SPD, no longer think that all Social Democrats are fanatics and traitors. Most Social Democrats will admit, if pressed, that whatever the weaknesses of the Christian Democrats, they are not hidden fascists, scheming to abolish democracy at the first opportunity and to establish another dictatorship. The Greens, at their worst, are no more than vegetarian and pacifist Pol Pots, genuinely well meaning, genuinely confused.

But what of the constant invocation of fears, and the frequent manifestations of hypochondria in public life? After her long stay in Germany, Madame de Staël noted that Frenchmen talk about their misfortunes, however grave, in a light-hearted way; Germans, on the other hand, tend to communicate them, for, as one of their proverbs has it, 'suffering shared is suffering reduced' (*Geteiltes Leid ist halbes Leid*). The articulation of fears, like whistling in the dark, may be a way of releasing tension.

Germany is on the move again, but in what direction? Neither to great glory, nor to a collapse. The age of manifest destinies has gone, the dimensions of the world stage have changed, the part played by Germany has become more modest. Her freedom of movement, like that of everyone else, has become more restricted. All things considered, there is now not only more freedom in Germany than ever before in her history, but also more common sense and moderation.

There is a great deal of hypochondria about, but also an essential toughness, an unwillingness to surrender without a major struggle to the threats facing the country at home and abroad. Germany may need these resources in the years to come.

Index

Adenauer, Konrad, 104, 200
administration, 'tertiary sector', 24–5
agriculture, farming, 24, 26–8, 192
air traffic, 32
Albertz, Pastor Heinrich, 134
Alexis, Willibald, 21
Alt, Franz, 208n.
alternative lifestyle, 65–7
Anderson, Hugh, 11n.
Angst, see fear
anxiety, *see* fear
Arbeiterbund, 57
architecture, building, 33–5, 44
Arendt, Hannah, 100
Arminius, 143–4
Aron, Raymond, 101
Augsburg, 202n.
Austria, 11, 217

Baedeker, 21–2, 32
Bahr, Egon, 158, 165, 212, 213
Bahro, Rudolf, 158, 162
banks, 180
Bavaria, 182
Beilstein, 46
Belgium, 171, 183, 217
Berlin, 18, 19, 34, 35, 37–41, 48, 53, 62
    East Berlin, 39–40
BHE, 151
Bielefeld, 31
Bildungskatastrophe, 74
birthrate, 23
Black Forest, 45
Bloch, Ernst, 110
Böll, Heinrich, 103–4, 105, 107, 107–8,
    128, 130
Bonn, 103–4

Born, Nikolaus, 76
Brandt, Peter, 167
Brandt, Willy, 105–6, 129, 151, 165, 212
Brecht, Bertolt, 43
Bremen, 34, 181, 202–3
Brentano, Clemens, 37
Brentano, Heinrich von, 104
Breslau, 18
Britain, 14n., 47, 111–12, 125, 130, 141,
    145, 169, 172–3, 183, 189, 195
Bruder, zur Sonne, zur Freiheit, 92–7
Buber, Martin, 81
Büchner, Georg, 74
building industry, 180
Bultmann, Rudolf Karl, 11

canals, 33
cars, car industry, 30, 32, 35, 47, 178–9,
    184, 186
Castro Fidel, 110–11
Catholics, *see* Roman Catholics
CDU, *see* Christian Democrats
Chamberlain, Neville, 7
chemical industry, 29–30, 177, 179–80,
    184
Christian Democrats (CDU), 54, 104, 105,
    129, 136, 200, 202–3, 205, 206, 208,
    210n.
Church Council (EKD), 131, 132
cinema, films, 43, 55–6, 113–21, 164
cities, 18–19, 20, 33–7, 44, 168–9
    biggest, 18
    conurbations, 22–3
    medium-sized, 30–1
    most popular, 48
    see also individual cities
Clark, Kenneth, 8n.

class, 23–5, 48
Claudius, Hermann, 97–8
coalmining, 24, 28–9, 178
Cold War, 54, 121, 124–7, 170, 211
Cologne, 18, 30, 35, 202*n*.
Communist Party, 98, 101*n*., 162
computers, 182
conscientious objection, *see* pacifism
Constance, Lake Constance, 44–5
countryside, nature, 20–1, 25–7, 44–5,
   144, 168

defence
   European Defence Community, 218–9
   spending, 47
   see also NATO
Denmark, 171, 217
Descartes, René, 7
Detmold, 91, 143
Deutsche Bank, 180
Deutsche Nationalzeitung, 147*n*.
Deutscher Almanach 1981, 101–2
divorce, 47
Diwald, Helmuth, 159
doctors, *see* medicine
Dortmund, 18
Dostoevski, Fyodor, 37
Dresden, 18
drink, alcoholic, 47
drugs, 61–4
Duisburg, 29, 30, 34
Dürer, Albrecht, 8
Düsseldorf, 18, 34
Dutschke, Rudi, 84, 126

East Germany, 16, 40, 129, 194, 213–15
Eastern Church, 10–11
Eastern Europe, 221
   see also Sonderweg; Soviet Union
   economy, 24–5, 175–96
   economic miracle, 104, 106, 112, 175–6
   see also agriculture; industry; transport;
      work education, 68–74
EEC, 213
Eichberg, Henning, 153*n*., 162*n*.
Einstein, Albert, 74
EKD, *see* Church Council
electrical industry, 30, 31, 177, 178, 184
electronics, 186–7
Ende, Michael, 17*n*.
Entfeindung, 133

Enzensberger, Hans Magnus, 51, 104,
   105
Erhard, Ludwig, 23, 104
Essen, 18, 30, 197, 202*n*.
Esslingen, 31
Europe, European unity, 144–5, 172–3,
   218–19, 220–2
exports, 177, 186

Falklands war, 172
Farben (IG), 29–30, 179
farming, *see* agriculture
fascism, 86–7
   see also Nazism
Fassbinder, Rainer Werner, 114, 115,
   117–18, 119
FDP, *see* Liberal Party
fear, *Angst*, anxiety, *Weltschmerz*, 5–16,
   137–9, 198–9, 224
   problems of definition, 14*n*.
films, *see* cinema
foreign workers, 118, 154, 155, 190, 191
France, 14*n*., 47, 111–12, 125, 130, 141,
   145, 169, 172–3, 183, 195, 217
Frankfurt, 18, 19, 30, 33, 35, 43–4, 66
Free Democrats, 73
Freiligrath, Ferdinand, 91
Friedensforscher, 132–3
Friedrichs hafen, 44
Fuchs, Gerd, 161–2

Gaiser, Gerd, 113
Gaulle, Charles de, 218
Gaullism, 219*n*.
Gaus, Günter, 138, 158, 219*n*.
Gelsenkirchen, 30
Germany
   geographical position, 217
   national characteristics: conformism,
      99; exaggeration, excess, 50–1;
      extremism, perfectionism, 13, 55;
      heroes, heroism, 7, 137; history,
      sense of, 50; order, 50;
      Romanticism, 85–6; values, change
      in, 79–80, 137
   north and south, 31, 180, 182, 183
   partition, reunification (*see also* East
      Germany), 12, 39–40, 125, 170, 173,
      212–15
Giessen, 30
Glotz, Peter, 101, 139

GNP, 176
Goethe, J. W. von, 37, 73–4, 141
Gordon, Rev. Ernest, 135*n*.
Göttingen, 30–1
Grass, Günter, 105, 129, 130
Greece, 217
Green party, 8, 51, 57–9, 98, 200–201, 204, 205*n*.
Grenier, Richard, 117
Grimm, Hans, 22
Gruppe 47, 103, 104–5
Gütersloh, 31

Haarmann case, 115
Hamburg, 18, 33, 35, 48, 181, 182
Hamelin, 87–8, 202*n*.
Hanover, 34
Harnack, Adolf von, 11
Heimat, 144–5, 167–9
Heine, Heinrich, 74
Heinemann, Gustav, 131
Heisenberg, Werner, 74
Herzog, Werner, 114, 115, 116, 117, 118, 164
Hesse, Hermann, 17, 60, 74
history, study of, 77
Hitler, Adolf, 28, 32, 42, 86, 103, 121, 197–8
Höfer, Werner, 208*n*.
Hofmannsthal, Hugo von, 74
Holland, 171, 217
Huch, Ricarda, 101–2
Huizinga, Johan, 86
Humboldt, Wilhelm von, 68
Hungary, 6

industry, 28–33, 175–6, 177–88, 195, 207
inflation, 188
Ingolstadt, 30
intellectuals, 99–142, 168, 199
Iran, 110
iron and steel, 29, 30, 178, 183–4
Italy, 125, 141, 151, 183

Japan, 179, 186, 189, 195
Jaspers, Karl, 86, 105
Jens, Walter, 129
Johnson, Rev. Hewlett, 134
Jugend '81, 77*n*.
Jugendbewegung, 52

Kaiserslautern, 34
Kandinsky, Wassili, 43
Keller, Gottfried, 37
Kiel, 202*n*.
Klee, Paul, 43
Koch, Klaus, 11*n*.
Köppen, Wolfgang, 103–4, 164
Krupp, 177–8
Kursbuch, 105

Länder, 22
Lattmann, Dieter, 129
Leber, Georg, 135
Leinemann, Jürgen, 138*n*.
Leipzig, 18
Lenin, 43
Lenz, Siegfried, 129
Liberal party (FDP), 200, 203*n*., 210*n*.
libraries, 36
literature, 128
living conditions, 33–7
Lommel, Ulli, 115, 116–17
Löns, Hermann, 27
Löwenthal, Gerhard, 208
Luek, Ernst Dieter, 208
Lukács, Georg, 110
Lukanga Mukara, 17, 52*n*.
Lüneburg Heath, 27
Luther, Martin, 9–10

machine-tool industry, 177
Mann, Thomas, 42, 43, 74, 91, 146, 161, 167
Marcuse, Herbert, 153
Marx, Karl, 24, 74, 91, 135*n*.
Marxism, 109–13, 121–8
media, 12–13, 136–7, 207–9
    see also cinema
medicine, doctors, 14*n*., 45–6, 193–4
mergers, 184–5
Meysenbug, Malwida von, 91
Mies van der Rohe, Ludwig, 34
missiles, 16, 58, 108, 126, 204, 210
    see also NATO; nuclear war
Moselle, 46
MSI, 151
Munich, 18, 30, 34, 35, 41–3, 48, 182
Münster, 34

names, personal, 48*n*.
national anthem, 171

nationalism, *see* patriotism
NATO, Western Alliance, 58, 112, 131,
    145–7, 155, 171, 204, 210–13, 217–
    22
Nazism, Nazi party, 17*n*., 28, 40, 41, 58,
    85, 86–7, 95–6, 97, 103, 112, 114,
    116–17, 121–4, 168
    since 1945, 147–57, 158–62
neutralism, 7, 58, 77, 146–7, 170, 217,
    219
New German Film (NDF), 114–21
New Left, 56–7, 66
New Right, right-wing extremism, 148,
    152–7, 159–60
New Ulm, Minnesota, 144
Niemöller, Martin, 131
Nixdorf, Heinz, 182
Nobel prizes, 73
Nölle-Neumann, Elisabeth, 80*n*.
Nordrhein-Westfalen, 182
Nowotny, Friedrich, 208
NPD, 147, 151
nuclear war, fear of, 7–8, 58, 98, 132–3
    see also missiles

O'Brien, Bernie, 14*n*.
Ohnesorg, Benno, 53
oil companies, 180
Oldenburg, 30, 202*n*.
Ollenhauer, Erich, 151

Paasche, Hans, 17, 52*n*.
pacifism, peace movement, conscientious
    objection, 7, 89*n*., 107–8, 131, 132–
    3, 154–5
parties, political, 76, 200–206
    see also individual parties
Patriotism, nationalism, 145, 157–63,
    169–71
Paul, Jean, 37
peace movement, *see* pacifism
Pied Piper, 87–8
Piwitt, Hermann, 164
Poelzig, Hans 34
Pohrt, Wolfgang, 163–4, 164–5
Poland, 212
politics, 13, 76
    see also parties
population, 22–3, 47, 222
prices, 195
Protestants, 11, 23, 131–5

psychoanalysis, 110
public opinion polls, 48, 75, 80*n*., 156,
    172, 189

Radikalenerlass, 109
Radin, Leonid Petrovich, 93
railways, 32, 181
Reagan, President, 211*n*., 212
Reichstag, 40
religion, churches, cults, 9–11, 23, 48,
    59–61, 131–5
Remer, General Otto, 162
Rentschler, Eric, 114*n*.
Reutlingen, 31
Rhine, 19–20, 29–30, 33
Richter, Hans Werner, 103
right-wing extremism, *see* New Right
Rilke, Rainer Maria, 17, 74
roads, 32
Roman Catholics, 10, 23, 131
Rote Armee Fraktion (RAF), 54–5, 56
Rothschild, Th., 102*n*.
Rhur, 18, 29, 30, 37, 197
Russia, *see* Soviet Union

Scharoun, Hans, 34
Scherchen, Hermann, 94–5, 96
Scheringer, Lieutenant, 162
Schiller, J. C. F. von, 74
Schlöndorff, Volker, 114, 118, 120
Schmid, Thomas, 160–1
Schmidhäuser, Ulrich, 133*n*.
Schmidt, Helmut, 5, 129, 200
schools, 67–8, 69–70, 71*n*., 73
Schopenhauer, Arthur, 88*n*.
Schroeter, Werner, 114, 115
shipping, shipbuilding, 33, 180–1, 182
shops, shopping, 35–7
Siemens, 31, 178
Sinnkrise, 13, 84–5
SINUS Institute, study, 156, 210–11
soccer, 28–9, 47
'social defence', 132–3
Social Democrats (SPD), 129, 200, 202–7
    and America, 211–12, 220
    coalitions, 58, 105–6, 108–9, 126, 200
    and German rearmament, *Bundeswehr*,
        146, 210
    and industry, unions, 191, 206–7
    Radikalenerlass, 109
    songs, 97

and students, youth, 54, 135–6, 203, 205–6
and television audiences, 208
Sölle, Dorothea, 134
Sonderweg, 133, 145, 174, 197–8, 209
songs, 92–8, 102*n*.
South Sea islands, 77
Soviet Union, Russia, 209–10, 215, 221
   German attitudes to, 108, 111, 145–6, 163, 166, 169, 173, 210–16; *see also* Cold War
Sozialgeschichte der deutschen Literatur von 1918 bis zur Gegenwart, 101–2
Spartakus, 57
spas, 45–6
SPD, *see* Social Democrats
Spengler, Oswald, 43
Spiegel, Der, 5
squatting, 66–7
SRP, 147, 151
Staël, Madame de, 21, 224
Stamokap, 123
steel, *see* iron and steel
Stendhal, 37
Stern, Annemarie, 102*n*.
Strauss, Franz Josef, 41
students, 51–2, 53–4, 56–7, 58, 151–2, 156, 203
   see also universities
Stuttgart, 30, 33, 34
suicide, 6
Sweden, 47, 169, 217
Switzerland, 6
Syberberg, Hans Jürgen, 115, 116, 118

Tätowierung, 55–6
taz, 65
television, 207–9
terrorism, 50, 54–6, 89, 154
tertiary sector, *see* administration
Teutoburg forest, 44, 143
textile industry, 180
Thatcher, Margaret, 172
Third World, 110–13, 127
Thyssen, Fritz, 122

trade unions, 188, 206–7
transport, 31–3
   see also cars; railways; shipping
Trier, 46
Trotsky, Leon, 43
Twain, Mark, 21, 37

unemployment, 176, 182, 183, 190–3, 195
United States of America, 47, 125–6, 130, 141, 186, 189, 195, 216–22
   anti-Americanism, 54, 58, 77, 111–13, 126–7, 145, 146–7, 161, 163–7, 169–70, 171, 204, 210–12, 220–2
universities, 68–9, 70–3
   see also students

VEBA, 178
Vereine, 167–8, 169*n*.
villages, village life, 25–7

Wader, Hannes, 164
wages, 195
Wald, James 159*n*.
Walser, Martin, 104, 112–13, 130, 167
Weerth, Georg, 91
Wehnert, Herbert, 151
Weimar Republic, 53, 223–4
Weiss, Peter, 128
welfare, 193–5
Weltschmerz, *see* fear
Wenders, Wim, 114, 115, 120
Wenn wir schreiten Seit' an Seit', 97–8
Western Alliance, *see* NATO
Wiking Jugend, 154–5
wine, 46
Wir Selbst, 153*n*., 162*n*.
Wolfsburg, 30
women, 47–8
work, attitudes to, 79–80, 188–90
World Council of Churches, 135*n*.

youth, 49–90, 170, 171, 172, 205–6
   see also students

Zuse, Konrad, 187